In Search of Tusitala

GAVIN BELL was born in Lanarkshire, Scotland, and educated at Hutchesons' Boys' Grammar School, Glasgow. He followed his father into journalism, as a reporter for Scottish newspapers, before joining Agence France-Presse in Paris. For almost twenty years he was foreign correspondent with Reuters and *The Times*, covering stories in more than sixty countries from bases in Europe, the Middle East, the Far East and Africa. This is his first book.

GAVIN BELL

In Search of Tusitala

TRAVELS IN THE PACIFIC AFTER
ROBERT LOUIS STEVENSON

PICADOR

First published 1994 by Picador

This edition published 1995 by Picador
an imprint of Macmillan General Books
25 Eccleston Place, London SW1W 9NF
and Basingstoke

Associated companies throughout the world

ISBN 0 330 34245 2

1 3 5 7 9 8 6 4 2

A CIP catalogue record for this book is available from
the British Library

Typeset by CentraCet Limited, Cambridge
Printed and bound in Great Britain by
Cox & Wyman Ltd, Reading, Berkshire

*This book is for
my mum and dad
without whom, of course,
it would never have
been written*

ACKNOWLEDGEMENTS

There are no laws that say people should be kind to strangers in their midst. Stevenson was aware of this, and observed: 'We are all travellers in the wilderness of this world, and the best that we find in our travels is an honest friend.'

In this respect, I was fortunate. Among many others, who will probably never have the opportunity to read this book, I am grateful to the following for their hospitality and friendship:

Captain Colin Mundy and the officers and crew of the MV *Wellington Star*, for a safe and enjoyable passage to the South Seas; in the Marquesas, Eliane and Jean Derrien, Jean-Claude and Joelle Thibeaux, Hiti and Catherine Teremihi, Philippe Trillaud the barefoot judge, and Yvonne Katupa and her son Maurice were rays of light in a gloomy landscape; in the Tuamotus, Daniel Snow the *Tusitala* of Fakarava, and Christian Petron, Cyril Isy-Schwart, and Yves Lefevre, the intrepid divers of Rangiroa, shared wonderful stories and adventures; in Tahiti, Roger Gowan and Michel Tevaarauhaka and their wives, Giles Artur and Dominique Maury at the Musée Gauguin, Colin Stenhouse, and Heidy Baumgartner helped me to discover traces of the island's evanescent charms.

In Hawaii, Roland Crisafi, the last white resident of Hookena, Bernard Schwind, Fe Carpenter, and Olivia Breitha in Kalaupapa, and Robert Van Dyke, Rasa Clark, and Elke Marsh in Honolulu provided a wealth of material and memorable experiences; in Kiribati, Teataake Bwebwetaake and his family and friends showed me a way of life I had only dreamed of, and Bill and Sandy Rowstron and Simon Diffey brought a welcome touch of home; in Samoa, Salesi Lelaulu and Helen Macdonald gave me food for thought and shelter for a weary body, and Rachel Dillon helped recapture the magic of Stevenson's *Treasure Island*.

My gratitude is also due to Gillon Aitken who set me off travelling hopefully, and Peter Straus who helped distil the best of my experiences on my return.

Finally I am indebted to Judy Meddis and Pete Kerr, old friends, who calmed the fevered brow of a despairing author with sympathy and encouragement when it was needed most.

LIST OF ILLUSTRATIONS

ITINERARIES

ROBERT LOUIS STEVENSON
On the yacht *Casco* (June 1888–January 1889)
and the schooner *Equator* (June–December 1889)

On the *Casco:* San Francisco – Marquesas (Nuku-Hiva – Hiva-Oa) – Tuamotus (Fakarava) – Tahiti – Hawaii (Oahu).

On local Hawaiian steamers: Oahu – Hawaii – Oahu – Molokai – Oahu.

On the *Equator:* Oahu – Gilbert Islands / Kiribati (Butaritari – Abemama) – Samoa (Upolu).

On local Samoan steamers: Upolu – Tutuila – Upolu.

GAVIN BELL
on ships and planes (July 1992–March 1993)

San Francisco – Tahiti – Marquesas (Hiva-Oa – Nuku-Hiva – Uapu – Hiva-Oa – Fatu-Hiva – Hiva-Oa) – Tahiti – Tuamotus (Fakarava – Rangiroa) – Tahiti – Hawaii (Oahu – Hawaii – Oahu – Molokai – Oahu) – Kiribati (Tarawa – Butaritari – Tarawa – Abemama – Tarawa) – Western and American Samoa (Upolu – Tutuila – Upolu).

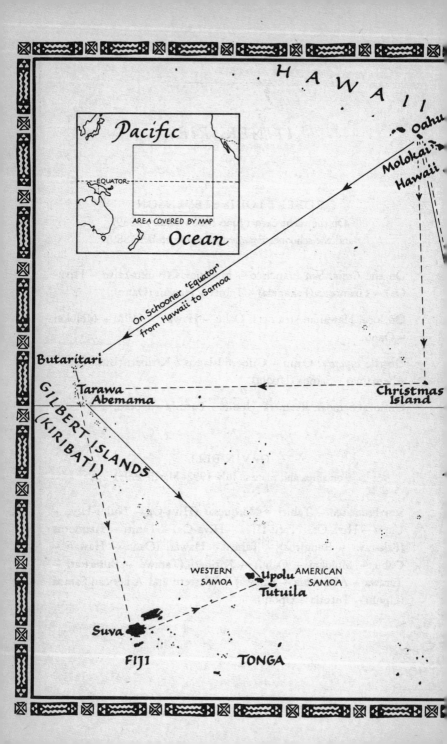

Pacific

EQUATOR

AREA COVERED BY MAP

Ocean

HAWAII

Oahu

Molokai

Hawaii

On Schooner 'Equator' from Hawaii to Samoa

Butaritari

Tarawa
Abemama

GILBERT ISLANDS
(KIRIBATI)

Christmas
Island

WESTERN
SAMOA

Upolu

AMERICAN
SAMOA

Tutuila

Suva

FIJI

TONGA

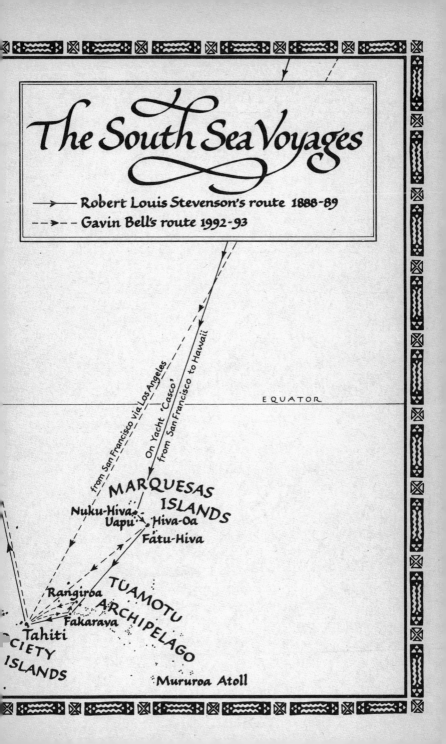

The South Sea Voyages

→——— Robert Louis Stevenson's route 1888-89

--->---- Gavin Bell's route 1992-93

EQUATOR

from San Francisco via Los Angeles

On Yacht 'Casco',
from San Francisco to Hawaii

MARQUESAS
ISLANDS

Nuku-Hiva
Uapu · Hiva-Oa

Fatu-Hiva

TUAMOTU

Rangiroa

ARCHIPELAGO

Fakarava

Tahiti

CIETY
ISLANDS

Mururoa Atoll

In Search
of Tusitala

'Stevenson was so vivid and attractive as a person, so picturesque in his travels and his ways of life, so copious and entrancing in his essays and his letters, so pleasing as a poet, that the general figure of him has somewhat overshadowed his stature as a novelist . . . [yet] next to Dumas, he is perhaps the best of all the romantic novelists . . .'

— *John Galsworthy*

'I think that Stevenson will remain in the history of literature not so much as a novelist, an essayist, a critic, but as a unique and ever delightful figure, a man who, whether he was writing romances, short stories, travel sketches, letters, or poems, illuminated every page with the curious magic of his personality and style.'

— *J. B. Priestley*

'This climate; these voyagings; these landfalls at dawn; new islands peaking from the morning bank; new forested harbours; new passing alarms of squalls and surf; new interests of gentle natives — the whole tale of my life is better to me than any poem.'

— *R. L. Stevenson*

'The coral waxes, the palm grows, but man departs.'

— *Tahitian proverb*

PROLOGUE

I admire and bow my head before the romance of destiny

IT IS DIFFICULT to imagine the tranquillity of a pine forest by moonlight when there are tracer bullets coming through your bathroom window.

I tried anyway. It had been a bad day in Beirut, and self-styled Rambos were still dismantling the city and its inhabitants in the name of various gods and freedom struggles as darkness fell. My duties as a Reuters correspondent were over for the day, and seeking respite from the madness I opened an old book I had bought on a recent trip to England. It was a collection of travel sketches by various authors, entitled *The Lore of the Wanderer*, and I began reading at random an account of a night spent in a pine forest in southern France.

This is what I read: 'I have not often enjoyed a more serene possession of myself, nor felt more independent of material aids . . . and yet even while I was exulting in my solitude I became aware of a strange lack. I wished a companion to lie near me in the starlight, silent and not moving, but ever within touch. For there is a fellowship more quiet even than solitude, and which, rightly understood, is solitude made perfect. And to live out of doors with the woman a man loves is of all lives the most complete and free.'

I considered these romantic sentiments in the light of my own situation. The noise of war reverberated around my apartment, a refrain of mindless savagery and suffering; and suddenly I was weary of it all. The stillness of that remote forest glade seemed curiously more real, and infinitely more appealing, than the mayhem outside my window.

The passage was an extract from *Travels with a Donkey in the Cevennes*, and it was my introduction as an adult to Robert Louis Stevenson. I knew little about the man, and the sensitivity of his prose pleased me; his musings struck a sympathetic chord in one who shared his love of nature, and his enthusiasm for wandering off the beaten track.

A year later, I lay beneath the stars on the slopes of Mont Lozere in the Cevennes, lulled by tiny rustlings in the pine forest around me. I had a bicycle, a sleeping bag, and the company of a young woman with whom I was fleetingly in love. We were pleasantly tired after a long day on country roads, and had dined simply but well at a wayside inn. A silent community of spirit between us dispelled the need for conversation, and I luxuriated in a rare sense of freedom and contentment. I mused on a line of poetry: 'What is this life, if full of care we have no time to stand and stare . . .' In the deepening shadows, my imagination fancied the lean figure of a man, dressed in the fashion of a century before, drawing on a pipe and writing his journal. He seemed to turn towards us, and with a smile nod his approval.

This first encounter with the spirit of Stevenson left a deep impression. After being transferred by Reuters to Paris, I was drawn repeatedly to his old haunt in the artists' village of Barbizon, in the forest of Fontainebleau. There I would wander for hours, alone with my thoughts and a volume of Stevenson's essays or letters, before repairing to a local *auberge* for lunch. Later I joined *The Times*, travelling over much of the Indian sub-continent, the Far East, and Africa with notebook and camera, recording the curious behaviour of humanity; but a colleague had given fate a nudge by finding a complete set of the *Tusitala* edition of Stevenson's works in a second-hand bookshop.

RLS thus became a familiar literary companion, and the more I read the more intrigued by the man I became. Sheltering from Russian mortar fire in an Afghan guerrilla base, I read the youthful essays of *Virginibus Puerisque* by candlelight; returning to Java after being scared out of my wits by an ill-tempered volcano near Sumatra, I found peace on *The Beach of Falesa*; tedious hours in the Angolan bush with UNITA guerrillas were enlivened by the adventures of *The Master of Ballantrae*.

I enjoyed swashbuckling romances like *St. Ives*, which reminded me of Dumas and his gallant musketeers, and understood the dark violence of the Celtic character finely drawn in other Scottish novels, but I was attracted above all by the personality of the author which came through in his essays, letters, and travel sketches.

Here was a man I could admire and for whom I felt a strong empathy. A fellow Scot, traveller, writer, and francophile, he was a romanticist whose spirit flew above Victorian conventions, Calvinism, and chronic illness; passionate and almost boyish in his enthusiasms, he had a lively sense of humour, and of the absurd, with the ability to laugh at himself. He was as down to earth as Burns and more stirring in his writing than Scott. Even at the height of his powers and fame, there was no pompous self-assurance; he took his craft more seriously than himself. Describing narrow escapes from shipwreck and bouts of crippling illness, he would lapse into broad Scots, the 'weel-kent' language of Burns, to make light of his perils. In short, here was a man I would have loved to spend a few hours with swapping reminiscences of good books and foreign lands.

The idea of following Stevenson's blithe spirit to the South Seas was little more than a vague notion until I met a Samoan chief in Namibia. Lelei Lelaulu introduced himself at a reception for United Nations personnel supervising the territory's transition to independence, and we quickly discovered a mutual interest in RLS. 'Well, Gavin, you may be interested to know that the land on which Stevenson built his home in Samoa originally belonged to my family, and that the present occupant is a relative of mine,' he said. 'When are you coming to visit us?'

I learned later that Stevenson's house had become the official residence of the head of state of Western Samoa. Amid the tinkling of glasses, I felt a gentle nudge in the small of my back, and construed it to be the finger of fate.

Two years passed before fate finally lost patience and propelled me on my way to Samoa in the form of a summons from the managing editor of *The Times*. After years of globe-trotting, I was to be recalled from Johannesburg to London and assigned to home news reporting. I looked around the suppressed bedlam of a newsroom close to edition time, and wondered whether I could be content with reporting a labour dispute in Sheffield or a by-election in Dorking. I thought it unlikely, and said so. An hour later, I left Mr Murdoch's bleak citadel in Wapping with the assurance of a satisfactory pay-off, and a jumble of emotions veering between anxiety and excitement. As I walked for the last time along the grimy highway leading to the city, with a stream of trucks thundering past me, I recalled a remark by Stevenson shortly before he sailed for the South Seas: 'I admire and bow my head before the romance of destiny.' I smiled and stepped out with a new sense of purpose, oblivious to the noise and bustle of the city around me. Within a few days, I was back in South Africa working my notice, and enquiring about shipping schedules in the Pacific.

Although nowhere in Scotland is far from the sea, there is no seafaring tradition in my family. As a child, my only nautical adventure almost ended in disaster when my father inadvertently steered a 'wee oarie boat' into the path of a steamer on the Firth of Clyde. The memory of his strained face as he paddled furiously to escape the huge vessel bearing down on us deterred me from venturing on the high seas for years to come.

Nor did far-away places with strange-sounding names figure large in my family's history. On my return from Beirut, my grandmother asked me where I had been.

'That's nice, Gavin, where's that?'

'In the Middle East, Grannie.'

'Aye, ye're just the same as yer uncle Jimmy. When he was a laddie he went away tae England.'

My gran's perception of a distant place was Glasgow, fourteen miles from her home in Lanarkshire.

Fortunately my father had a fine library, which suggested there were worlds worth exploring beyond the range of the tramcars which rattled through the cobbled streets of Glasgow to such exotic destinations as Auchenshuggle. By the time RLS enticed me to the South Seas with his tales of ruffians, wizards, and cannibals, he was summoning an inveterate wanderer.

I was aware of potential pitfalls. J. C. Furnas, complaining about a deluge of fanciful nonsense written about Oceania, once growled: 'More thousands of words of swill have been written per square mile of dry land about the islands than about any other geographical entity.' The *Pacific Islands Yearbook*, in debunking the perennial myth of a Polynesian Eden, offered sensible advice: 'Those of us who seek to understand the Pacific Islanders would be doing them and ourselves a service if we began by expunging the term "paradise" from our vocabularies.'

Having observed *coups d'état* and nuclear tests in the Pacific as a foreign correspondent, I did not expect to find any tropical paradise, and I was prepared to be deeply suspicious if I did. Life in the South Seas was precarious and frequently brutal in Stevenson's day, and from my limited experience the passage of the twentieth century did not seem to have improved matters much. There would be, as there were for RLS, sights and characters to delight and dismay.

The figure which beckoned me back to Polynesia was slight and lean in stature, and sallow in complexion, with large brown eyes shining with the unnatural luminosity of the consumptive, lank dark hair, and a restless temperament – by all accounts the only time he sat still was when he was writing – generally courteous and humorous, given to outbursts of anger, always curious and eager to learn. His conversation, like his demeanour, was animated and amusing, interspersed with French, broad Scots, and Samoan.

Enraptured by his first sight of the Marquesas, he wrote:

The first experience can never be repeated. The first love, the first sunrise, the first South Sea island are memories apart and touch a virginity of sense.

He was an incurable romantic, who found true happiness in weeding his garden on a high plateau 'beautiful beyond dreams' (Samoa), and moral beauty in a leper colony (Hawaii). Repeatedly drawing parallels with the highland clans of eighteenth-century Scotland, he was fascinated by the Pacific Islanders and their societies; he respected and admired them, and in return their kings and commoners became devoted to him. To the Samoans who knew him affectionately as *Tusitala* (writer of tales), he cut a dashing figure eloquently portrayed by his friend, W. E. Henley:

> The brown eyes radiant with vivacity –
> There shines a brilliant and romantic grace,
> A spirit intense and rare, with trace on trace
> Of passion, impudence, and energy.
> Valiant in velvet, light in ragged luck,
> Most vain, most generous, sternly critical,
> Buffoon and poet, lover and sensualist:
> A deal of Ariel, just a streak of Puck,
> Much Antony, of Hamlet most of all,
> And something of the Shorter-Catechist.

There was also a touch of Don Quixote in the gaunt figure who took up his pen in a crusade against incompetent colonial administrators in Samoa. Lloyd Osbourne, the stepson who shared Stevenson's life in the islands and who collaborated with him on several novels, summed up this side of his character thus:

'Intolerant of evil; almost absurdly chivalrous; passionately resentful of injustice; impulsive, headstrong, utterly scornful of conventions when they were at variance with what he considered right.'

Yet curiously, many of Stevenson's strongest opinions were not expressed in his books. He was, for example, like his contemporary Ibsen, a strong advocate of women's rights. Osbourne recalled: 'In those days of large families, the accepted right of men to breed their wives till they died filled him with loathing . . . the obligation for women to be attractive at any age and in any circumstances appeared to him also as not the least of their many disabilities.' It was the same with social reform: 'No socialist ever used the word "bourgeoisie" with more contempt than he. He thought that the lower classes and the higher could alike be fired by high ideals, but that the mass of the middle class was almost hopelessly antagonistic to human advancement. Its unreasoning self-satisfaction, its exploitation of the helpless, its hypocritical morality, its oppression of women, its intolerable attitude towards art and literature, were all to him a series of inexcusable offences.' Osbourne concluded: 'I imagine he thought there was no audience for such opinions. The Victorian era, superficially at least, appeared set in an unaltered mould; nothing seemed ever destined to change. It was as idle to rage as though one were buried in a dungeon . . . I doubt not that Stevenson turned to romance with an immense relief.'

The intensity of Stevenson's life and the quality of his work is all the more remarkable given that he was perpetually stalked by death. Generally assumed to be suffering from tuberculosis, for months at a time he was not permitted to wear a coat, lest the raising of his arms should bring on a haemorrhage. Osbourne provides a haunting portrait of these periodic bouts of illness: 'The truly dreadful part of his life was the uncertainty of its tenure; the imminence always of a sudden death. He would put a handkerchief to his lips, perceive a crimson stain, and then sooner or later there might be a haemorrhage of the lungs, with all its horror and suspense, and its subsequent and utterly dejecting aftermath of having to lie immovable for days and nights on end. The mental agony was beyond expression; one wonders how he ever bore up against it.'

ROBERT LEWIS BALFOUR STEVENSON emerged into the grey half-light of a Scottish winter in a small stone house on low ground to the north of the water of Leith in Edinburgh on the 13th of November, 1850. (The spelling, but not the pronunciation, of his second name was changed from the Scots form to the French when he was about eighteen, apparently because of strong distaste for an acquaintance of that name. In adult life, he was addressed by family and friends as Louis.) Two years later, an attack of laryngitis presaged a lifetime of illness.

The only child of a family of distinguished lighthouse engineers – his father Thomas perfected the revolving light and had the bright idea of using louvre-boarded screens to protect meteorological instruments – young Louis dutifully studied civil engineering at Edinburgh University. But he was more interested in creating and writing for magazines, invariably carrying two books in his pocket – one to read and the other to write in. There was much exciting contemporary literature to read, and to discuss with his friends. Flaubert was in print with *Madame Bovary*, Dickens was at the height of his powers with *A Tale of Two Cities* and *Great Expectations*, and Dostoevsky had recently completed *Crime and Punishment*. Stevenson's father eventually permitted him to follow literature as a career, provided he read law and was admitted to the Scottish Bar as an alternative. Louis duly passed his final examination, was called to the Bar, made one singularly incompetent appearance before the Court of Session, and set off for England and France to seek inspiration for his preferred craft of writing.

In the autumn of 1876, he vaulted through the open window of an inn at Grez near Paris with a dusty knapsack on his back, to the amusement of his friends and the consternation of a dark-haired American woman sitting quietly in a corner. This was Fanny Van de Grift Osbourne, who had come to Europe to escape from an unhappy marriage, to further the education of her son and daughter, and to paint. Unsmiling Victorian photographs do not flatter her, portraying a thick-set woman of dark complexion, vaguely masculine with her hair cut short, and altogether severe in appearance. However, Stevenson fell in love with her and followed her three years later to California, where they were married in the summer of 1880.

The couple returned to Europe, and *Treasure Island* appeared in 1883, followed by *The Strange Case of Dr Jekyll and Mr Hyde* and *Kidnapped* three years later. Stevenson's best-known book began with the drawing of a map, with a pen and a shilling box of water-colours, to amuse Fanny's twelve-year-old son Lloyd on a rainy September morning in a cottage near Braemar in Aberdeenshire. To the youngster's delight, Stevenson added features such as Spy-Glass Hill and three red crosses denoting the site of buried treasure, and assured him it was a lair of pirates. 'Oh, for a story about it,' the boy said. Stevenson pocketed the map and strolled thoughtfully away; on the next day Lloyd was summoned to his stepfather's bedroom to hear the first chapter of a story called 'The Sea Cook', which became *Treasure Island*.

The allegorical tale of Jekyll and Hyde came to Stevenson in a dream. One night Fanny was wakened by cries from her husband, and believing he was having a nightmare, she wakened him. 'Why did you wake me? I was dreaming a fine bogey tale,' he said. In a fever of excitement, he wrote the first draft in three days. When Fanny criticized the work, he burned the entire draft, and completed a second in three days more. The finished version was ready for his publishers within six weeks.

Stevenson was thus a celebrated author when he retired to a

sanatorium at Saranac Lake near the Canadian border in 1887 in an attempt to improve his failing health. A favourite family diversion during the winter nights was planning a yachting cruise, to be financed by a legacy that Stevenson had received from his father's estate six months before. 'If this business fails to set me up,' he wrote to a friend, 'well, £2,000 is gone and I know I can't get better.' In the spring Fanny found and chartered a vessel from an eccentric Californian millionaire, and on the 28th of June the Stevenson household sailed from San Francisco into a primitive world known to few Europeans, many of whom had been consigned to the cooking pot as the dish of the day.

In an account of his voyages, *In the South Seas*, Stevenson penned a self-fulfilling prophecy:

Few men who come to the islands leave them; they grow grey where they alighted; the palm shades and the trade wind fans them till they die, perhaps cherishing to the last the fancy of a visit home, which is rarely made, more rarely enjoyed, and yet more rarely repeated.

Stevenson had every intention of returning to Europe, and frequently made plans for doing so, but he fell under the spell of the islands and eventually settled in what is now Western Samoa. He never saw his native land again. Three years later he died of a cerebral haemorrhage, at the age of forty-four, and was buried near the summit of a hill overlooking his island home.

THIS BRIEF SKETCH of Stevenson is intended to serve only as an introduction to my quest for traces of his passage among the more remote communities of French Polynesia, Hawaii, Kiribati, and Samoa. Scholars of RLS may find little in my book to add to their store of knowledge, but that is not my intention; I happily leave biographies and other retrospective works on the centenary of his death to academics. My goal was rather to focus on the most eventful episode of Stevenson's life, by retracing his two principal voyages among exotic islands where he led his family into a *Boy's Own* adventure story as daring and thrilling as any of his novels. At the same time I hoped to convey something of the magic of his personality. It was a literary odyssey to find *Treasure Island*, and the spirit of its creator.

ONE

To travel hopefully is a better thing than to arrive

QUEEN ELIZABETH STREET on the Bermondsey side of Tower Bridge in central London is an unlikely place to begin an odyssey. It is a drab commercial area of decaying buildings and empty warehouses, but among them I found what I was looking for: a smart red-brick façade which stood out among its neighbours with the air of a gentleman surrounded by ruffians. A large red flag with a blue star on a white circle was flying above the main entrance, suggestive of the consulate of some obscure banana republic. It was the head offices of the Blue Star Shipping Line.

After numerous faxes to agents in London, New York, and Papeete, I had come here to buy a ticket for voyage number 1,379 of the *California Star*, a container ship due to leave San Francisco in a few weeks and to arrive in Tahiti 'on or about' the 29th of July – by a happy coincidence, my birthday. In seeking to emulate as closely as possible Stevenson's two principal voyages in the Pacific, I had hoped to sail directly from San Francisco to the Marquesas, his first landfall; but these islands were evidently so remote and little frequented that they were served only by local freighters and light aircraft from Tahiti. Thus it was to the evanescent paradise of Bougainville and Cook that I was initially bound.

In an upstairs office of the Blue Star building, a helpful young woman issued me with a ticket, luggage tags, brochures depicting unexpectedly luxurious accommodation, and a warning: 'The schedules are subject to change. Do keep in touch with us before you leave, won't you?' I promised I would, and walked down the staircase, admiring framed photographs of Blue Star vessels at sea. At the reception desk, I heard a Scottish captain chatting to a secretary: 'Aye, there's been some funny weather about the doldrums right enough.' My heart beat a little faster, and I recalled a remark by Stevenson:

I will never leave the sea, I think; it is only there that a Briton lives . . . life is far better fun than people dream who fall asleep among the chimney stacks and telegraph wires.

Riding a grubby commuter train from London Bridge to Waterloo, in my mind's eye I was already standing on the heaving deck of a cargo ship, an old sea dog watching some funny weather developing in the vastness of the Pacific. It seemed too good to be true. It was.

Two weeks later, the Blue Star lady called me in Glasgow to tell me the *California Star* had changed her route, and would be calling at Fiji rather than Tahiti; was this a problem? It certainly was, being nowhere remotely near where I wished to go, and I asked whether she knew of any other shipping company which could help me. She called back with the depressing news that she could find no accommodation on any vessel on my route for months. Having already purchased my flight ticket to San Francisco, I decided to set off as planned, and try to make alternative arrangements when I got there. I drew comfort from one of Stevenson's maxims: 'To travel hopefully is a better thing than to arrive.'

Before leaving Scotland, I spent a day in Edinburgh searching for vestiges of Stevenson's early life. My quest was not particularly fruitful. A brass plaque outside an imposing Georgian residence at 17 Heriot Row, where Stevenson spent his childhood, declared firmly: 'This is a private house. Not a museum.' A cardboard sign tied loosely to park railings opposite the house suggested a literary museum in the Lawnmarket might be more rewarding. Lady Stair's House is a pretentious seventeenth-century miniature château, replete with turrets, beneath the ramparts of Edinburgh Castle, in which mementoes of Scotland's most illustrious men of letters are displayed. As museums go, it is fairly unimpressive, with a prim *Upstairs, Downstairs* approach: while Burns and Scott are accorded commodious apartments, RLS is confined to two small rooms in the basement.

I had fondly imagined being ushered into the quiet sanctum of an RLS society, and browsing through rare editions of Stevenson's works in a book-lined study. Instead, I found myself peering at an extract of a birth certificate, old photographs, and a sparse collection of oddments in glass cases such as a pipe, a fishing rod, and riding boots. Where was the 'spirit intense and rare' of Henley's poem? This was all dead stuff, with no attempt to breathe life into them, so I went back upstairs where I spotted an old poster advertising an RLS exhibition more than a decade before. I asked an attendant whether I might buy one.

'Ah havenae sold wan o' these posters for years. Naebody's interested.'

'Well, I am, how much are they?'

'Ah dinna ken, is a pound a'richt?'

Before leaving, I asked whether there was an RLS club or society. He rummaged for an old notebook and found a contact number for a law firm handwritten in pencil. I decided to give this august society a miss, and headed back to Glasgow to pack my bags.

SCOTS ACCUSTOMED TO dreary weather are fond of joking that they consider themselves lucky if summer falls on a weekend. I evidently picked the wrong weekend in June to begin my travels. Rain was sweeping across the tarmac at Glasgow airport as I boarded an American Airlines flight to Chicago, with a connection to San Francisco; actually the aircraft was a silver time capsule. Hurtling in pursuit of the sun, with no sense of changing time or space, I was to be deposited in a strange place almost four thousand miles away while my watch would insist that only two hours had elapsed.

TWO

San Francisco is a city beleaguered with alarms

IT IS SAID THAT if you get tired of walking around San Francisco, you can always lean against it. This is almost literally true. The whimsical jumble of Victoriana, mock-Romanesque, and Spielberg sci-fi meanders over forty hills, clinging improbably to inclines worthy of black runs in an Alpine ski resort. In this roller-coaster city there are streets where ranks of vehicles parked facing the sidewalk appear to defy gravity. One has the suspicion that a push on the car at the top would send the lot cascading to the bottom with a satisfying crunching sound. I don't actually like cars very much. They are like people. Individually, a well-made car can be pleasing; in great numbers they are a disaster.

The air of permanence suggested by soaring towers, neo-Gothic castles, and ornate cathedrals that look as if they have been transplanted from Bolivia is of course illusory. For San Francisco is flirting, in its inimitable friendly, funky way, with disaster.

Stevenson spotted the incongruity when he first arrived in the city in 1879 to be reunited with Fanny and to marry her.

The sandy peninsula . . . shaken to the heart by frequent earthquakes, seems in itself no very durable foundation. San Francisco is a city beleaguered with alarms . . . earthquakes are not only common, they are sometimes threatening in their violence; the fear of them grows yearly on a resident; he begins with indifference, ends in sheer panic; and no one feels safe in any but a wooden house.

Nowhere else in the world, he added, was the art of the fireman carried to so nice a point.

On the morning after my arrival, I flicked through the *San Francisco Examiner* to check on whether my hotel was likely to disappear into an abyss. In its regular 'Earthquake Watch' column, it reported that Los Angeles had moved half an inch to the north-west as a result of an earthquake measuring 7.5 on the Richter scale in the Mojave Desert. (Palm Springs, closer to the epicentre, shifted four inches.) The best story was about a plan to store seventy-seven thousand tonnes of radioactive waste in the bedrock of a mountain at a nuclear weapons test site. The Department of Energy assured the public that the area was relatively free of seismic activity, and there had been no major tremors there for ten thousand years. A few days later, a quake measuring 5.6 shook the mountain and blew out the windows of the Department of Energy building six miles away.

The odds in favour of the 'Big One' hitting within twenty years, and dispatching fifteen thousand people to their maker (according to the scientific pundits), had no effect that I could see on the kaleidoscope of humanity in the streets of San Francisco; but the firemen were busy, and provided arguably the most splendid sight in the city. I was pleased to see the *pompiers* admired by Stevenson had reached the zenith of their art, hurtling through the streets on wonderful red and chrome machines in a cacophony of wailing sirens and blaring horns. I never actually saw any burning buildings, so maybe they were just rehearsing; a glorious vision of the holocaust without the heaving earth.

By a lucky coincidence, I found my hotel was located in the downtown area around the corner from 608 Bush Street, where Stevenson had rented the cheapest accommodation he could find while waiting for Fanny across the Bay in Oakland to secure a divorce. It was not a happy time for the little-known young author. Lonely, ill, and poor, he scratched away at 'Prince Otto', a short story, *The Amateur Emigrant*, an account of his journey to California, and some essays, notably one on Thoreau. His finances permitted only one square meal a day, leading to malnutrition exacerbating his lung disorder. The man was simply wasting away. On Boxing Day he wrote to Sidney Colvin, his closest friend, then a Professor of Fine Art at Cambridge University.

For four days I have spoken to no one but my landlady or landlord or to restaurant waiters. This is not a gay way to pass Christmas, is it? and I must own the guts are a little knocked out of me.

By April his condition had deteriorated, as he related in a letter to another friend.

For about six weeks I have been in utter doubt; it was a toss-up for life or death all that time; but I won the toss, sir, and Hades went off once more discomfited. This is not the first time, nor will it be the last, that I have a friendly game with that gentleman.

It was in his workman's lodging in Bush Street, destroyed by the great earthquake and fire of 1906, that Stevenson first sketched out his requiem: 'Home is the sailor, home from the sea, and the hunter home from the hill.' Writing to Colvin, he said:

I may perhaps try to write it better some day; but that is what I want in sense. The verses are from a beayootiful {sic} poem by me.

The scene of these morbid preoccupations had become the San Miguel men's haircutting salon. By the adjacent entrance of a seven-storey apartment building, a plaque with gold lettering commemorated Stevenson's brief sojourn. A lady leaving the building told me: 'Yeah, I know the guy. We used to have a picture of him in our lobby, but somebody stole it.'

In the salon, I settled into the creaky comfort of an old-fashioned barber's chair and asked Robert San Miguel, a thick-set native of Los Angeles, whether he knew anything of Stevenson. 'Sure, wanna hear a ghost story? I got a letter for him a few years back. From Ronald Reagan.' Now I was aware of Mr Reagan's difficulties in orientating himself on the planet, but this seemed to be pushing the caricature a bit. The barber insisted: 'Seriously, it was from the White House, addressed to Robert Louis Stevenson, 608 Bush Street, thanking him for sending a birthday card to the President. Somebody had a sense of humour, huh? Ya think it was Stevenson?' I agreed it was a prank worthy of Stevenson, and was buoyed by the thought that at least there was a kindred spirit in the city.

I searched in vain for Donadieu's restaurant in Bush Street, where Stevenson carefully measured out half a bottle of wine with his lunch to keep within his budget of fifty cents for the meal. The site had become a vacant lot, between an art gallery and an empty office building, ignored by tourists flooding into Chinatown around the corner in a jostle of loud T-shirts and video cameras. A large woman with a Midwestern drawl was filming her husband, and speaking into the microphone: 'Well, here we are in Chinatown, just walking around. We're on a walking tour . . .' I had no more luck in finding the erstwhile home of the Reverend William A. Scott at 521 Post Street, where Stevenson in his thirtieth year married Fanny, some twelve years his senior, on the 19th of May, 1880. Nothing stands between number 501, which is an expensive restaurant, and number 545, which is a luxury hotel. The good Reverend Doctor Scott's house disappeared, along with twenty-eight thousand other assorted buildings, in the 1906 earthquake.

Opinions about the marriage vary: some of Stevenson's associates were dismayed by his liaison with what they considered a wilful and devious woman determined to control his life and work, but Colvin considered her a staunch companion, a shrewd critic of Stevenson's work, and an efficient nurse. Stevenson himself seemed to have no reservations. Two years before his death, he wrote:

As I look back, I think my marriage was the best move I ever made in my life. Not only would I do it again; I cannot conceive the idea of doing otherwise.

Whatever her personality, she was no classic beauty. In a

letter to J. M. Barrie from Samoa, Stevenson drew a fond but hardly flattering portrait of his wife.

She runs the show. Infinitely little, extraordinary wig of grey curls, handsome waxen face like Napoleon's, insane black eyes, boy's hands, tiny bare feet, a cigarette, wild blue native dress, usually spotted with garden mould . . . is always either loathed or slavishly adored — indifference impossible.

SOMERSET MAUGHAM found San Francisco to be the most civilized city in America, full of delightful people; Kipling said it was a mad place, inhabited for the most part by insane people whose women had remarkable beauty: the truth lies somewhere between the two. By and large it is a relaxed, tolerant society, liberal and loopy, with room for people of all races, creeds and eccentricities. The large (and influential) gay community gives it an amusing and vaguely theatrical air. Even the panhandlers, begging for pennies with paper cups, are generally colourful and courteous; one senses these are serious kings of the road, with the dust of a thousand weary miles on their sneakers and cowboy boots. The wooden clapboard houses with ubiquitous bay windows look warm and inviting; they make you want to live there.

I did not leave my heart in San Francisco, I left it firmly where it belongs in Scotland; but I found it to be by far the most charming of American cities. Listen to this: while I was there, California was suffering from its worst economic crisis since the Great Depression; the *New York Times* reported that the state was reeling from earthquakes, drought, fires, floods, recession, cutbacks in military spending, and race riots. Yet a bus company near San Francisco spent $1,300 to have its administration building diagnosed by an expert in feng shui, the Buddhist practice of arranging surroundings to promote harmony and prosperity. To deal with flickering lights and a water leak, he recommended rearranging the furniture, painting a grey fence green, and mounting banners on top of the building to draw up the vital energy of nature.

In one of the yuppie singles bars in Pacific Heights, where mating games are played out to a cacophony of rock music and giant television screens, there is a sign with 'rules for beginners' which sums up the ethos of the bar, and perhaps the city. It says: '1. Talk – don't touch. 2. Ask – don't insist. 3. Leave the four-letter words in the street. 4. If you don't get good vibes, move on.' I stayed for a while.

One evening a large man came into the Edinburgh Castle, a cavernous tavern on Geary Street offering British beers, fish and chips, and mediocre bagpiping by a spindly caricature of Harry Lauder. The man was wearing a multi-coloured kaftan, an impressive beard, and a headband around shoulder-length hair, from which protruded a small stick with gold-coloured streamers. Nobody, except me, paid him the least attention. He walked purposefully up to the bar, ordered a McEwan's Export, and downed it slowly in one; he replaced the glass on the counter, gazed at it reflectively for a moment, and turned to me and said in a rich baritone: 'Life is like that.' I nodded sympathetically, for want of anything intelligent to say, and he turned away and strode out. I felt like applauding.

Meanwhile I was working my way through almost a hundred steamship companies and agencies listed in the San Francisco Yellow Pages directory. Since my destination was French Polynesia, I began with a long shot by calling the French trade commission. I was told snootily by an American woman in bad French: 'Try a shipping company. We don't have that kind of information here.' Jens Jensen of the Polynesia Line was more helpful, saying he might be able to arrange passage for me on a ship leaving in a month's time; but I was impatient to leave, so I called a few yacht clubs in the hope of finding an eccentric millionaire as Fanny had done.

'Not this time of year,' a voice at the San Francisco Yacht Club said. 'Getting close to the typhoon season. They've all gone, or they're heading back.' I even tried the Longshoreman's Union, where I was told: 'It's not so easy to travel like that any more. It's kinda gloomy.' Eventually I found myself hitched to Blue Star again. Passenger accommodation on all their vessels was fully booked until the end of the year, but the captain of the *Wellington Star*, due to sail for Papeete in two weeks, came to the rescue by offering me his purser's cabin. Accordingly I was issued with another ticket, more luggage tags, four pens, a pack of playing cards, and a baseball cap all bearing the Blue Star logo – and the familiar warning to check for changes in schedule.

I drove down the peninsula to visit old friends in San Jose, an English journalist and his wife with whom I had shared a previous life in Florida as a young reporter on the *National Enquirer*. Paul and Jenny Bannister are kind people who live in a nice suburban house with all the home comforts I had left behind. I was already beginning to experience the loneliness of the long-distance writer, and it was good to be enveloped by the cosiness of their hospitality and familiar British accents.

Attracted by names on my map, I returned to San Francisco the next day by heading towards Santa Cruz and then turning north up Bear Creek Road, past Mustang Mesa, and down into Ben Lomond (pop. 3,050). It was a delightful drive along a high forest road, with spectacular vistas of mountains clad in Douglas fir, oak, and hazel rolling down to the Pacific. By a stream in Ben Lomond I found a fanciful miniature castle, with turrets and ramparts, which owed more to Disney than *Macbeth*: I half expected to see Donald Duck emerging with a blood-stained dagger.

Sitting outside a coffee shop near by, I was joined by an interesting character. A lean young Dutchman with one tooth, a straggly beard, ill-kempt long hair topped by a baseball cap worn backwards, and wearing a dirty yellow T-shirt, jeans, and sandals, introduced himself in a laconic manner. He earned a living by making Indian peace pipes and sculpting figures from soapstone for tourists. He told me about a peace festival in Oregon when five thousand people had hiked four miles to a camp high in the mountains to spend a few days listening to music and smoking dope: 'No hard drugs, no liquor, no trouble, no cops. Best thing was, spring comes at different times at different altitudes. Saw spring over and over again as we climbed. Real trippy.'

He paused reflectively. 'Ya been to the Big Basin? Ya otta go, man. Big trees. Real big trees.' With this advice, he sloped off with a one-tooth grin. I like big trees more than big cities, so the next day I left San Francisco again and cruised along the aptly named Skyline Boulevard through the Cruz Mountains to the Big Basin Redwoods State Park.

Rambling through woods has always been one of my favourite pastimes. I know of nothing mankind has created which compares with the vibrant natural beauty of trees and flowers; but nothing had prepared me for the giant redwoods of California. It was like someone who likes mountain streams discovering Victoria Falls. These sylvan columns soaring more than three hundred feet into the sky are stupendous; one walks among them in silence, awed by their size and the stillness which they instil at human level on the forest floor. Even the fauna flitting through the undergrowth seem hushed by an aura that is almost spiritual. American Indians revered the redwoods, and avoided settling among them; it would have been like living in a cathedral. I understood that. I wish I had known a few of those Indians.

By the park headquarters there is a raised cross-section of a redwood which was more than two thousand years old when it was felled in 1934. It is three yards in diameter. Somebody had

had the ingenious idea of fixing small brass plates on the wood, commemorating events in human history and thus measuring our presence in terms of the tree's growth. The birth of Christ is near the centre, with the signing of the Magna Carta in 1215 a couple of feet outwards. Drake's landing in California in 1579 is three inches from the edge, and the declaration of American independence almost two centuries later is one and a half inches from the edge. The mathematics may have been suspect, but one could not ignore the perspective, and I left the park with a sense of humility.

Driving thoughtfully back towards San Francisco, my reverie was broken by the horn of a white Cadillac blaring its impatience to overtake me on the narrow mountain road. As I pulled into the side, I reflected that the driver's life-span would be measured by a redwood at less than two inches. I considered that about right.

THERE WERE TWO other places I wanted to visit before leaving California – a museum devoted to Stevenson in the wine-growing Napa Valley, seventy miles north of San Francisco, and a mountain beyond where he and Fanny spent their honeymoon in the bunkhouse of an abandoned silver mine. The Silverado Museum, in a large white cottage by the public library at St Helena, puts the basement in Lady Stair's House to shame. It is a lively exhibition of more than eight thousand items which changes with varying displays; during my visit the central theme was *Jekyll and Hyde*, with pictures of Spencer Tracy and John Barrymore playing the leading roles in an early Hollywood version.

The original nameboards of the two vessels in which Stevenson made the voyages I was about to retrace were there; the lead soldiers with which he played with his stepson, the desk at which he worked, and more than a hundred books from his library in Samoa were all exhibited in a homely and informative manner.

I was also drawn to an oil painting of a street scene at the artists' colony of Grez-sur-Loing. It was painted by Fanny in 1876, the year she met Stevenson in the village, and it served a useful purpose three years later. Not having $100 to pay for the divorce from her American husband, she presented her lawyer with the painting instead. To the untrained eye, it is remarkably good.

This treasure trove of RLS memorabilia is cherished and presided over by elderly ladies enthused by the 'spirit intense and rare' so lamentably lacking in the Edinburgh collection. It was founded by Norman H. Strouse, an American bibliophile, who had been enchanted by *The Silverado Squatters*, Stevenson's account of his honeymoon: by the time Strouse retired as a company chairman, he had accumulated a large private collection of Stevensonia which formed the nucleus of the museum when it opened in 1969.

I tried to have a chat with Ellen Shaffer, the curator, but it proved difficult. We were repeatedly interrupted by telephone calls from researchers, writers, and others enquiring about Stevenson's life and work. Ms Shaffer showed an impressive depth of knowledge in her replies to even the most esoteric queries about relationships in the author's family. I tried to imagine the poster-seller in Edinburgh explaining the marital problems of Stevenson's stepdaughter, but I gave up.

After buying a few postcards, I drove on up through the vineyards of the narrowing valley towards Mount St Helena, which dominates the landscape with a bulky profile not unlike Ben Nevis (like Stevenson, I confess that during my travels I was often struck by features reminiscent of Scotland). The Robert Louis Stevenson State Park, historical monument no. 510, is reached from the summit of Highway 29 which snakes over the shoulder of the 4,343-foot mountain. Warned by signposts of western black-legged ticks, which carry a nasty infectious disease, I dutifully tucked my trousers into my socks and began hiking up a narrow, winding trail through a dense forest of pine, fir, and oak.

After about a mile, I reached a small clearing dominated by a rocky bluff, with a steep scree leading up to a fissure in the rock-face, the entrance to the old Silverado mine. Views of the valley were obscured by the trees, and the spot had a forlorn and gloomy air. This would not be the first time I would wonder at Stevenson's resolve to wander far off the beaten track, ignoring the stalking shadow of illness, in his quest for peace of mind and inspiration. At least he found the latter here: Mount St Helena is said to have served later as the model for Spy-Glass Hill of *Treasure Island*.

A small monument in the shape of an open book marks the site of the cabin where Stevenson and Fanny, accompanied by her twelve-year-old son, piled hay for bedding and set about clearing the area of poison oak and rattlesnakes. At last Stevenson was with the 'companion to lie near me in the starlight' he had yearned for in the Cevennes, although Fanny and her son rather spoiled the idyll by sickening with diphtheria. I browsed around the clearing for a while, but Stevenson's spirit was long gone, and I picked up no sense of his having been there. Vaguely disconsolate, I walked back down the trail as rain began to whisper through the silent trees, and headed back to San Francisco.

By the time Stevenson returned to California eight years later to embark for the South Seas, his reputation as a novelist was well established. In the San Francisco library, I found on a roll of microfilm a brief report of his departure in the *Daily Examiner* of Thursday, the 28th of June, 1888: 'The yacht *Casco*, bearing the Robert Louis Stevenson party, sailed out this morning with the tide. The voyage will last until next January. A large number of friends went down to section 1 of the seawall yesterday afternoon to bid the popular novelist and his wife goodbye.'

THREE

It is singular to come so far and to see so infinitely little

BY ALL ACCOUNTS the *Casco* was a handsome vessel. A 74-ton fore-and-aft schooner with lofty masts, white sails and decks, and glittering brasswork, she sat like a bird on the water. Her saloon was fitted luxuriously with silk and velvet in gaudy colours, but she had been built for cruising in Californian waters, her one pump was inadequate and almost useless, and she was unfitted for hurricane weather.

There was of course no radar or communications with meteorological stations to warn of tropical storms, no satellite navigation system to fix her position on the globe, no radio for transmitting a distress signal: she depended entirely on sextant, compass, unreliable charts, and the weather-eye of her captain. Negotiating the treacherous shoals of the Tuamotu archipelago in the *Casco* with the charts of the day would have been like an astronaut threading his way through an asteroid belt with a map of the London Underground.

Stevenson was not enamoured by this precarious life at sea at first. From Tahiti, he wrote to Colvin:

The sea is a terrible place, stupefying to the mind and poisonous to the temper, the sea, the motion, the lack of space, the cruel publicity, the villainous tinned foods . . . but you are amply repaid when you sight an island, and drop anchor in a new world.

By the time the *Casco* reached Hawaii four months later, however, the tone of his letters to Colvin had changed.

I cannot say why I like the sea; no man is more cynically and constantly alive to its perils; I regard it as the highest form of gambling; and yet I love the sea as much as I hate gambling. Fine, clean emotions;

*a world all and always beautiful; air better than wine; interest
unflagging; there is upon the whole no better life.*

Fanny turned a brave face towards the perils of the deep, but
she did not share her husband's enthusiasm, as she confided in a
letter to a friend.

'I hate the sea, and am afraid of it – though no one will
believe that because in time of danger I do not make an outcry –
nevertheless I am afraid of it, and it is not kind to me.'

My thoughts of the *Casco* and her adventurous passengers were
interrupted by the strident bell of a mobile crane on the dock,
signalling the imminent departure of the *Wellington Star*. Passing
north-west of Santa Catalina island, we set a south-westerly
course of 212° for the next two and a half thousand miles at a
steady eighteen knots.

The Pacific Ocean is the greatest single geographical entity on
earth, extending over almost a third of the planet's surface; it is
one-fifth larger than all the land area put together. It is thus a
very big place, and it can be very scary. In response to my
questions about navigation and the sea, Richard Lough, the first
mate, gave me a copy of *The Mariner's Handbook*, a hefty tome
full of information about gigantic rogue waves, underwater
volcanoes, and various other unseen hazards. For a landlubber on
his first ocean voyage, it is the equivalent of reading a ghost
story in a haunted castle.

Standing on the bridge with Richard, I looked out across
these problematic waters and was reassured to see that for once
the Pacific was living up to its name. All around, as far as the
eye could see, the world was entirely flat and devoid of life. Not
a fish, not a bird, not a sign of mankind beyond our lonely ship
disturbed that vast panoply of sea and sky.

As the *Casco* laboured through calms and squalls on her
passage to Polynesia, Stevenson recorded in his diary:

*In impudent isolation, the toy schooner has ploughed her path of snow
across the empty deep, far from all track of commerce, far from any hand*

of help . . . now to the sound of slatting sails and stamping sheet-blocks, staggering in the turmoil of that business falsely called a calm, now, in the assault of squalls, burying her lee-rail in the sea . . . flying fish, a skimming silver rain upon the blue sea; a turtle fast asleep in the early morning sunshine; the Southern Cross hung athwart in the fore-rigging like the frame of a wrecked kite – the Pole Star and the familiar Plough dropping ever lower in the wake: these build up thus far the history of our voyage. It is singular to come so far and to see so infinitely little.

'And what you see now,' Richard said, interrupting my thoughts, 'is what you'll see for the next eight days, which is f— all.' His words were barely out when my attention was drawn to what appeared to be a water-spout off the port bow. An instant later, an enormous black shape exploded entirely out of the water, span lazily in the air, the sun flashing on a white belly, and plunged back into the sea in a tumult of foam and the lingering image of a huge tail. 'Apart from the odd sperm whale, of course,' Richard added.

Our new friend cavorted around us for about twenty minutes in a spectacular display of maritime gymnastics, before bidding us farewell with a somersault and double twist I adjudged to be worth 9.9 (his tail spoiled a clean entry). I would like to say something here about our habit of slaughtering these creatures. It seems we have been hunting them to the verge of extinction for seven centuries to produce such indispensable consumer goods as corset stays, umbrellas, and buggy whips. (Whaling was first established in the Bay of Biscay, conferring on the Biscayan variety of Right whale the dubious distinction of becoming the first species to be exterminated.) Yet there are no products derived from the carcasses of these inoffensive creatures that cannot be duplicated, or improved upon easily and inexpensively, from synthetics and other sources. It seems insane. In the history of this pointless butchery there have been a few satisfying victories for the whales, however.

The *Société des Oceanistes* records that on the 20th of November 1819, the British whaler *Essex* sighted a pod of whales in the Pacific and sent her boats out among them. An eighty-five foot monster, correctly identifying the *Essex* as the principal antagonist, charged her at full speed and struck her with the impact of a cruise missile. After recuperating from the stunning blow, the whale charged again and completely stove in the ship's bows. There was barely time to save some navigating instruments and a little bread and water before the hull settled down One of three boats carrying the whalemen was never seen again; the others were sailed over three thousand miles by their starving crews who ultimately resorted to cannibalism before the survivors were rescued. I think the final score was something like Moby-Dick 12, Essex 0.

DAYS PASSED IN A HAZE of idle contemplation and wonder at new visions of the planet I call home as the *Wellington Star* ploughed her lonely furrow towards empty horizons. I calculated we were traversing the Pacific twenty-seven times slower than I had flown across the Atlantic, and considered this sedate progress far more agreeable. I had no fixed routine: when the skies darkened I would retire to the lounge with a book – apart from Stevenson's letters I was reading Joshua Slocum's *Sailing Alone Around the World*; when the weather was fair I lay on the 'monkey deck' above the bridge, a nest of brilliant white metal plating, with only passing clouds and navigation instruments for company. There were none of the cramped conditions of a small craft, and none of the enforced gaiety of a cruise ship: I had solitude such as I had rarely known when I wished it, and companionship when I preferred. We skirted hurricanes, and steamed through calms and squalls with equal nonchalance, and my affection for this fine old ship grew daily.

One of my favourite pastimes was standing in the darkened

wheel-house at night with the officer on watch, admiring the ghostly luminescence of moonlight on restless seas, and examining charts of the islands I was bound for. I liked Sam's company best. A policeman in north Yorkshire for twelve years, Sam had been invalided out of the force after being battered to within an inch of his life by three burglars. He had then returned to his first love, the sea. He was a calm, soft-spoken man. One sensed that if a sea monster reared up over the bows of the ship, he would tell it politely but firmly to move along now, like a good chap. The hours I spent with Sam talking about books, navigation, the sea, and life in general are among the fondest memories of my Pacific travels.

Our first sight of land after ten days at sea was a dark smudge on the horizon off the starboard bow. As we passed it at a distance of seven miles, I discerned through binoculars a low-lying group of thickly wooded islets. This was Tetiaroa, twenty-five miles north of Tahiti. In the heyday of the Pomare family, the last monarchs of Tahiti, it served as a pleasure resort and as a pre-nuptial retreat for young women of chiefly families, who went there for fattening and to live in the shade of enormous *tuu* trees so their skins would become fair. The only early European explorer known to have visited the atoll was Captain Bligh, in his vengeful quest for mutineers from the *Bounty* in January 1789. In 1904 the Pomare family gave the atoll to a Canadian dentist in recompense for his dental services, and his stepdaughter subsequently sold it to Marlon Brando. I considered visiting it, although Stevenson had never gone there, but on learning the actor had built a tourist resort amid the *tuu* trees, I decided to give it a miss.

Meanwhile a small fishing boat, the first sign of life, had bobbed into view, and the radio began crackling in French. A rusty old coaster rolled by, bound for the outer islands; a fresh breeze scented with earth and flowers sprang up, and it seemed as if the waves were doffing their white caps in greeting. Then the great mass of Tahiti rose out of the sea, its volcanic peaks hidden in clouds, offering a grand panorama of hazy green land sloping up to jagged peaks that looked like a crude medieval crown. Captain Samuel Wallis of HMS *Dolphin* was the first European to discover this splendid vista, in 1767: with haughty disregard for a Polynesian society which had been living there for more than a thousand years, and quite reasonably assumed it belonged to them, he took possession of it in the name of King George III. Louis Antoine de Bougainville, the French navigator, came along a year later and was moved by the beauty of the island and its people to name it La Nouvelle Cythère, after the birthplace of the Greek goddess of love.

Our first emissary from this mythical paradise was a young Frenchman with a two-way radio, who scrambled up a rope ladder from a pilot boat to guide us through the reef, and past a small flotilla of yachts, to our berth beside a huge container ship from Le Havre. The *Wellington Star* shuddered slightly as she touched the dock at Papeete, and then was still. Colin Mundy, our affable captain from Dorset, invited me to join him in his cabin for a farewell drink as he completed the paperwork.

The first words Stevenson heard when the *Casco* arrived at the Marquesas in July 1888, were spoken by a white trader in a canoe, who said: 'Captain, is it permitted to come aboard?' The first words I heard in Tahiti came from an enormously fat American in a loud shirt, who was waving my passport in Colin's cabin and demanding rudely: 'Where's your onward ticket?' When I said I did not have one, he turned to a Tahitian immigration official, and in heavily accented French declared with finality: 'We can't land him. He doesn't have an onward ticket.' I explained the purpose of my trip, and said I hoped to find a ship bound for Hawaii after completing my research in French Polynesia. In shocked tones, he blurted: 'You can't travel to foreign countries like *that*.' I was tempted to say I would travel where I liked any way I damn well pleased, but I kept silent; I supposed officialdom was on his side, and I also had a sneaking suspicion he was right. The little Tahitian offered a few helpful suggestions to get around the problem, all of which were dismissed by the American, who was now sweating profusely. Finally I produced a credit card, which presumably established my credentials as a man of means who could be relied upon to post an $850 'repatriation deposit' with the immigration authorities. '*Qu'est-ce que je fais?*' the Tahitian enquired. '*Debarques-le,*' the American replied curtly.

In the end, Jim Hostetler, for such was the name of the shipping agent who loved onward tickets, was helpful and offered to drive me to my hotel. Crawling in heavy traffic along the waterfront, he told me he lived in the hills out of the capital. 'This place is a dump,' he said. 'I never come here unless I have to.' I had fond memories of a reporting assignment here seven years before, but I had to admit the town – the only place worthy of the name for thousands of miles in any direction – looked pretty seedy. Colin had come along, and we bade farewell at the entrance to my hotel, a couple of miles along the coast from Papeete. It was the same place I had stayed at as a Reuters correspondent *en route* to a story on the nuclear atoll of Mururoa, and I was pleased to be recognized by a smiling receptionist. I had chosen the Hotel Tahiti as a base again because it was quiet, and had a dilapidated charm which I preferred to the glamour of the more modern tourist hotels.

After dinner, I strolled on to the jetty to watch the *Wellington Star* departing for New Zealand. A water-skier was skimming across the lagoon, and four outrigger canoes were etched against a stunning sunset over the serrated peaks of Moorea, regarded as one of the most splendid sights in the South Pacific. Twilight was fading before I saw tugs nudging my old ship from her berth; I had told Colin I would be watching and waving goodbye, and as she steamed towards the breakwater the blue star on her funnel was suddenly illuminated and the night was rent by a long blast of her horn. Colin wrote to me later that the light had been to enable the pilot to regain his boat, but that the horn, as I had fondly imagined, had been for me.

I stood for a long time, thinking of my cabin, and friends on board sitting down to supper, until the lights of the good ship *Wellington Star* dwindled and disappeared over the horizon. It was an emotional and suddenly lonely figure who left the darkened jetty to begin his quest in earnest.

FOUR

*The Marquesan beholds with dismay the approaching
extinction of his race*

I SERIOUSLY THOUGHT I was about to die. The small
aircraft in which I was a cowering passenger was bucking and
whining in dense cloud in its fifth attempt to find a runway high
in the mountains of Hiva-Oa.

Hit by a vicious cross-wind, it slewed to one side, and
through the murk I caught a glimpse of a wild valley far below,
with the highest waterfalls I had ever seen cascading from
vertical cliffs. The next thing I saw was a sheer rock face, at a
crazy angle directly in front of us; I had barely time to reflect
that my first sight of the Marquesas could be my last, when the
aircraft's engines screamed and there was an almighty bang.

The day had begun well, with no foreboding of a brush with
eternity. In seeking to follow Stevenson's itinerary as closely as
possible, I had decided to head immediately for the island of
Nuku-Hiva in the Marquesas, his first landfall. The only vessel
with a fixed schedule to these islands almost a thousand miles
north-east of Tahiti was not due to sail for two weeks; two other
freighters were at sea, and their schedules were subject to the
whims of local commerce and uncertain weather. Thus I found
myself with a dozen other passengers in a twin-prop ATR-42 of
Air Tahiti, climbing into a cloudless sky above Papeete and
banking over the lagoon on course for a cluster of extinct
volcanoes in the northern reaches of French Polynesia.

Four months before, the port engine of a brand-new Dornier
of Air Tahiti had caught fire as it was approaching Nuku-Hiva.
The pilots switched off the starboard engine by mistake, failed
to restart it, and the aircraft plunged into rough seas – in which

the co-pilot and nine passengers died. An inquiry found the crew had been hung over from a drinking session the night before. I paid close attention to the pilots on my flight as they walked towards the aircraft, but they seemed at least to be steady on their feet.

As we reached our cruising height, I looked idly at the waves beneath us and estimated the wind at force four, and was proud of my new expertise. After about an hour, we passed over a few atolls of the Tuamotus, which would be my next destination; pale green patterns of coral shimmering in an empty ocean, encompassing enormous lagoons and dotted with clumps of coconut palms barely above sea level. The remainder of the flight passed uneventfully until we approached the island of Hiva-Oa, where we were to make a brief stop *en route* to Nuku-Hiva.

In contrast with the brilliant blues of the surrounding sky and ocean, Hiva-Oa was a dark mass swathed in rainclouds. I was mildly surprised when we flew into this gloomy shroud and then out again on the other side. When the manoeuvre was repeated and we were heading into the turbulent darkness for the third time, I began to become uneasy. By the time we were circling the island for a fourth attempt, I was distinctly nervous, and asked the flight attendant what was the problem. He said the landing strip was on a high plateau surrounded by mountains, and helpfully raised his arms in an expressive gesture to indicate the towering nature of the mountains concerned. Quite unnecessarily, he added that landing on this craggy island in poor visibility was a risky procedure. I noticed the other passengers had begun reading the emergency instruction cards.

There are seasoned travellers who seem perfectly relaxed in an aircraft which is bucking like a wild mustang. They affect to smile and joke among themselves, oblivious to the craven fear of those around them: I am not among them. As a war correspondent, I discovered in myself a fierce desire to live; but on the ground there is usually somewhere to hide, if not to run. In this mid-air bucking bronco I was helpless, at the mercy of whimsical fate and maniacal pilots whom I grew to despise. I imagined them sitting in the cockpit, hunched in tense concentration, still wearing their dark glasses to look cool. Who were these lunatics? What were they trying to prove? I pictured the inscription on their tombs, after they had decorated a Marquesan mountain with bits of their aircraft and passengers: 'They died with their wings on.'

It was on the fifth roller-coaster ride, buffeted by strong winds, that the screaming engines and a loud bang signalled we had cleared a sheer cliff and slammed on to the runway. As the aircraft slowed and I relaxed, my teeth began chattering. At this point a barefoot Polynesian Venus, with a mass of dark hair tumbling over tanned shoulders, materialized from the mist and walked towards us with a divine smile. This ethereal vision posing as a ground hostess seemed to be walking on air. If we had crashed, I was prepared to accept the consequences.

The tension on board eased when about a dozen passengers got on, most of them women and girls, and the cabin was filled with laughter and the scent of flowers. Our departure was less traumatic than our arrival, although I studiously avoided looking out of the window as we flew off the edge of the cliff. Our landing on the coastal runway at Nuku-Hiva was relatively smooth, but my journey was far from over.

Nuku-Hiva is a volcanic mass about twenty miles long by twelve miles wide, supporting a population of little more than two thousand, some coconut plantations, a lot of jungle, and not much else. The airport was perched on the north-west corner of the island, and Taiohae, the main village and my destination, was far away on the south coast. There are no roads worthy of the name anywhere in the Marquesas, so I was offered the choice of a five-minute helicopter ride or a boat trip which would take between two and four hours, depending on the weather. I glanced at clouds brooding over sombre mountains in the distance and then at the sea, which seemed relatively calm, and decided to trust my fate, like Stevenson, to the ocean; if anything went wrong, I reasoned, I could swim better than I could fly. This was a mistake.

An old yellow bus was standing in the drizzle outside the terminal building, and I clambered on board with a few other passengers for a two-mile ride down to the local harbour. We bumped and splashed along a rutted track through undulating scrubland, crawling over small streams of murky, ochre-coloured water. The landscape was bleak, and weird formations of tortured black rock testified to volcanic upheavals. On my map, the area was designated *Terre Deserte*, which seemed appropriate; in all the western coastal area of about forty square miles not a single habitation was marked. An ominous buzzing drew my attention to a large, venomous-looking insect drifting up and down the centre of the bus as if considering which of us to attack. Eventually a barefoot boy swatted it into oblivion.

At the harbour, two vessels lay by a worn stone jetty: a rusty old ferry and a small speedboat. I was relieved to see we were boarding the larger vessel, which was soon chugging past a succession of craggy headlands broken by ravines plunging steeply into the sea. Anything further from the postcard image of a smiling South Sea island would have been difficult to conceive. There were no palm trees swaying gently by calm lagoons here. This was an iron-bound coast in conflict with heavy seas, stark and brutal, as daunting as the wildest regions of northern Scotland; I found myself almost wishing it was Auld Scotia, and I could hop in a car and drive home to Glasgow.

I was beginning to feel hungry, but declined the offer of an unappetizing mess in a tin pot on a dirty Primus stove. A crewman was helping me to ignite the stove for coffee with a pair of pliers (the control button was broken) when there was a scraping noise, a babble of excited voices, and the engines slowed. There were not supposed to be any reefs in the vicinity, but given the events of the day so far, I assumed we had struck one and were now in peril upon the sea. In fact the noise had been a fishing reel on the stern playing out to a hooked fish, which eventually got away.

As we rounded a point, we came to an enormous cliff with a serrated pinnacle at one end; together they formed a towering black theatre, but the only actors were gulls screeching across the upper circle and waves heaving and crashing into the stalls. It was a kind of maritime version of Dante's Inferno. This was a grim, Stygian shore that glowered at us, daring us to venture closer. I averted my eyes from this chilling sight and turned to see a wall of low pressure closing in from the sea; apparently it would be a race between the boat and the storm to reach port.

The ferry had begun rolling heavily in a beam sea when the fishing reel screamed, and to my despair the engines slowed again. It was now night, and pitch dark. Another life and death struggle ensued, and this time death triumphed. A flash of silver beneath the waves at the stern emerged as a large tuna, which was promptly harpooned in the head, dragged aboard, and clubbed with a wooden baton. As the hooks and harpoon were removed, a foam of blood and entrails sloshed around the writhing creature; I was reminded of the practice in Nelson's day of painting the gundecks of men-of-war red, so that crews would not be sickened by the bloodshed. I think I would not have made a good gunner.

I was sitting alone in the passenger lounge, feeling cold, tired, and hungry, and wishing earnestly I was somewhere else, when a crewman tapped me on the shoulder and said in halting French: 'You no feel good?'

'I no feel good,' I admitted.

'OK, Taiohae maybe five minutes.'

I considered the import of 'maybe', but soon a few lights appeared around a headland, the first sign of human life I had seen throughout the boat trip. Rain was drizzling across dim harbour lights as I disembarked at a gloomy quay. There should have been a sign declaring: 'Abandon hope all ye who enter here'. I expected a gaunt figure on a black coach to address me in guttural tones: '*Komm, mein Herr,* ze Count is expecting you.' At that moment, a flash of lightning would illuminate the towers of a ruined castle, and an unseen orchestra would strike a dramatic flourish.

In fact, I was met by nobody. A few trucks drove off with my fellow-passengers and their belongings, and I was almost alone when a man offered to give me a lift to my hotel. We had an interesting conversation:

'Are you from Taiohae?'

'Yes.'

'Are you a fisherman?'

'Yes.'

'How long has it been raining?'

'About one year.'

'Oh.'

In the Hotel Moana Nui, a motel-like building on the seafront, I was shown to a small room with green walls, two single beds, and a cloud of insects buzzing around a naked light bulb. I regarded it gratefully. After unpacking, I stepped into the shower and was startled by a jet of cold water shooting into my midriff from a broken hose.

In the bar downstairs, a few Frenchmen were drinking with local women at rough wooden tables, but nobody paid me any attention; not so much as a smile or a nod. I ate alone, overcoming my squeamishness concerning the late tuna to devour a bowl of raw fish marinated in lime juice: I also became a little mellow on a bottle of beer and a half-bottle of wine. The bar was festooned with shell necklaces and a large portrait of smiling Polynesian girls in bright sunshine, which I regarded sceptically. A corpulent white lizard with pink feet was slouching around a neon light in the hope of a grilled mosquito. He should have come to my room; he would have had a banquet, and I would have had some company.

After dinner, I stood by the open door looking at sodden trees glistening in the light of a single street lamp, and listening to the dull roar of the surf. A mangy hound regarded me dolefully. I made encouraging sounds and kneeled with outstretched hand; he approached me cautiously, I stroked him, and he came closer until his head was pressing against my chest in mute companionship, two bedraggled spirits comforting one another.

On retiring I tossed and turned, the rain, the surf, and bass notes from a tape player in the bar beating into my jangled nerves. Then I heard noises in the night. First it was an aircraft, its engines whining as it circled the bay, searching for a place to land. Then I heard a voice, more distinctly, crying with a mixture of anguish and despair. It was so real I hastened to the window, but there it became only an echo. Had I really heard someone calling? Stevenson said Marquesans were obsessed with death and malevolent spirits: had I imagined a voice from the grave? Doubting my own senses, I returned to bed and fell into fitful sleep as the insects began acquiring a taste for Scots blood.

Perhaps the weather had something to do with it; when the rain ceased, the sky remained overcast, the air humid and oppressive. Perhaps it was the land; wild mountains scarred by erosion, and abysmal valleys that looked as if they had been gouged out of the volcanic rock by a demented deity. Perhaps it was the people, who seemed curiously subdued. Whatever the reason, I sensed a melancholy pervading Nuku-Hiva. It was hardly surprising, since this was an island which had risen almost literally from the grave.

When Herman Melville deserted from the American whaling ship *Acushnet* in 1842 and sought refuge among the natives of the Taipi Valley, he found a happy band of savages seemingly devoid of cares, griefs, and sickness, apart from the odd altercation with a neighbouring tribe. Sensing disaster, he viewed with misgiving the arrival of European ships: 'Fatal embrace! They fold to their bosoms the vipers whose sting is destined to poison all their joys . . . Ill-fated people! I shudder when I think of the change a few years will produce in their paradisaical abode.'

By the time Stevenson turned up in 1888, the population had been decimated by foreign diseases, famine, and desultory warfare, and Melville's 'secluded abode of happiness' had become a vale of deserted dwellings haunted by cannibal spirits. In the space of a single generation, the population had dwindled from fifty thousand to less than six thousand. Observing suicidal tendencies among the survivors, Stevenson wrote:

The Marquesan beholds with dismay the approaching extinction of his race. The thought of death sits down with him to meat, and rises with him from his bed; he lives and breathes under a shadow of mortality awful to support; and he is so inured to the apprehension that he greets the reality with relief . . . he seeks instant refuge in the grave.

A century later, under the mixed blessings of French colonialism, the population of Nuku-Hiva is slowly recovering. As in Stevenson's day, the men are generally more handsome than the women, being tall and muscular with fine features, the women tending to be heavier and duller in appearance. Most live in coastal hamlets, earning a modest living from subsidized copra production and discovering the dubious delights of a consumer society. A young traveller who had spent a week walking from the airport told me he had been astonished to find natives in the bush watching French soap operas on satellite television.

Strolling along the seafront at Taiohae, which has the only paved road on the island, I mused that the general aspect of the village could have changed little since Stevenson saw it: a low straggle of white-painted wooden bungalows and stores with corrugated-iron roofs running along the shore of a horseshoe-shaped bay and into the foothills, all enclosed by a formidable wall of mountains. A deep silence was disturbed only by the murmur of the sea, the crowing of cocks, and the occasional splutter of a vehicle. Four-wheel-drive jeeps and trucks are the sole practical form of motorized transport on the island; I never saw a car, and only once heard a vehicle horn being sounded, by an impatient Frenchman, which evoked an appropriate response from a local pedestrian.

Two barefoot youths walking along the road, oblivious to the rain, smiled at one another as I passed. Fishermen were wading into the bay with their nets, and the sound of their laughter carried across the water. It all seemed peaceful and harmonious, and yet I was not a happy wanderer. Something intangible in the rude landscape and the quiet behaviour of the people summoned images of the past, as if the spirits of a lost generation were saying: tread softly and keep your happiness to yourself.

'If you spend only a few weeks here you will understand nothing,' the animated little Frenchman told me. 'You have to live here, it takes time.' He had dropped into the bar of the Moana Nui for a drink, an erstwhile bank manager who had left France to settle on a neighbouring Marquesan island, cultivate a vegetable farm, and father children by a local woman. 'They have a lot of qualities we have lost in Europe,' he said. 'Most of them can still be happy living off the land, but the slavery to money has begun. Before, the women used to do their washing in the rivers, now they all want washing machines.' The locals I spoke to did not like this man. 'He talks shit,' one of them informed me.

At the eastern end of the village is a small hill overlooking the bay. Stevenson occasionally walked up it, past an old fort which served as a prison, to a club where a handful of whites played billiards, drank absinthe, and discussed the affairs of the day on 'one of the most agreeable verandas in the tropics'. Among the French officials and German and Scottish merchant clerks was a drifter who sparked Stevenson's interest with a curious tale of unrequited love. He had fallen in love with a high chiefess, who declared she could never marry a man who was not tattooed. He duly submitted himself to weeks of excruciating pain to be adorned from head to foot in the approved manner, and presented himself to his beloved a new man: the fickle lady laughed in his face and rejected him on the grounds that he looked ridiculous. Stevenson concluded:

For my part, I could never see the man without a kind of admiration. Of him it might be said, if ever of any, that he had loved not wisely, but too well.

The fort, the agreeable veranda, and the tattooed lover were long gone by the time I strolled up a rocky path through a copse of trees to the grassy summit. All that remained was a circular hole leading down through stonework to the old sewers. I sat for a while, my only companion a tethered horse grazing on the mound, looking at the sea and the mountains and wondering at man's infinite capacity for making a fool of himself in affairs of the heart.

ONE ASPECT OF Marquesan life had not changed. When M. Delaruelle, the French Resident, escorted Stevenson on a visit to the prison, they found it empty. That day being a holiday, the gaoler had quite reasonably given the inmates the day off to go hunting for goats in the mountains. It seems M. Delaruelle was accustomed to the whimsicalities of his little realm, and found the incident amusing.

The same enlightened attitude prevails today. Serious crimes being virtually unheard of, islanders charged with minor offences are tried and sentenced in accordance with French judicial procedures, committed to prison, and then set free to do public works. Their day begins at around 6.30 a.m. when the gaoler arrives to have coffee with them, and then they go around the village or into the hills mending roads and fixing fences. 'I told the judge we don't really need this stupid prison,' the mayor informed me, 'and he agreed with me. But he said he couldn't do much about it on his own, so it stays where it is.'

The new gaol, which looked like a copra shed with bars on the windows, lay at the eastern end of the village near the old administration building. As I passed by one day, I noticed four figures sitting on the steps outside. They turned out to be Emile the warden, a man convicted of cultivating cannabis, and the prisoner's wife and infant son. They were having lunch. I remarked that it seemed like a fairly relaxed prison. 'Yes, it's not bad,' the prisoner agreed. 'It's like a hotel with home cooking.' Emile said he thought the prison served a useful purpose. 'You know, the men who come here are not really bad. It's better than sending them to Papeete, where it would be hard for them to be away from their families, and they could get into bad company.' In following days I often passed the prison, and Emile and his charge waved to me. One day the erstwhile marijuana planter was sitting on his own. 'If you see my wife, tell her Emile's brother caught some fine fish last night,' he called. I promised I would.

In the administration building, an elegant two-storey villa dating from 1846 and said to be the oldest building in French Polynesia, I was pleased to discover a worthy successor to M. Delaruelle in Jean-Jacques Fort. An old Africa hand, he ran his little outpost with a genuine concern for local cultural values and a lively sense of humour. A small, lean man with a prominent nose and mischievous dark eyes, he looked like a Gallic Mr Punch. After paying him a courtesy call, I was invited to attend a reception for the baptism of his latest grandchild at his residence, a rambling colonial compound by the seashore. Having waded up the driveway in a downpour, I arrived with shoes and trousers sodden and caked with mud; I thus presented a dishevelled figure when M. Fort put his arm around my shoulders on the steps of his patio, and introduced me grandly to his assembled guests as a friend who had been unfortunate in his place of birth and choice of profession, but who had the good grace to learn the language of Voltaire rather better than he had mastered that of Shakespeare. Rarely has a man's native land been slighted and his ego flattered with such diplomatic *savoir faire*.

I enjoyed mingling with the French and Marquesan guests, the music of a local band, and the rare pleasure of a fine Bordeaux, but it was a formal occasion which offered little insight into native life. It was Hiti the fisherman who introduced me to Polynesian hospitality.

If the population of Nuku-Hiva declines again, it will not be the fault of Hiti Teremihi and his wife Catherine. In fifteen years of marriage, they have produced nine healthy, good-looking children, including a trio of little girls with liquid brown eyes and impish smiles that would light up the heart of darkness. I was trudging through heavy rain towards my hotel, after a walk to the western promontory of the bay, when Hiti offered me a lift in his pick-up truck. We stopped at a store to buy eggs, and he emerged with a couple of beers and offered me one. 'Come to my house,' he said simply.

We climbed a muddy, deeply rutted track to a wooden bungalow he had built in the foothills above the village. Catherine, a plump, jolly woman, served us coffee and home-made cakes on the veranda. Hiti told me he came from Tahiti, but he preferred living in the Marquesas. 'I don't like Papeete,' he said. 'Too many people and cars and noise, and rushing around all the time. Here it is quiet and peaceful.' He provided for his family by diving for lobsters in murky seas infested with hammerhead sharks, which I did not consider a particularly peaceful occupation. I asked him if he ever had close encounters with these predatory rivals. 'The sharks don't bother me too often, but yesterday a big one, more than four metres, circled my boat.' Was he afraid? 'Yes, I was afraid he would flip me over and I would lose my catch,' he said. Sometimes I think of

Hiti's wiry figure sliding alone into dark waters, with a lamp powered by a car battery on his boat, as a dorsal fin cruises towards him. It puts a new perspective on buying lobster in the local supermarket.

I asked Catherine about the great chiefs and tribes of the Marquesas, renowned for their tattoos and prowess in battle. 'They are all gone,' she told me. 'There are none left any more, but there are books. We can read about them in books.'

One of the most colourful characters in the old books is Kooamua, the last cannibal high chief of Nuku-Hiva, who led a desperate war against the French. Stevenson met him and was impressed by his formidable presence, describing him as a dusky Gladstone. It occurred to me that Kooamua had no more relevance to Catherine than Charles Edward Stewart has to the average Scot today.

On leaving Hiti, I made the mistake of admiring his fine collection of seashells. He promptly presented me with a prize specimen, a large ridged conch in delicate hues of orange and purple, and pressed two smaller shells on me for good measure.

MY ANTIPATHY TOWARDS the Marquesas gradually faded. The longer I stayed, the more I was reminded of the Western Isles of Scotland; the harsh landscapes and rough seas, the turbulent histories, the insular character of the people. At first they seemed withdrawn and wary of strangers, but treated with courtesy and respect they showed the same generosity of spirit I had known in Hebridean crofting communities. Stevenson reached the same conclusion, and added that he considered tattooing more becoming than 'the ignoble European practice of tight-lacing among women'.

There were few tattoos or corsets in evidence at a *soirée dansante* in the local market that Saturday night, but there was a lot of finery adorning remarkably pretty girls. The dance hall was basically a concrete floor with a dilapidated roof supported by wooden pillars, which had been swathed in palm fronds for the occasion. I had hoped for a band, but instead a disc jockey wearing a baseball cap backwards on his head was playing rock music and Polynesian melodies. In time-honoured fashion, the boys spent most of the time at the bar noisily recounting memorable exploits at fishing and football. I was standing alone admiring the girls waltzing to a local tune when I felt a tug at my trousers, and a voice said: 'You should pick a girl to dance with and take her to your room.' I looked down to see one of Hiti's scamps, precocious in jeans and T-shirt, regarding me with sparkling eyes. 'And what should I do there?' I asked. She smiled impishly and disappeared.

A minute later, she returned with a beautiful half-caste girl, a fragrant vision of long dark hair and slender legs in a black miniskirt. 'This girl will dance with you,' Hiti's child-woman announced. We waltzed around the floor in a close embrace, and I wondered idly whether a few tattoos might improve my prospects of romance. I was on the point of suggesting a stroll in the moonlight, possibly in the direction of my hotel, when I caught the eye of a youth regarding me fixedly. I had seen that look before in Glasgow pubs. 'That is my boyfriend,' my partner informed me. 'He is going to be a soldier in the French Army.' I returned to the bar to learn more about Marquesan fishing and football.

One of the most curious guests to dine aboard the *Casco* was Vaekehu, an old cannibal queen. Stevenson thought she was charming, and struck up a friendship with her son Stanislaos Moanatini, a local chief. I found Keo Pahuatini, a direct descendant of Stanislaos, sitting alone in a wooden chair in the middle of a large, sparsely furnished room of his bungalow, gazing out of open french windows at the sea. He looked like an old chief waiting to follow his tribe to the last hunting ground. I had noticed before this propensity of Marquesans to sit for hours, staring vacantly into space, but I never fully understood it. 'I am at peace,' or 'I am thinking of the past and the future,' was all they would say.

I asked Keo if I might speak with him. He motioned me to a chair on the veranda, where he joined me. He had never heard of Stevenson, but he did know a lot about the Marquesan aristocracy of the day. 'Stanislaos was not Vaekehu's natural son, you know. He was the son of her sister by the same man and she adopted him. My grandmother was his daughter. Temoana was the husband of Vaekehu. They lived at Hakaihu, which is now known as Pua, but that is wrong. Hakaihu is the name of the valley and Pua is the name of the people, but only the old ones remember this.' Keo said all of this without looking at me, gazing into the middle distance as if he could see the richly tattooed old Vaekehu in his mind's eye.

I asked him if he had seen many changes in the Marquesan way of life. 'Yes, it is not as before. In the old days there were no cars, only horses, or you travelled by foot. If you came from another valley, people would greet you and offer you food and shelter. Now people live like the Tahitians, like the French, like you. If you don't have money you don't eat, and everything is expensive now. And few people remember the old stories. They are not interested in their ancestors any more, they just live for today and tomorrow.' When I left Keo, he walked back into his house and resumed his place in the middle of the room, staring impassively at a changed world.

The tombs of Vaekehu and Stanislaos lie together on a small rise overlooking the bay, near a monument to Melville and his companion Richard Tobias Greene, known as Toby. The latter is an impressive wood sculpture, tracing the shipmates' trek through the mountains, with photographs of the two men fixed behind glass. Toby looks like a slim version of Oscar Wilde: Melville, bearded and wearing a frock-coat and high winged collar, looks supercilious, as well he might, having deluded early readers of the authenticity of his work (he claimed to have spent four months in Taipivi, in fact he was there for less than a month).

The white-painted slabs on the hill above the remains of Vaekehu and Stanislaos have no inscriptions or any other distinguishing features. One senses that eventually they will crumble into the earth, and nobody will care.

Before leaving Taiohae, I went to see the mayor, an articulate, powerfully built man at ease in shorts and a loose shirt, and asked him whether his people were happy. 'That's a good question,' he said. 'One thing is certain, the people are attracted by what they do not have. Life in the Marquesas is generally easy, there is no lack of food or the basic necessities, but we have begun to live beyond our means and have come to depend on France. I think by and large our people are fairly happy just now, but the deeper we get into the consumer society the more difficult life will become.'

I asked whether the Marquesans shared the aspirations of some parties in Tahiti for independence. 'In your opinion,' the mayor said, 'if you live on an island of two thousand people and you are surrounded by big countries like America, Australia, and New Zealand, what can you do? A little archipelago lost in the Pacific, do you think it can survive alone? No, we do not wish for independence. We know we have nothing to gain from it.'

I noticed that he had a beautiful wooden desk, intricately carved in the Marquesan manner, and on top of it was a computer. A French presidential portrait regarded the scene with paternal indulgence – traditional culture and silicone chips with a dash of French dressing. Having acquired a taste for French bread, the Marquesans know which side it is buttered on; pass the subsidies and the song-sheets for 'La Marseillaise'. . .

*

I WAS KEEN TO VISIT Stevenson's first landfall, in the Bay of Anaho on the north side of the island, but getting there was problematic. The mountain tracks were washed out, no boats were available, and it seemed too far to walk in a day. Also there was no guarantee of accommodation. The remaining options were by horse or helicopter to the village of Hatiheu in an adjacent bay, which Stevenson had also visited and where there was a modest *pension*.

Having experienced the temperament of the local horses, which tended to shy at small streams as if they were raging torrents, I shuddered to think of them prancing around narrow cliff paths in stormy weather, and decided to fly. The dark blue helicopter of Tahiti Conquest Airlines looked a bit frail for flying through mountains obscured by rainclouds. I checked my French map, the equivalent of an Ordnance Survey, and noticed a lot of blank spaces on our route, marked *nuage* or cloud. I briefly considered walking instead, but the pilot was already climbing aboard and I supposed he knew what he was doing. We took off fully laden with five passengers and an engineer. Taiohae slipped quickly beneath us, and we began climbing towards the surrounding mountains.

For some time we seemed to be getting closer to the cliffs without getting any higher. Alain, the pilot, turned to explain: 'We're carrying extra fuel, and it's hard to get her up when she's so heavy.' After buzzing ineffectually beneath a col for a moment, we veered off to the right and flew through a lower gap with about twenty feet to spare. The ground fell away sharply on the other side, and we passed over a high plateau with no sign of life other than the glistening ribbon of a muddy track. This was the land of the Hapaars, the erstwhile neighbours of Melville's Taipis; for more than a century it had been forlorn and deserted, the domain of wild pigs and chickens.

When we flew over another ridge, the ground abruptly

disappeared. It took an instant for my brain to register that it was now more than a thousand feet below, a dark green mass of jungle. I looked up to see an opaque curtain of rain before us, a dark wall of water advancing ominously between craggy peaks. 'We can't fly through that, can we?' one of the passengers asked nervously. Alain made no reply, and I noticed the engineer was staring at the instrument panel. Then it seemed we were flying through a car wash. This was a bit unnerving, considering this washing machine was airborne. Happily Alain's navigation was as unerring as his flying skills. Through the murk I glimpsed a narrow gap in a wall of rock directly ahead of us, we clattered through it, and the clouds cleared to reveal the Bay of Hatiheu spread beneath us.

All that remains of the community viewed by Stevenson is a statue of the Virgin Mary high on a pinnacle of rock at the western end of the bay. The rest was destroyed by tidal waves at 11 a.m. on the 1st of April, 1946. Yvonne, the widow who owned the Pension Hinakonui where I was staying, was eight years old at the time. 'We had gone to the next bay at Anaho for the day, and I was fishing with some friends,' she told me. 'I remember there was very fine rain, but no mist. Suddenly the sea went down, as if it was draining away, and I ran up the hill to tell my parents. About ten minutes later there was a roaring sound and a huge wave came and smashed all the houses. It went back very far, then another wave came, and then a third. They were moving very quickly but they weren't breaking. When we went back to Hatiheu, it wasn't there. Everything was gone or in ruins.'

It says something for the resilience, or perhaps the fatal attraction, of this community that people still live here given its track record for unforeseen disasters. The valley once teemed with five tribes, numbering around ten thousand people, until a cholera epidemic introduced by a foreign vessel virtually wiped them out.

There is a savage beauty about the place which is almost intimidating. The usual cluster of wooden bungalows with ubiquitous corrugated-iron roofs lines the shore, beneath a wall of mountains; at the western end rises a series of fantastic needles of rock swathed in dark green vegetation; in the absence of a reef, the bay is a restless expanse of grey water with strong currents. Less than two hundred people were making a living from fishing and copra when I was there, and the population over the ridge in Anaho was a mere fifteen.

After lunch I borrowed an umbrella and went for a stroll in the rain. The village seemed deserted, but I spotted a group of people at one end of the bay and walked along a muddy track towards them. I had assumed they were fishermen, but I found a beefy man and five youths slaughtering two goats. The shore was awash with blood and a dirty brown froth covered the surface of the water as various items of the unfortunate animals' internal plumbing were brandished and hurled into the sea. One youth, for reasons best known to himself, was hacking with a sharp knife at a horned skull in which dead eyes stared at him balefully. In the background, the pinnacles of rock on the other side of the bay looked like broken teeth. It was a sickening and melancholy sight; I turned away and looked out to sea, feeling lonely. I reflected that Stevenson had been fortunate in having the company of his family and the crew of his yacht in this wild place.

I had another problem. My arms and legs had come to resemble the volcanic topography of the island, being a mass of infected sores. The culprits were microscopic vampires known to scientists as *Simulium buissoni*, to other interested parties as blackflies, and to Marquesans as *no-nos*. They rank among the world's worst blood-sucking pests and carriers of disease – in Africa they are responsible for 'river blindness' – and Nuku-Hiva is infested with untold millions of them. The good news is they are not found on beaches. The bad news is the beaches are the domain of their white cousins, *Styloconops albiventris*, which are equally voracious. During my visit, a team of French entomologists was waiting patiently for the rain to stop so they could pour chemicals into mountain streams to eradicate the blackflies. They had been waiting for three months.

One of them explained to me the difference between the *modus operandi* of mosquitoes and blackflies. The former are like flying hypodermic needles, inserting suckers and withdrawing blood with surgical precision; the latter chew and tear at flesh to drink the blood, leaving ragged wounds susceptible to infection. Marquesans eventually become immune to the insect saliva that causes irritation, but there is no respite for the unsuspecting traveller. In 1904, a severe infestation forced French administrators to move lock, stock, and wine-barrel from Nuku-Hiva to Hiva-Oa. To be on the safe side, they stayed there for forty years. The French expert obligingly showed me a reference work on the subject by a member of the Natural History department at the British Museum. Referring to social and economic disruption caused by these vermin, the author notes: 'The experience of being continually bitten, unable to step outside without soon oozing blood from countless bites, is a demoralizer with few equals.'

I heartily endorse this view. On my first night at Hatiheu, I had a beautiful dream. I was lying in a darkened room, between crisp, clean white sheets. Every so often a nurse would come to my bed and silently bathe my arms and legs in a cooling solution. I was awakened from this reverie by the infernal screeching of a cock outside my window in the middle of the night, to find myself scratching a profusion of insect bites behind my right knee. A thin trickle of blood was staining the sweat-soaked sheets.

My only companion in Hatiheu was Yvonne's son, Maurice. An intelligent, sensitive young man, he had abandoned medical studies in Papeete on the death of his father to return to Nuku-

Hiva to help his mother. He had visited the United States, Chile, and New Zealand, but he said that one day he would marry and raise a family in Hatiheu. 'This is my home,' he told me. 'I am secure here. It is quiet and peaceful, I have the sea in front of me and the river beside me. What more do I need?'

One night, by the light of a gas lamp in the *pension*, he showed me his most prized possession: a large illustrated volume of the cultural history of the Marquesas, *Die Marquesaner und Ihre Kunst*, by Karl von den Steinen, first published in 1928. Gazing at photographs and sketches of tribal chiefs, their tattoos and artefacts, he said: 'I wish I had lived then. I often sit on the stones by the sea and dream of living then.' He pointed out one figure with pride: a handsome, sturdy man of about thirty, standing self-consciously in profile for the camera, wearing a skirt and shoulder-covering of human hair and an ornate headdress of feathers and palm fronds, and carrying a staff with an emblem of what could have been either a turtle or a giant spider. 'This man was my great-great-grandfather Kooamua, the last cannibal of Hatiheu,' he said.

'Stevenson met this man and thought highly of him,' I said. 'Would you like to hear what Stevenson said of him?' Maurice's eyes shone eagerly, as if I was summoning his ancestor from the grave, as I read a passage from *In the South Seas*:

We had been but three days in Anaho when we received the visit of the chief of Hatiheu, a man of weight and fame, late leader of a war upon the French, late prisoner in Tahiti, and the last eater of long-pig in Nuku-Hiva. Not many years have elapsed since he was seen striding on the beach of Anaho, a dead man's arm across his shoulder. 'So does Kooamua to his enemies!' he roared to the passers-by, and took a bite from the raw flesh. And now behold this gentleman, very wisely replaced in office by the French, paying us a morning visit in European clothes. He was the man of the most character we had yet seen: his manners genial and decisive, his person tall, his face rugged, astute, formidable, and with a certain similarity to Mr Gladstone's — only for the brownness of the skin, and the high chief's tattooing, all one side and much of the other being of an even blue.

Maurice said: 'Tomorrow I will show you the secret high place of Kooamua.'

It was raining when Stevenson, accompanied by a French priest and a schoolboy guide, struck into the forest above Hatiheu in search of the cannibal high place. Tropical showers roared overhead, but in the dank heart of the wood only a few drops penetrated the dense foliage. Coming upon a huge banyan tree, Stevenson found the sloping earth paved in terraces, as far as the eye could see, framed by a crumbling parapet which had contained the main arena. He imagined drums throbbing and a crescendo of dancing and singing as the priests sanctified the brutish feast.

And yet it was strange. There, upon the spot as I stood under the high, dripping vault of the forest, with the young priest on the one hand, in his kilted gown, and the bright-eyed Marquesan schoolboy on the other, the whole business appeared infinitely distant, and fallen in the cold perspective and dry light of history . . . I beheld the place with no more emotion than I might have felt in visiting Stonehenge.

Stevenson shared European repugnance at cannibalism, but he questioned the moral basis for it.

Sentiments are outraged . . . and yet we ourselves make much the same appearance in the eyes of the Buddhist and the vegetarian. We consume the carcasses of creatures of like appetites, passions, and organs with ourselves; we feed on babes, though not our own; and the slaughter-house resounds daily with screams of pain and fear . . . rightly speaking, to cut a man's flesh after he is dead is far less hateful than to oppress him whilst he lives.

A century later, it was raining again when Maurice drove me in his jeep up a muddy trail above Hatiheu and parked beside a forest. Scrambling through the skirting bushes, we entered a lofty twilight world of deep green hues illuminated by shafts of light filtering through the leafy canopy high above us. The tropical downpour faded to a dull whisper, and the splatter of a few drops on black volcanic rocks half-buried in the forest floor. Although the cannibal lair was now an archaeological site, there were no signposts or discernible paths leading towards it. Maurice skipped over the moss-covered rocks and shallow brooks with ease; stripped of his jeans and T-shirt he would have looked every inch the Marquesan warrior hurrying to a clan gathering. Large spiders scampered from fallen tree trunks as I scrabbled for a hold, and I was startled by the scream of a wild pig when I blundered into its refuge.

And then, there it was. The paved terraces had collapsed, but their remnants lay in a jumble of boulders by a fast-flowing stream. I walked among them, touching them, and examining petroglyphs of men, fish, and insects worn smooth with age. The sacred banyan stood a few yards away, a magnificent specimen swathed in a tangled mass of aerial roots sprouting from the trunk fifty feet above the ground. This venerable lord of the forest went up for ever. I felt like Jack standing beneath the Beanstalk. Maurice said it was estimated to be six hundred years old, and then he showed me something Stevenson had not recorded. Obscured by undergrowth at the base of the tree was the entrance to a narrow pit like an old well, about twenty feet deep, its slimy stone walls still intact.

'This is where the victims were kept,' Maurice said. 'Guards were posted on the rocks around to watch them until the day of the feast.' I tried to picture the wretches awaiting their fate, but like Stevenson I found the dreadful images of men dining *al fresco* on their brethren had faded in the mists of time. Yet it was a relief to emerge from the oppressive stillness of that gloomy arbour, and find that the rain had stopped.

So far I had been back-tracking on Stevenson's itinerary in the Marquesas, but by hiking over a ridge from Hatiheu to Anaho I would come to his first landfall. From this point I could retrace precisely his voyages through the Pacific. The skies cleared as I set off on a rocky path up the wooded hillside, and shafts of sunlight transformed the grey landscape. At first I was accompanied by a chattering burn, sparkling amid bursts of colour from brilliant flowers; a bird as white as snow cried and flew off at my approach; when I stopped to quench my thirst a large butterfly, a dark velvety brown with exquisite blue and white markings, settled briefly on my shoulder. The woods were alive with birdsong, and for the first time since leaving the *Wellington Star* I began to enjoy myself.

After a couple of weeks in Nuku-Hiva I had become sceptical and a little weary of Stevenson's superlatives, but I had to admit the prospect of Anaho from above was superb. To the east a narrow, hilly peninsula stretched out to sea, enclosing a large bay of calm water; the forest was a green carpet running down to the shore, where it was edged with the pattern of a coconut plantation; a tin roof was visible among the palms, from which a thin stream of smoke curled into the morning haze. The only sounds were the wind sighing across a rock face above me, the chirruping of unseen birds, and the occasional bleat of a goat far below. A lone yacht bobbed at anchor in the bay; for all that had visibly changed since Stevenson's visit, it could have been the *Casco*.

The first sign of life at the bottom of a steep, narrow path was a low stone wall and a corrugated-iron hut from which I heard children's voices. Strolling past a few simple wooden dwellings along the shore I heard other voices, but saw nobody. I stopped by the church, a low thatched hut with a sandy floor and tree stumps for seats. A white cloth lay on a small table, and what looked like an old ship's bell was fixed to a block of wood at the entrance. The only communicant was a dog scratching itself; it growled as I approached, I growled back, and it slunk away.

An open-walled thatched hut offered shade, and I sat on the concrete floor and opened a lunch packet Yvonne had prepared for me – delicious sandwiches of river shrimp, egg, and cucumber, washed down with fresh coconut milk. Still nobody had appeared; whether I had passed undetected or simply unheeded, I had no idea. I rolled a cigarette, exhaled luxuriously, and looked out across the bay, recalling the very different reception accorded Stevenson and his party.

Having permitted the resident trader Mr Regler and the local chief to board the *Casco*, Stevenson was unnerved when they were followed by dozens of muscular natives wearing knives and tattoos and little else, who proceeded to swarm over the ship demanding absurd prices for island curios in a tumultuous babble.

There was no word of welcome; no show of civility; no hand extended save that of the chief and Mr Regler . . . I own I was inspired by sensible repugnance; even with alarm. The ship was manifestly in their power; we had women on board; I knew nothing of my guests beyond the fact that they were cannibals . . . and as for the trader whose presence might else have reassured me, were not whites in the Pacific the usual instigators and accomplices of native outrage?

Perhaps it was the buxom lady who lifted her dress, and, with cries of wonder and pleasure, rubbed her bare bottom on the velvet cushions of the *Casco*'s saloon, who broke the ice. At any rate, Stevenson was soon sharing coconut milk and a pipe with the folk of Anaho, and engaging in high debate (with Mr Regler as interpreter) about the misdeeds of the French, the Panama Canal, and the geographical position of San Francisco.

I looked around me. Nothing stirred, save the occasional goat scrunching around fallen coconuts, so I went to explore the western end of the bay. The merest suggestion of a path led me to a plantation where I found an old man who had spent twenty-five years building houses at the French Pacific nuclear test site on Mururoa Atoll. I tried to engage him in high debate about the misdeeds of the French, but he wasn't interested. 'They provide work,' he said.

Returning via the hamlet, I came across a man in ragged

T-shirt and shorts dismantling an old jetty. 'When I was a child there were about fifty people living in Anaho,' he told me. 'We used to walk every day to school in Hatiheu, and when we came home we would call down to our mothers from the top of the ridge to prepare our food, and they would hear us. Life was good then.' So what about now? 'Copra prices are low, but it's OK, we don't need much to live here.' I walked back up the trail to Hatiheu, reflecting that life was barely surviving in Anaho and the spirit had gone out of the place. Nobody had even offered to sell me an island curio.

At dinner that night, my limbs were on fire under constant attacks by blackflies. No sooner would I quench the flames on one limb with lotions when there would be a fresh outbreak on another. Maurice was unsympathetic: 'That is why there are so few tourists. It's just as well, too many tourists would not be good for the Marquesas.'

It was my last evening in Hatiheu and the sky was full of stars, so I braved the *no-no* nightfighters for a stroll by the shore. As I gazed at the heavens, a shooting star flashed down behind the black buttresses framing the bay. It was a magical scene, and like Stevenson in the Cevennes I felt a longing for a companion to lie near me in the starlight. But I was not alone. Through the trees, I saw Maurice sitting motionless on a stone bench looking out to sea, framed by the dark outlines of palm fronds. Was he dreaming of the past, or wondering about an uncertain future? I left him to his reverie, a lonely relic of a forgotten race of warriors and cannibals.

THE WEATHER HAD CLEARED sufficiently to allow me to return to Taiohae by land, in a municipal Land-Rover conveying a man with a chest infection to hospital. From the summit of the pass through which Alain's helicopter had flown a few days before, I beheld for the first time Melville's valley of

Taipi – a long, lush vale sloping down to the sea, enclosed by a horseshoe of green mountains laced with waterfalls. A hamlet was visible in a coconut plantation far below.

When Jack London visited the valley in 1907, he found only about half a dozen wretched inhabitants afflicted by leprosy, elephantiasis, and tuberculosis. He also encountered a lot of blackflies: 'There is no past nor future when they fasten upon one's epidermis, and I am willing to wager that Omar Khayyám could never have written the *Rubáiyát* in the valley of Typee – it would have been psychologically impossible.'

I had been advised it would be worth straying from Stevenson's itinerary to visit Mgr Lecleach on the neighbouring island of Uapu. He had recently retired as Bishop of the Marquesas, and was said to be an authority on the history and culture of the islands. The *Aranui*, a 2,000-ton mixed cargo and passenger vessel, was due to leave Nuku-Hiva for Uapu the next day, so I went to the harbour as soon as she arrived. I was offered a mattress on the after-deck, or an air-conditioned cabin which was considerably more expensive; deciding that I had suffered enough from oppressive heat and villainous insects, I chose the latter and luxuriated in my first hot shower for two weeks.

Like the *Wellington Star*, the *Aranui* had been built in Bremen. In her white livery she was a handsome vessel, with comfortable passenger accommodation and three cranes forward for her principal business of moving cargo. Hostesses gave lectures on the history and customs of the islands she visited during her sixteen-day voyages out of Papeete, and led excursions ashore; tourists could thus enjoy a taste of adventure in the outer reaches of Polynesia without any of the discomforts of actually staying there. In the afternoon, we sailed around the coast to off-load cargo at Taipivi, and allow the passengers to make an excursion. I remained on the poop deck, splashing around in a small plunge pool, and entertaining a gaggle of Polynesian children with what I thought was a reasonably good impression of the Loch Ness

Monster. One little girl could not swim, and cried for me to carry her into the pool. With this lovely soft-skinned creature laughing in my arms, and the sun mocking the brooding cliffs of Nuku-Hiva, I was stirred by an emotion I had not felt for some time. It was happiness.

At dinner that evening, I shared a table with an electrician from Los Angeles, a Swiss insurance salesman, and a telephone engineer from Kansas. They were friendly and gregarious men, but I felt uneasy in the hubbub of conversation after weeks among reticent Marquesan islanders, and went on deck as soon as the meal was over to find we had anchored off Uapu in darkness. Nothing was visible save a few scattered lights on shore. The seamen were casting lines for fish attracted by the ship, and I was intrigued by an intermittent silver flashing around the hull, which turned out to be flying fish whizzing over the inky water like big dragonflies. The steady hum of the ship's auxiliary power was soothing, and the air was fresh and cool. However briefly, it felt good to be at sea again.

FIVE

The fit signboard of a world of wonders

THERE SHOULD BE SIGNS in Uapu saying: 'Here be Dragons'. A few *Tyrannosaurus rex* footprints would not be amiss, either. It is that kind of place. Imagine a volcanic mass rising from the ocean, with a central ridge of mountains dominated by a series of pinnacles; gigantic needles of rock soaring into the heavens like Celtic standing stones, hundreds of feet high; and everything save these monoliths swathed in tropical forest. It looks like The Land that Time Forgot.

From the deck of the *Casco*, an excited Stevenson saw this weird landscape appearing on the horizon at dawn on the 28th of July, 1888:

. . . like the pinnacles of some ornate and monstrous church, they stood there, in the sparkling brightness of the morning, the fit signboard of a world of wonders.

From the deck of the *Aranui* little more than a century later, I watched our whaleboats ferrying goods to a coastal hamlet beneath these awesome spires with the same sense of wonder. This was Hakahetau, the home of Mgr Lecleach; I had arranged to be put ashore and rejoin the ship in the main settlement of Hakahau later in the day by hiking through the mountains. Two youths lounging by the quay directed me along a rocky beach to a path lined by flowering bushes, which led past a pretty little church to a cottage of wooden hardboard panels on a hillock. A villager was stretched out asleep on a stone in the garden, with his wife and naked infant son sitting beside him; a young girl was raking leaves around flowering shrubs. I had telephoned in advance, and Lecleach was expecting me: a small, stocky Breton with silver hair, he welcomed me with a smile and a firm handshake and led me into a sparse room with a library of mainly religious works.

'Stevenson's observations were fairly perceptive, allowing for the fact that they were coloured by his romanticism,' he told me. 'But people today who say the Marquesans are like Europeans have understood nothing about them. Mentally, they are totally different and they mask their feelings. My predecessor lived in the islands for forty years and admitted he could never explain their behaviour.' Lecleach said there was a dark side to the Marquesan character, which he illustrated with a story. Not long before, a man had fallen out with his sister and ordered her to leave his house. She refused, but he insisted and warned her to be gone by the next morning. The next day she was still there, so he told her to say her prayers. When she had finished, he shot her dead with a hunting rifle. His lawyer pleaded in mitigation that his ancestors were warriors, and he was sentenced to only a few years in prison.

Lecleach agreed the Marquesans' enigmatic behaviour could be attributed partly to their history of tribal warfare and cannibalism and the degradation of their society in the late nineteenth century. It seems that a popular recreation for warriors in olden days was to set off in canoes in search of people fishing alone in other valleys; women were prime targets. The idea was to sacrifice them to the gods, and feast on the leftovers. Inevitably, there were reprisals. 'They remain enormously distrustful,' Lecleach said. 'Their philosophy may be summed up by a saying, "*ia oe ta oe*", which means mind your own business.'

The Western work ethic and coveting consumer goods are relatively new concepts in these remote islands, but they have had a profound effect. Polynesians used to consider work an illness, not a virtue, and anybody who cherished money was regarded as sick. Lecleach said there was still no Marquesan word for 'work', and the word for 'dance' was used instead; but men clearing the bush for the municipality were dancing to the tune of £500 per month, and teachers earned three times this amount. Hence the proliferation of jeeps, motor boats, televisions, and washing machines. 'You have noticed they do not smile much. There is no depression here, but there is gravity. They are not unhappy, no such word exists in their language, but there are anxieties and drunkenness which undermines their self-control.'

When Stevenson sailed past Uapu on his way to Nuku-Hiva, French priests were translating the Bible into Marquesan, but the population was declining so rapidly they gave it up on the assumption that soon there would be nobody left to read it. They were almost right: by 1926 there were barely two thousand souls left in all the islands. With the population having recovered to about seven thousand, Lecleach has completed the translation. He had also, I discovered later, designed the Marquesan flag. Another of his schemes was an association to preserve and promote Marquesan culture. 'It is not an easy task, when we are subjected to Western television, music, and fashions,' he said. 'But of course you will be following Stevenson to Western Samoa. There you will find a fine race of people who have preserved their way of life admirably.'

The *Aranui* had left Hakahetau by the time we had finished talking. The good monseigneur gave me an apple and a glass of water, and I strolled through the village towards the road for Hakahau. A young man walking towards me, the only figure in the main street, did not look up as I passed, but I was observed curiously from doorways. The road of beaten earth rose gradually around a headland, and then hugged the coast over and around bluffs, with occasional views of the pinnacles to my right and deserted coves and beaches to my left. Other than the road I was travelling on, there were no signs of human life. It was about twelve miles to the main settlement, and I was enjoying the solitude and the exercise; but when an open truck approached me about halfway, I accepted a lift. It was just as well. As we climbed up to a bleak plateau among the mountains, which included the highest peak in the Marquesas, the scenery disappeared behind a hissing wall of torrential rain. I was deposited, a bedraggled figure soaked to the skin and caked with mud, at a restaurant where the tourists had gathered for lunch.

I MADE ONE OTHER departure from Stevenson's itinerary in the Marquesas, to visit the island of Fatu-Hiva. In Nuku-Hiva I had met Philippe Trillaud, a fresh-faced young circuit judge from Savoie, whose jurisdiction extended over a swath of French Polynesia about the size of Western Europe. He called himself 'the flying judge'. In civil cases, he put the islanders at ease by adopting an informal approach: usually he wore a casual shirt and shorts, a flower behind his ear, and no shoes. Apart from being well informed about Marquesan society, and having a fund of amusing anecdotes about island justice, he was a pleasant companion; when we met again on my arrival in Hiva-Oa and he suggested I accompany him to Fatu-Hiva to hear a land dispute, I readily agreed. It was decided we would sail to the island on the *Aranui*, and return to Hiva-Oa on a municipal *bonitier* (tuna boat).

Fatu-Hiva is the southernmost island in the archipelago. It is also the wettest. Formed by the remnants of two volcanoes in the shape of a crescent, it is about eight miles long by four miles wide, with a population of less than four hundred. In the 1930s the Norwegian ethnologist Thor Heyerdahl and his young bride lived in the jungle there with no modern conveniences in an attempt to return to nature; after a promising start, they were eventually driven out by the rain, venomous insects, skin disease, and the hostility of natives. His subsequent *Kon-Tiki* raft expedition across the Pacific must have seemed like a pleasure cruise by comparison.

From the *Aranui*, Fatu-Hiva appeared one night as a row of

six street lamps beneath a dark mass of mountains, with staccato bursts of the surf rifling the shore like machine-gun fire. In the morning, a church, a few houses, and a soccer field were visible through fine rain sweeping down a green valley; a group of figures in yellow oilskins was huddled by a small quay. There is no tourist industry anywhere in the Marquesas, and consequently there are no souvenir shops. When local women came on board the *Aranui* to sell *tapa* – parchments from the bark of banyan, mulberry, and breadfruit trees, painted with ancient designs and tattooed warriors – the tourists descended on them like sharks in a feeding frenzy. I left on the first available whaleboat to join Philippe and his Marquesan clerk Pierre in the court-house of the village of Omoa.

We assembled in a large room in a modern bungalow and sat around a table with three islanders, all of us in casual shirts, shorts, and bare feet. The petitioners rolled cigarettes, lit up, and produced documents from plastic bags for the inspection of the court. Outside, rain drizzled from clouds above a verdant mountain. Proceedings were briefly interrupted by a whirlwind of snarling fur which swept in through an open door; Pierre restored the decorum of the court with a well-aimed kick at the canine disputants. During a break, Pierre explained that the men were demanding compensation from the commune for the erection of electricity poles and an irrigation channel on their land at the head of the valley. 'They're asking far too much, and they don't pay their electricity bills anyway,' he said. 'The problem is they went to Tahiti to work and joined the independence movement, and they've been causing trouble ever since they came back.'

I left this barefoot justice to run its course, and joined a party of the more energetic tourists for a hike to the only other settlement, at Hanavave. French soldiers had carved a trail through the mountains between the two communities, but there was no sign of it having been used by anything other than unshod horses; the islanders apparently preferred to travel by outrigger canoe, which was quicker. A strenuous climb up the winding trail was rewarded by a splendid view of the Baie des Vierges, a narrow canyon formed by stupendous crater walls falling in serrated, razor-backed ridges to the coastal hamlet of Hanavave. It looked like a dark, hellish place, but it was pleasant enough down in the valley were we found a muddy track meandering through coconut plantations by the side of a swift-flowing stream. I plunged into a rock pool, and enjoyed drifting in its swirling eddies after the heat and exertion of the hike. At the shore I finally took my leave of my fellow-passengers on the *Aranui*, and made arrangements to return to Omoa by canoe.

None of the villagers seemed keen to take me, but eventually a fisherman agreed to make the fifteen-minute trip for the equivalent of £20. It seemed expensive, but it was late afternoon and I had no desire to walk back over the mountains alone. An ancient, frail-looking craft with paint flaking from its sides was dragged from a shelter, and a plug wrapped in plastic was inserted in a drain-hole in the hull; a rusty 15 h.p. engine was then attached to a piece of wood by the stern. I regarded these proceedings dubiously. As we waded into a heavy swell beneath overhanging cliffs, one of the tourists pointed his camera at us and called: 'Smile, Gavin, this might be a famous last picture.' My humour was not improved by the sight of Emile the boatman muttering a silent prayer and crossing himself as we spluttered past the *Aranui* towards the open sea.

In the event the sea was relatively calm, and we chugged around the coast without incident until we came to the bay of Omoa, where it suddenly became choppy. Huge waves were exploding against the quay with immense power, rocking us with their recoil, and Emile said: 'We try somewhere else. You fall in there, you finish.' His expressive gesture of slicing his hand across his throat was unnecessary. I suggested running the

canoe up the stony beach, but Emile said we would capsize
before we reached it, and he steered instead for the other side of
the bay, where waves were rising and falling by about five feet
against the rocky shore. 'You think you can jump there?' Emile
asked. I said I would try, there being no apparent alternative.
He looked doubtful, but edged the canoe in, waited for a wave
to lift it near the top of the rocks, and shouted: 'Jump!' I
scrambled up a rock to safety, to the alarm of a colony of crabs,
as the succeeding wave pulled at my legs. When I looked back,
Emile was a dark silhouette waving farewell on the shimmering
silver sea.

NATURE PRODUCES IMAGES of stupefying severity
and sublime beauty in the Marquesas; the bewildered traveller is
constantly being confronted by one or the other. The moon rises,
or a boat rounds a headland, the kaleidoscope turns, and a
dazzling new pattern emerges. I came upon one of its most
enchanting sights on an evening stroll through Omoa village,
when I was attracted by the sound of singing from the church.

Beneath a wooden roof in the shape of an inverted whale boat,
almost the entire village was gathered for evening Mass. The air
was fragrant with *leis* draped around religious statues, and the
singing accompanied by a guitar was delightful; there was a
happy cadence and purity of tone in these devotions which I
came to associate with the South Seas, far more moving than the
monotonous mumbling of European congregations. Outside,
two palm trees were etched in perfect symmetry against a
crimson sunset, and a lone star twinkled above them. I walked
down a path by lamplight to the beach, where the dark outlines
of cliffs ran out to sea, their ridges spiked with palm trees.
Looking back, a thin sliver of moon directly above the church
created a circle of bright light suffused with all the colours of
the rainbow; the windows of the church emanated a warm, rosy

glow; the lilting melodies from within drifted on the evening breeze. A more exotic scene could not be imagined. It was absurdly beautiful, and I reflected that Stevenson had missed the jewel in the dark crown of the Marquesas. As I strolled back, people were coming out of the church whistling and singing softly to themselves; from each one I received a smile and a friendly *bonsoir*.

'The important thing here is not to lose face. If you do, you're lost.' Philippe was explaining the subtle art of applying French justice in Polynesian societies without causing offence. 'The problem is we have two societies with very different ways of thinking. You have to be careful, to juggle with sentiments, be very diplomatic, and try to find consensus and compromise.' To illustrate the point, he told me a story of a man on an atoll in the Tuamotus who had stolen a neighbour's pig and eaten it. The man admitted the offence, but being a fisherman he had no money to pay a fine or compensation. 'I knew that in the Tuamotus people eat dogs, so I asked the defendant if he had any dogs. He said he had, so I asked the plaintiff if he would accept a dog in exchange for his pig. He said he would, but he wanted more than one. Quite arbitrarily, I suggested four. Both men agreed, and they went off together to choose them. This was duly noted in the court documents, thereby settling a feud which could have festered for years. But I sometimes wonder how such a judgment would be received in France.'

Boarding the *bonitier* for our return to Hiva-Oa was difficult due to a heavy swell running against the quay, but when we reached the open sea the helmsman told me: 'Weather good, sea calm, you very lucky. This is rare.' Calm is a relative term in the Pacific; traversing the Humboldt current in a following sea in a small boat is an interesting experience. The horizon frequently disappears behind five-foot waves travelling a good deal faster than the boat, resulting in a maritime roller-coaster that would be the envy of any amusement park. The rear deck was dominated by a large fishing reel secured by bolts. Other fishermen I had met scoffed at this addition, asserting that any self-respecting big game fish would shear the bolts and wrench the mechanism from the boat, along with a good section of the hull. Looking at the fixtures, I tended to agree. It was thus with some trepidation that I viewed the crew putting the boat about with excited cries when they spotted a flock of frigate birds wheeling and diving into a shoal of tuna. Happily no fish were deluded by our bait of brightly coloured streamers, and our suspect engineering was not put to the test.

A fine rain was falling as we approached Hiva-Oa and tied up in the small harbour of Tahauku. A few minutes later, we were driving into the valley of Atuona, described by Stevenson as 'the loveliest, and by far the most ominous and gloomy, spot on earth'.

SIX

At all hours of the day they strike the mind with menacing gloom

NOTHING MUCH HAD CHANGED. The village of Atuona now boasted a sports field, two modern warehouses, and a large satellite dish, but it remained an insignificant settlement in a landscape of melancholy grandeur. The vale behind rose gradually to the escarpments of a bowl of mountains three thousand feet high, effectively sealing the valley from the rest of the island; it invoked claustrophobia on a grand scale.

As at Nuku-Hiva, Stevenson remained on the *Casco*, making visits ashore and receiving guests on the yacht. I rented a small bungalow from the municipality in the centre of the village, and began planning my first expedition. Looking up from my map, it seemed as if the mountains were on fire. Wisps of cloud were curling among crevices and swirling across their pitted faces like fumes from the volcanic cauldrons which created them. I regarded them with mixed feelings. They had a wild beauty, but they were also hard and daunting, and I was about to traverse their flanks. From a similar viewpoint, Stevenson wrote:

Tahiti and Hawaii can offer no such picture of abrupt, melancholy alps . . . at all hours of the day they strike the eye with some new beauty, and the mind with the same menacing gloom.

Undaunted, he ascended the valley on horseback in the company of a French missionary as far as a newly opened graveyard, where he admired the craftsmanship of its dry-stone walls and reflected on the honour Marquesans bestowed on their dead. Unable to find a horse or a guide, I followed him alone on foot.

A concrete road wound out of the village of wooden bungalows and followed a shallow river towards the mountains. I passed a youth dressed in shorts, sandals, and a crimson eye-shade, wired for sound from a portable tape-player and apparently oblivious to his surroundings, including me. The road ended at a crossing-point over the river which had collapsed, resulting in a swift current and a waterfall. According to my map, a path marked 'uncertain' which I assumed to have been taken by Stevenson began a few yards back. Accordingly I retraced my steps, found a muddy trail in the undergrowth, and struck up through dense vegetation. The path ascended steeply and soon I was pausing to admire a panorama of mountains and the sea, but there was no sense of bucolic peace; beneath a lowering sky there was a brooding disquiet about the scene. It was as if I had entered a lair of prehistoric creatures. There should have been signs saying beware of low-flying pterodactyls.

I continued climbing, and at the top of a hillock I came upon the crumbling remains of the dry-stone walls admired by Stevenson, but it was now a bleak and gloomy place. A few rusting iron crosses rose starkly from uneven ground, where rectangles of black rock covered the graves. Curiously the earth was sparsely vegetated, as if the wild grasses were loath to take root in such a desolate place. It was Boot Hill beneath a broken volcano. The roof of one tomb, cracked and mouldy with age, had either collapsed or been broken through at one end, and I peered in. On a ledge halfway down lay the remnants of a wooden oar; on the earthen floor was a pile of what appeared to be thigh bones and a pelvis. Unless the occupant had been a contortionist, which seemed unlikely, his remains had clearly been disturbed, but by whom or for what reason I was never able to discover.

I mused that these grisly fragments might once have carried a man to a cannibal feast, but I had no sense of disturbing a sacred site; it seemed so ancient that one felt even the spirits of the dead must have departed long before. Yet as I sat on the graveyard wall jotting down my impressions, I gave an involuntary shudder when a wind sighed up from the valley and moaned through the mountains. I looked up to see clouds whirling into spectral forms across a vertical cliff looming over me; behind me the shattered crypt stared at the darkening sky like a malevolent one-eyed beast. It was a classic setting for a Dracula film, lacking only thunder and lightning.

I went on, vowing to ensure I would not have to pass this way again after nightfall. The path became abruptly narrower, with the foliage pressing in on both sides and forming a canopy which further diminished the light. Something lightly brushed my hair; I looked up, but the nearest branch was at least three feet above me. I presumed it was a spider's web and pressed on. A few minutes later the wind increased in strength, and the clouds became seriously menacing. It was now late in the afternoon, and I was uncertain how much further I could go before dusk forced me to retrace my steps. Cravenly I turned back, telling myself that given sunshine and a cheery companion I would venture further one day. (In the event, the clouds clung doggedly to the mountains for the remainder of my stay on Hiva-Oa, and the expedition was not repeated.) I turned to face the sea, hurried past the cemetery, and after a few twists and turns gratefully beheld the village nestling in the valley below.

The sound of guitars from houses among the trees restored my spirits, and cries of laughter led me down a path to the river. In the soft gloaming, urchins were launching themselves from the bank at the end of a rope attached to a tree, and plunging with excited squeals into a clear pool, a picture of innocent happiness. Watching their lithe brown bodies emerging from the river, I thought of the sombre burial ground above them, and mused on the brief intensity of life. My decision to turn back had been a wise one: as I lingered by the river bank the heavens opened, and by the time I reached my bungalow I was drenched to the skin.

IN THE SOUTH SEAS is far from being Stevenson's best book. Writing to Henry James from Samoa, he admitted:

I am continually extending my information, revising my opinions, and seeing the most finely finished portions of my work come part by part in pieces. Very soon I shall have no opinions left. And without an opinion, how to string artistically vast accumulations of fact?

There are fine descriptive passages and amusing anecdotes in the book, but there are episodes which are frankly dull, and those on Hiva-Oa are among them. An account of a plantation having been destroyed by tidal waves before his arrival, and of petty rivalries between two local chiefs offers little material for retracing his adventures. Fortunately, I had another source of inspiration. Thirteen years after Stevenson, another ailing European arrived on Hiva-Oa, in September 1901, and made his home there.

'Today I am wiped out, defeated by misery and mostly sickness . . . I think that here, this really savage element, this complete solitude will give me, before dying, a last spark of enthusiasm which will rejuvenate my imagination and make the conclusion of my talent.'

The man who penned those words was Eugène Henri Paul Gauguin.

Having left two child-wives and an infant son in Tahiti, contracted syphilis from a prostitute in Paris, and suffered a broken ankle in a scuffle with sailors in Brittany, Gauguin limped into Atuona to face further disappointment. Instead of the naked cannibals and master craftsmen he had hoped to find, he came to a dispirited community intent on drinking itself to death.

The house that Gauguin built in the centre of the village surpassed in size and splendour anything that had been seen in the Marquesas. Forty feet long, eighteen wide, and two storeys high, it had a wood-carving studio, a kitchen, and a dining-room on the ground floor, and a small bedroom and a large studio upstairs. The entrance to the upper floor was surrounded by painted wooden panels, with a lintel on which the shocked missionaries read: *Maison du Jouir*. At first the House of Pleasure lived up to its name, drawing natives with its rum and claret to gape at the strange pictures on the walls and spend half the night carousing; but they deserted Gauguin when the outraged Catholic bishop denounced their wild parties, and local gen-darmes conspired to make his life a misery.

The house is no longer standing, but municipal workmen have created a faithful reproduction near the original site. The building of woven bamboo with a palm-thatch roof is light and airy, but that is all it contained when I visited it. There were plans for showing exhibits from Paris, but I could not imagine there would be long queues at the door. None of the locals I spoke to showed the least interest in their island's most illus-trious former resident. Yet standing alone in the studio, with soft light filtering through the plaited roof, it was easy to conjure images of the artist, demented by illness and hostile French officials, drowning the angst of his last days in absinthe. It was in an identical room that his native neighbour Tioka called to see him on the morning of the 8th of May, 1903. Receiving no answer, Tioka climbed the stairs and found Gauguin lying in bed with one leg over the side. He resorted to a traditional method of confirming death and bit Gauguin's head. The artist remained lifeless, and Tioka intoned an ancient Marquesan death lament.

The next day four native pall-bearers carried the coffin to a Catholic cemetery in the outskirts of the village. There were no funeral orations, and no flowers. The administrator of the Marquesas sent a report to his superiors in Papeete, in which he said: 'I have requested all creditors of the deceased to submit duplicate statements of their accounts, but am already convinced that the liabilities will considerably exceed assets, as the few pictures left by the late painter, who belonged to the decadent school, have little prospect of finding purchasers.' Gauguin completed about eighty pictures, at least thirty of them considered masterpieces. Two of his greatest works, *L'Appel* and *Contes Barbares*, were painted in Atuona.

There are no signposts to Gauguin's grave. After asking directions, I followed a trail leading up a hillside behind the gendarmerie, turned on to another unmarked path, and came to a small cemetery overgrown with weeds and long grass. In an obscure corner, a rectangular tomb of black volcanic stones lay beneath a frangipani tree, whose fragrant blossoms had almost covered the inscription: *Paul Gauguin 1903*. On a stone pedestal was a small figure of a woman, a copy of one of the artist's sculptures. The memorial was erected by another painter in the 1950s, who had found only a decaying wooden cross among a few scattered stones, and had raised funds from the local authorities to renovate the site. It seemed curious that France, so proud of her culture, had raised no better monument to one of her greatest artists.

A FEW WEEKS LATER in Tahiti I met a German woman who had lived in the Marquesas with her French husband for ten years. 'There are two things a foreign woman can do in the Marquesas,' she told me. 'She can explore new possibilities in herself, or she can go crazy.' This remarkable woman learned to speak French and Marquesan fluently, to ride horses, and to fight off sharks in spear-fishing expeditions. During her stay, three French women failed to discover new possibilities in themselves and went crazy. There are few foreigners resident in the Marquesas, but I had cause to be grateful to one of them. For all the passing friendships I had made, I felt lonely and depressed by the rude landscapes and the sultry weather. The spirit of Stevenson had eluded me, I was weakened by bouts of food poisoning, and three blackfly bites had become badly infected, requiring a daily change of dressings in the local clinic. Enter Eliane Derrien, a diminutive Vietnamese woman with the power of healing.

During the twelve days the *Casco* was anchored off Hiva-Oa, its passengers were 'adopted' by a local chief called Moipu. Stevenson regarded him with undisguised loathing as 'an incurable cannibal grandee . . . his favourite morsel was the human hand, of which he speaks today with an ill-favoured lustfulness'. Eliane was an infinitely preferable foster-parent. Evacuated from Vietnam in the 1950s after the battle of Dien Ben Phu, she met her husband Jean, a former Vietnamese soldier, in France, and for five years they had lived in the Marquesas, where Jean was a telecommunications engineer. Eliane was a disciple of an oriental philosophy which believed in a divine power that cured illness and fatigue. She practised this technique by summoning the benevolent power with prayers, and directing it to afflicted areas of the body with a cupped hand. The running sores on my legs did not improve with her therapy, but they did not get any worse either, and I always left her home near my bungalow with a profound sense of well-being.

On the eve of my departure from the Marquesas, I was queasy from a severe bout of food poisoning, and unable to sleep because of loud music and drunken laughter from an adjacent bungalow. In the middle of the night a cock began crowing, and set off a crescendo of infernal screeching among its brethren. I was weary and irritable when I climbed on board Jean's jeep for a half-hour ride to the airport, but for once it was a fresh, bright morning, and a rainbow had banished the clouds from the mountains.

At the small airport, the lounge was filled with music and laughter, and children with flowers in their hair. It was the happiest gathering I had seen in the Marquesas. A French passenger remarked: 'It is because they are going to Tahiti.' The irrepressible Eliane bestowed last-minute gifts of croissants and chocolate, and as the aircraft gathered speed down the runway, I saw her directing a last ray of divine power towards me. We flew off the cliff and the plane banked over the bay of Atuona, but I did not look back: I was glad to leave this land of loud scenery and quiet people.

SEVEN

We spent the evenings in the moonlight . . . entranced and thrilled by stories of Tahiti and the Paumotus

I WAS AWAKENED BY sunlight streaming into my thatched hut. A few steps away the lagoon was flat calm, reflecting the delicate pink of the sunrise. A lone gull skimmed silently over the water, the only sign of life in a quiet panorama of sea and sky.

As I bathed in the tepid shallows, a thin stream of cloud hovered above a distant smudge of land. It hung seemingly motionless in perfect symmetry with the horizon, as if afraid to venture from its tenuous anchorage; the effect was of providing variety and perspective, rather than any serious attempt to obscure the sun. A wagging tail with a friendly dog attached to it flopped down beside me on the beach, and soon was fast asleep. The melancholy which had haunted me in the Marquesas dissolved in a haze of peace and contentment.

There are essentially two kinds of islands in the Pacific: 'high' islands formed by the summits of volcanoes, and 'low' islands where the mountains have sunk back into the depths, leaving formations of coral barely breaking the surface of the ocean. The Tuamotus, to which I had come, were of the latter variety: narrow strips of land around huge lagoons, the highest points rarely exceeding ten feet above sea level. From the air, they look like necklaces scattered carelessly over the ocean; on land, the effect is of being on a stationary aircraft carrier perilously low in the water.

When Stevenson persuaded the captain of the *Casco* to set a course for these remote atolls north-east of Tahiti, it was against the latter's better judgement. The area had an infamous reputation among mariners as the Dangerous Archipelago, due to treacherous currents swirling among a maze of badly charted reefs; the coastal waters and the lagoons teemed with sharks, and the natives were deemed equally uncivil. France had formally extended its authority over the seventy-six islands of the group more than thirty years before, but the inhabitants of dozens of them were still regarded as savages and cannibals, and navigators were warned to treat them with the 'greatest prudence'.

The prospects of the *Casco* coming to grief in this maritime graveyard were considerable: but due to their isolation and lack of economic resources, the islands remained outposts of dreams and visions in the vastness of the Pacific, a compelling lure for an adventurous author. Sailing into this time-warp, the Stevenson household promptly became lost. Having missed their destination of Takaroa by thirty miles, they fetched up at Fakarava to find a superstitious population haunted by demons.

For the first time on their voyage they lived ashore, in a small house by the lagoon which they found delightful: but on the wilder ocean side of the atoll Stevenson was impressed by a very different aspect.

The beach is accursed and deserted, the fit scene only for wizardry and shipwreck, and in the native belief a haunting ground of murderous spectres . . . when the living ate the dead, horrified nocturnal imagination drew the shocking inference that the dead might eat the living.

No ghouls were immediately apparent as I approached Fakarava in a twin-prop of Air Tahiti, but I did see monsters: by the outer rim of the atoll, two whales were clearly visible a few feet beneath the surface, blowing fountains of water into the air. It was a splendid welcome to an enchanting island.

Local guidebooks listed no accommodation in Rotoava, the main village where Stevenson had stayed, so from Papeete I had called the agent for Air Tahiti to seek his help. An indistinct voice on a crackling line said: 'OK, no problem. I'll meet you at the airport. My name is Williams.' The plane scrunched along a gravel runway and taxied towards a *fare*, a kind of open, thatched hut, where I found Mr Williams in a red T-shirt and shorts issuing tickets for the onward flight to another atoll. A few people were lounging against pick-up trucks waiting for friends and relatives, smiling and chatting in bright sunshine. Nobody seemed in any hurry to go anywhere. Time slowed, and I sat on my bags and removed my watch. I felt I would have no use for it in Fakarava.

Eventually Mr Williams emerged and I climbed into the back of his truck for a short ride along a white track of beaten coral to Rotoava. On my right, the lagoon shimmered in myriad hues of blue and green, and through palm groves I heard the sound of the surf beating on the ocean shore barely a hundred yards to my left. The village appeared as a cluster of wooden cottages and stores around a stone jetty, with a school, a sports field, and a church. Mr Williams stopped to converse with a middle-aged man, then turned to me: 'This is Daniel Snow. You can stay with him.' Daniel was not expecting guests, but he took me to his home, a rambling bungalow in a back lane, and invited me to make myself comfortable. His wife was visiting relatives in Tahiti, and he proposed that the next day we should move to huts they had built by the lagoon outside the village. 'It is more peaceful there,' he assured me. Rotoava was hardly a bustling metropolis, but I was happy to go along with whatever he suggested.

Over lunch I learned that my host was the *tavana*, or head man, of Fakarava and had held a senior position in the local administration for almost thirty years. He traced his ancestry to two traders, William Snow of Scotland and George Smith of Australia, who had come to the island in the mid-nineteenth century and married local women. I also discovered he was a direct descendant of Stevenson's closest companion on Fakarava. We had been discussing the location of Stevenson's house, and

Daniel asked to whom it had belonged. I told him Stevenson never found out who the true owner was, but that his most frequent guest was M. Rimareau Donat, a half-Tahitian who served as acting Vice-Resident. 'Ah, he was my great-grandfather,' Daniel said. 'Now I know where the house stood. The last people who lived there were my sister's family. Come, it's not far from here.'

Stevenson described the house as the best-appointed private residence on the island, a single-storey building of three rooms with verandas at the front and rear, just beyond the church in an oblong patch of cultivation. Fanny recalled that the two weeks they spent there passed in a gentle monotony of collecting seashells and admiring tropical fish in rock pools by the beach:

'The close of the placid day marked the beginning of the most agreeable part of the twenty-four hours. After a simple dinner, and a dip in the soft sea, we sat expectant of our invariable visitor, the governor of the island, M. Donat . . . we spent the evenings in the moonlight, sitting on our mattresses that were spread out on the veranda, the only chair being reserved for our guest . . . night after night we literally sat at his feet entranced and thrilled by stories of Tahiti and the Paumotus [Tuamotus], always of a supernatural character.'

The scene of Donat's ghostly story-telling had been demolished ten years before. A low stone wall, blackened with age and crumbling in parts, enclosed a garden choked with weeds and a profusion of old fruit trees; at the end of a narrow path, a flight of worn steps led to an empty space where the front veranda would have been; beyond were only the foundations of the house, which I measured at roughly twenty-five feet by twelve. 'It's a pity, it was a beautiful house made of fine red wood,' Daniel said. 'The last of the old colonial houses were knocked down two years ago. They were lovely houses with carved verandas. If it had been me I would have restored them, but now people want only modern buildings.'

By the light of day it was a derelict site of no particular interest, but when bathed in moonlight, it evoked haunting images of the past. I returned that night and sat on the garden wall, thinking of the Whistlers. They were members of an obscure religious sect in Fakarava in the last century, whose idea of a good night out was to summon spirits of the dead and exchange gossip about their neighbours. The spirits would communicate in aerial whistling, which would be translated by a medium. Although Donat was an intelligent, cultivated man, he was afraid of them. Fanny recalled:

'When Rimareau spoke of these people and their superstitions his voice sank almost to a whisper, and he cast fearful glances over his shoulder at the black shadows of the palms.'

Stevenson thought they were dreary and silly. One night he amused himself on a stroll by whistling a sea shanty outside a darkened house from which he heard low voices. With the first note, all conversation stopped; when he passed again on his return he found the lamp had been lit, but that the inhabitants were still silent.

I had no guess at the time at the nature and magnitude of the terrors I inflicted, or with what grisly images the notes of that old song had peopled the dark house.

Sitting alone outside Stevenson's old house, a breeze whispering through the palms and moonlight glinting on the gnarled branches of a dead kava tree, I considered it a perfect setting for ghostly manifestations; on my way home I whistled a few bars of 'Annie Laurie' outside a darkened house, but it had no noticeable effect: the occupants were watching a video.

The next morning Daniel and I moved half a mile out of the village, to where he and his wife had a smaller bungalow and a couple of thatched huts for visitors. The latter were simple one-roomed affairs of wooden panels resting on logs, with sloping roofs of dried palm fronds. Each had mattresses, a small table, a bookcase with a shell vase containing silk flowers, and an armchair. In the early afternoon, sunlight reflecting from the lagoon would project a bright, shimmering pattern on the opposite wall. Outside my door a fishing net was suspended between a palm tree and what looked like a small fir; a bench seat salvaged from an old car lay beneath; and a log resting on two tree stumps facing the lagoon completed a pleasing tableau. A seperate hut served as a kitchen, another as a shower and toilet, and an open thatched shelter with a low wall of woven bamboo was the 'restaurant'. There Daniel and I settled down like a couple of old cronies to share the cooking – he caught and fried the fish and I made pasta sauce – and swapped stories late into the night. Daniel proved to be a story-teller worthy of his ancestor Donat, and I enjoyed the sense of history repeating itself.

One night I asked him whether the islanders still believed in spirits. 'That's all finished now, nobody is really afraid of them any more,' he said. 'Still, there are some things that happen that you can't explain. I don't believe the old stories, but . . .' His voice trailed off. We were sitting at a small table by the lagoon. Daniel's dark features were illuminated by a hissing gas lamp, the trees were stirring in a light breeze, and from behind us came the steady crash of the surf. A flying insect blundered into the lamp and crawled broken-winged in the circle of light. I asked Daniel to continue.

'Well, near the pass into the lagoon there are the remains of an old village where there lived a warrior chief called Tahirivairu. As the guardian of the pass, he defended Fakarava from attack. The fighters on the other islands feared him. The site is overgrown with bush now, and the people say it is haunted. A few years ago a man from Tahiti decided to clean it up. The people warned him not to, but he went anyway. That night his testicles swelled to a huge size, and he died.

'Then another Tahitian man came and said he was going to clean the place. He was young and strong, and he was not afraid of the old legends. When he came back to the village that night he was completely crazy. He was waving a big knife and raving that Tahirivairu had appeared and told him he was the new guardian of the pass. We had to restrain him and the next day a plane with doctors came and took him back to Tahiti. The last we heard he was still in a lunatic asylum.' I knew I had to go there. Daniel knew it too, and he organized an expedition in an old truck with a neighbour and a Chinese store-keeper.

The lagoon of Fakarava is thirty-five miles long by twelve miles wide, big enough to hold all of Tahiti, but north of Rotoava the coral road runs for only five miles to the airport. We drove along the side of the runway by the sea, then a rough track took us through coconut groves which gradually gave way to dense bush. A little further we came to an abandoned plantation littered with decaying coconuts and fallen branches; bleached by the sun, they looked like skulls and thigh-bones on an ancient battleground. The track eventually gave out, and we continued on foot along the narrow shore of the lagoon until Daniel led us inland again to a scene of utter desolation. This had been the redoubt of Tahirivairu and his clan, as was apparent from the broken coral-works and rubble of black stones rising from the undergrowth. Haunting enough in itself, the place also bore the scars of a recent hurricane: huge palm trees uprooted by the fury of the winds and others snapped clean through the trunks, their broken stumps protruding from a morass of decaying vegetation. There was no birdsong here, only the dull roar of the ocean on both sides. Our two companions, who had been carrying on a lively conversation, fell silent. 'I have lived on this island for forty years and I have never been to this place,' the store-keeper said. The tone of his voice suggested he would not come back in a hurry. I commiserated silently with the old warrior chief over the desecration of his stronghold by forces more powerful than himself, and passed on.

The way being barred by tangled bush, we returned to the lagoon, which was deeper and more turbulent than at the village. I kept my eyes to the ground. If not hidden treasure, I hoped to find debris from a shipwreck, or other romantic relics from the sea; but even in this remote spot there was evidence only of mankind's carelessness in littering the planet with plastic bottles and beer cans. Suddenly Daniel called: 'Shark!'

Close to the shore, two small sharks were gliding through the shallows and a bigger cousin could be seen prowling a few yards further out. I discovered that a pebble chucked into the water caused the sharks to flash towards the spot, and a shower of pebbles resulted in a frenzy of confused darting. The best effect was produced by skimming a flat stone across the surface, a technique known to generations of Glaswegian urchins at Clyde coastal resorts as 'skiting'. I am adept at this esoteric discipline, currently holding the Bell family and all-comers record of sixteen 'skites'. This was clearly unknown to the sharks, who sped repeatedly after the stones in their eagerness to snatch the tasty morsels they believed were hopping along above them. I grew tired of the game before the sharks did, and pressed on. Soon the vegetation ceased, and we found ourselves on a flat headland of broken coral, like a quarry of shingle, gazing at one of the most turbulent stretches of water I had ever seen.

Lagoons in the Tuamotus have a restless habit of flowing out to the ocean and back again twice every twenty-four hours in a stupendous rush of water like the bursting of a huge dam. The *Casco* had sailed through the pass in a tranquil period between these movements; I was witnessing one of the flood-tides at its height. The current was going out, a massive body of grey water moving inexorably through the channel to clash with the indomitable power of the Pacific, producing a maelstrom of conflicting currents. Daniel's neighbour pointed to the headland opposite, more than a mile distant. 'Never mind the sharks,' he said. 'Nobody could swim across the pass. There are seven different currents out there.' I did not mention at the time that I was planning to scuba-dive through a similar pass at another atoll. Daniel would probably have put me down as another victim of the curse of Tahirivairu.

THE CONTRASTS BETWEEN the Marquesas and the Tuamotus could not have been greater. Instead of grey skies and dark clouds, there was an endless variety of soft and delicate hues: where there had been claustrophobia there was infinite space: there rocky crags had dominated the skyline, here the land was a mere sliver of palm trees between the sea and sky.

On the entire atoll there were less than three hundred people. They were courteous and friendly, with a lively sense of humour, and were forever poking fun at one another; in a month in the Marquesas, I had never heard anyone tell a joke. They were also generous in their affections. After a few days, Daniel announced that I had created a favourable impression. 'The people here make up their minds quickly about foreigners,' he told me. 'For instance the Frenchman is not liked. The people say he is loud-mouthed and tactless. The German couple take themselves too seriously and are not friendly. But everyone says that is a good man staying with me, he is calm and polite and always says hello to people who pass him.' It was the most gratifying compliment I could have hoped to receive.

Like the Stevensons, I began each day with a dip in the lagoon. It was like bathing in a giant aquarium; as I lay motionless in the clear shallows, I was surrounded by a shimmering rainbow of tropical fish. A few yards off shore, eight wooden poles marked the site of a fish trap. This was a scene of some interest. At any hour of the day gulls would be perched there, one to each pillar like diners waiting patiently to be served. Usually there was a vacant perch for late arrivals, but occasionally the fly-in restaurant was full and there were squabbles. Then a gull would flap off and glide low over the water, on the look-out for a take-away snack from near the surface.

In the evening, nature transformed its light brushstrokes of pallid hues into a tapestry of stunning grandeur. The sun sets quickly in the Tuamotus, dropping perceptibly below the horizon. The masterpiece is unveiled half an hour later, when, for about fifteen minutes, the western rim is suffused with streaks of orange and crimson. Higher in the sky, with a fine sense of symmetry, a lone star appears above the dead centre of the lagoon. Daniel said it was called *fetika poi-poi*, the morning star. Sometimes cloud formations borne by the trade winds drift into this scene like strolling players. Once I looked up to see a cloud in the perfect form of a flying fish, complete with eye, tail, and wings, cruising sedately over the lagoon. Beneath this vision the sky was a pale luminous green; above it a layer of gold melted into crimson, and then a deep blue where the lone star twinkled its nightly greeting.

It takes less than five minutes to stroll across the atoll from the lagoon, through the Tuamotuan Looking-Glass, into another world. The sense of insecurity is immediate and appalling: the tranquillity of the lagoon fades to an illusion compared with this vista of the world's biggest ocean surging against one of its tiniest specks of inhabited land. Through the brush, one emerges on to a deserted beach of shingle leading to a broad platform of barely submerged coral. Beyond and beneath it is the reef wall, against which the sea pounds ceaselessly with immense power. Behind, the palm trees on the edge of the plantations are like a ragged line of American Indians facing the cavalry, their long hair streaming in the wind: Fakarava's Last Stand.

One is reminded uncomfortably that no part of this fragile crown of coral stands much above the height of a man; and that any seismic wave worth its salt would sweep over the island as if it did not exist. In 1983, hurricane Orama battered Fakarava with twenty-foot waves, which inundated the plantations and formed a torrent between the ocean and the lagoon which cut off the village. A dozen houses were swept away in the maelstrom. The population survived by sheltering in the church and the municipal offices, both stone buildings on raised platforms of coral. The storm raged for three days, and each night Daniel and three youths crawled on their hands and knees between the places of refuge, half a mile apart, to share provisions and tend the sick. 'The fishing was good afterwards,' Daniel said.

One night after dinner I suggested a walk to the beach to view the sea by moonlight. Daniel readily agreed, and brought his gas lantern. On the way, I sketched to him the plot of *The Isle of Voices*, a mystical Stevenson tale of sorcerers who transformed seashells into dollars, which Fanny believed had been inspired by the beach at Fakarava and the stories of M. Donat. On our nocturnal walk, with the lamp projecting our shadows like giants stalking among the palm trees, it was easy to imagine Stevenson's supernatural characters lurking in the bushes. When we reached the deserted beach the shadows were so black and sharp that they seemed alive, and I jumped when a hermit crab scuttled across my feet. Suddenly Daniel gave a cry – I turned, startled – he had found a buoy washed up on shore. 'These are expensive to buy in Tahiti,' he said with satisfaction. 'Worth many dollars. So your story of the voices is true.' He chuckled at his joke all the way home.

THERE IS NOT MUCH motorized traffic in Fakarava. I counted half a dozen old motor scooters, possibly the same number of small trucks, an American jeep of World War II vintage belonging to a Swiss baker, and one car, a dilapidated Volkswagen which appeared to have a top speed of 15 m.p.h. Most of the population depended on their feet, and a fleet of sturdy bicycles. Daniel had a television, a video, a refrigerator, and a municipal boat, none of which was working. This hardly mattered, since electricity from the kerosene generator in the village did not reach our settlement on the outskirts. However, he had a spare bicycle which was working in a wobbly kind of way, and it was on this machine that I pedalled into the village to attend the Great Event.

Elections in the Tuamotus tend to be low-key affairs, in which politicians fly in from Tahiti to distribute hats, T-shirts, and extravagant promises in the hope of gaining a lucrative term in office, and then disappear until the next time. On this occasion, the polling had international implications. In accordance with French law, the hundred and seventy-three fishermen and copra workers on the electoral roll of Fakarava were called upon to vote in a national referendum on the Maastricht Treaty of European unity. As *tavana*, Daniel set a sterling example to the community. 'I'm not voting,' he declared. 'I don't understand it, and I'm not really interested.' However, as the senior official present, it was his duty to supervise the proceedings; it was the only time I saw him exchanging his T-shirt and baggy shorts for a shirt and long trousers.

A few people had gathered at the *mairie*, a single-storey building in the colonial style which Stevenson had noted as one of two spacious government bungalows in the village. (It had been built eight years before he arrived.) In a large room, the portraits of French presidents past and present looked down on a couple of tables and a row of empty benches with varying expressions of sternness (de Gaulle) and benevolence (Mitterrand). The walls were adorned with necklaces of nuts wrapped in brightly patterned cloth, and a tape machine was playing island melodies. The voting procedure was fairly simple. People took both 'yes' and 'no' voting slips, placed the one of their choice in an envelope which went into a Perspex ballot box, and threw the other into a waste basket. It was thus fairly simple to gauge the voting trend by peering into the basket. After an hour I counted seven rejected 'yes' votes, and one 'no'.

I wandered out to conduct a straw poll among men lounging in the shade of the veranda. A fisherman from the southern part of the atoll summed up the general view. 'I don't really know what it's all about,' he said, 'but I voted no because I don't want a lot of foreigners coming here and changing our way of life.' The men murmured their assent, and resumed their discussion of copra prices and the merits of various outboard engines. After the initial rush of eight voters in the first hour the pace slackened, and Daniel and his assistants retired to the rear veranda to watch a football match on the sports field.

When the polls closed (at the end of the soccer game), the contents of the ballot box were presented to four and a half officials – three men and a young woman with an infant on her knee; as the town clerk read out the votes, Daniel chalked them on a blackboard. There was momentary confusion when two envelopes were found to be empty, two contained both 'yes' and 'no' slips, and the slip in another had been torn in half; all were declared invalid, and the residue amounted to a 37–8 rejection of the treaty.

The few spectators left without comment, and the town clerk went to a radio telephone to send the result to Papeete. Makemo Atoll, with almost double the electorate of Fakarava, was heard to report: 'Zero votes.'

The radio crackled: 'Repeat, please.'

'Makemo, zero votes, nothing, nobody voted.'

'Are you sure?'

'This is the mayor speaking.'

'*Ah bon.*'

Daniel and I went to a neighbour's house to watch the result of the referendum being announced on French television: Paris had not waited for its Polynesian citizens to make their views known. Daniel said: 'We're so small it won't make any difference. We don't really matter.' Cycling home beneath the stars, the coral road illuminated by moonlight, I was happy to be on a little island that didn't really matter.

UNFORTUNATELY, THE TUAMOTUS were acquiring economic importance. Two Frenchmen who owned a pearl farm on a neighbouring atoll told me the islands were in the grip of 'black pearl fever', which had precipitated corruption and land disputes. The industry was dominated by Chinese–Tahitian millionaires who flew around their concessions in private jets. One of them reputedly controlled half of all Polynesian production, and sold his share to a Lebanese dealer in New York who styled himself the Black Pearl King.

The Frenchmen blamed the big producers for swamping the market with poor-quality pearls. In the rush for quick profits, they said, pearls were being harvested after a year instead of the normal eighteen months, the quality had dropped, and prices had fallen by half. 'The Chinese are like rats,' one of them said. 'They'll be the first off the ship if it starts to sink.' Daniel had been approached twice by Tahitian businessmen offering substantial bribes for pearl-farming rights on Fakarava. 'I told them to take a walk,' he said. But the tide was against him. Three years before, there had been no foreigners resident on the island. Now there were five, and they all had pearl farms.

I was intrigued by this black gold rush, and I was pleased when Daniel offered to take me on a diving expedition to inspect three thousand shells he was cultivating in the lagoon. Rowing out in his dinghy was a laborious business, as he had only one oar. I asked him why. 'A friend borrowed the other one,' he said. Then I asked if there were many sharks in the lagoon.

'Yes, many.'

'But only small ones, right?'

'Some small, some big.'

I donned a mask, flippers, and wet-suit and followed Daniel with some trepidation into the depths at a marker buoy. About twenty feet down, a string of copra sacks containing the shells was suspended in the gloom. The visibility was surprisingly poor, and I glanced around repeatedly, fearful of inquisitive sharks.

At the next buoy, some distance further out, we discovered the weight of the shells had dragged the retaining lines down to sixty feet, which was too deep. Daniel said he needed to attach another buoy. I knew my lung-power was not equal to his, so I followed him only halfway down and watched him descending out of sight. It was then, while I was in a state of suspended animation, that a large dark shape flitted across the limit of my vision. I turned quickly, but whatever I had seen had been travelling fast, because it had vanished. I felt a tightness in my chest, whether from alarm or lack of air I do not know, and I was relieved when Daniel came finning up towards me and we returned to the boat. On the way back, I asked him if he was afraid of sharks. 'They don't bother us much,' he said. Had he ever been attacked? He pointed to a dark scar on his leg and patted his buttocks. 'Here and here. They came suddenly, I can't think what got into them.' I wondered if the Black Pearl King in New York ever considered this aspect of his realm. I thought it unlikely.

When we returned, we discovered we had missed a great event, the first fire in the known history of Fakarava. The airport, or what there was of it, had burned down. Daniel immediately jumped into a neighbour's truck and went to investigate. A dripping wet-suit was hardly the best attire for a reporter in pursuit of a hot story, so I changed into shorts and pedalled after them. I was barely halfway when I met Daniel coming back: 'It's not worth going on, it's all over. The *fare* is burned to the ground.' It transpired that plantation workers had been burning rotten trees, and left them smouldering when they went off for lunch; the brush caught fire, and within minutes the airport hut was reduced to ashes. 'The best of it is, there was a big new fire extinguisher in the *fare*,' Daniel said. 'It was not even a month old, but instead the fire put him out.' He found this highly amusing.

STEVENSON NOTED WRYLY that foreigners were generally assumed to be impervious to homicidal wizardry in the islands:

I believe all natives regard white blood as a kind of talisman against the powers of hell. In no other way can they explain the unpunished recklessness of Europeans.

I sometimes wonder what the superstitious natives of the nineteenth century would have made of recent European activities on Mururoa. I had visited the atoll in the southern Tuamotus a few years before, on a reporting assignment. From the middle of its lagoon, a red and white drilling rig rises like a fairground helter-skelter, and deeply tanned young men foster the illusion of a holiday resort by cavorting on gaily coloured sailboards. Reality lurks a few fathoms down, where French engineers have bored repeatedly into the basaltic rock of a submerged volcano to create explosion chambers for nuclear warheads; a laboratory for mass destruction in an illusory paradise. Outsiders can only speculate what effect these cataclysmic bangs have had beneath the ocean, but the aftermath of an earlier series of atmospheric tests is there for all to see.

At the western extremities of the atoll, the tangled vegetation gives way to a tortured landscape of incinerated palms and shattered coral, battered by huge waves as if nature was trying to wash away the detritus of man's folly. At the last military checkpoint before this restricted area there is a wooden board, where you leave your vehicle identification tag and collect it when you return, to ensure nobody gets left behind after dark. It is a very spooky place. On the eve of the test I was to witness, I lay by the lagoon looking at the stars, enjoying a cool breeze rustling through the palms, and thinking about a nuclear bomb ticking beneath me. It seemed absurd. How could intelligent men tinker with Armageddon in a place the Creator had clearly designed for poets and lovers? Moonlight on Mururoa is the stuff that fantasies and nightmares are made of.

I was in a two-storey concrete blockhouse the next day when the bomb went off a mile away. A closed-circuit television camera at the detonation site went briefly insane, sending a blurred image of the earth heaving, but the tremor where we were standing was barely perceptible. I turned to a French colleague:

'Did the earth move for you?'

'*Pas vraiment,*' she replied.

As a climax, it was a bit of a disappointment.

By the time I returned to the Tuamotus, the tests had been suspended. This was viewed with mixed feelings by the locals, many of whom depended on the *Centre d'Experimentation du Pacifique* for work. In the village store in Fakarava, I met a young Tahitian who had been employed by the *CEP* as a labourer. While diving for pearl shells off Fangataufa, the site of atmospheric tests, he had seen fissures in the reef wall about two inches wide. 'The coral is wide open and the cracks are very deep,' he said. 'How can they say nothing bad can come from there?' But he was equally concerned about the islanders losing their jobs. 'My heart tells me the tests are bad, but my head tells me a lot of people with families to support depend on the *CEP* for a living. It is not an easy question.'

Inevitably, Daniel had a story to tell about unexpected fall-out from one of the tests. As usual, we were sitting by the shore after dinner contemplating the savour of fresh fish and the beauty of the lagoon it had come from.

'It happened on Niau, which is near here,' he said. 'A few years ago the French decided to build a lighthouse there. It was a fine tower with a powerful light, and on the last day all they had to do was to take off the covers and start the machinery. The workers were just getting into their truck when there was a big flash in the sky and a terrible noise like thunder. When they got to the lighthouse, which was far from the village, it was in ruins. Not one stone left standing. Of course they knew it was an atomic test and they laughed, but they were lucky. Can you imagine if they had been on the top when the bomb went off? The best of it is, the French engineers got medals because nobody was injured building the lighthouse. That's the French for you.'

Daniel was a natural story-teller. Listening to him by the light of his gas lamp, with the lagoon lapping at our feet, was the Polynesian equivalent of sitting around a peat fire in a highland croft and hearing the legends of the Celts and the Norsemen. One night I mentioned that I had seen whales blowing off the reef. 'I remember the last man who could speak with the whales,' he said. 'This is not a legend, it is actual history. I know because I saw him doing it once when I was eight years old.' I reached for my notebook, and wrote down this South Seas tale:

'About ten whales had come near the pass, and Tutavake the leader of whales went in a canoe to meet them. He was wearing a *pareo* and a crown of leaves and flowers. When he came to the pass, he stood up in the canoe and spoke to the whales in a loud voice. They gathered around him, and when he came back into the lagoon they followed him to a special beach chosen for the killing of whales. They came right up into the shallows. Then the people would try to push one on to the beach, but if he cried or struggled, they knew he was not to be killed and they would push him back into the water. They did this until they found one which stayed quiet, and followed the movement of the people pushing him. In this way, they knew he was the one to be killed. All the others were pushed back into the water. Tutavake died in 1961 and nobody took his place.'

It was after this story that I formally dubbed Daniel the *Tusitala* of Fakarava.

'What does it mean?'

'It means writer or teller of tales. It was the name the Samoan people gave to Stevenson.'

'I would like to read this man's book.'

On my return to Tahiti, I sent Daniel a French edition of *In the South Seas*. I like to think of him sitting by the lagoon, his old spectacles perched on his nose, smiling at the stories his great-grandfather related to Stevenson.

ON THE SURFACE, Fakarava had changed little since Stevenson sat entranced at the feet of Donat, but inexorably the lure of black pearls was undermining its tranquillity. About a hundred yards from Daniel's huts, wealthy Tahitians had built a house, the only two-storey structure on the island, from where they intended to manage a pearl farm. It was a pleasant enough building faced with wood, but from the lagoon it stuck out like a sore thumb on the shoreline where the other dwellings were barely perceptible among the trees.

One day the serenity of late afternoon was broken by bass notes from rock music throbbing over the lagoon from the Tahitian house. Daniel's brow furrowed, and for a moment he said nothing. Then he burst out: 'I don't understand these people. Already their music is too loud for us, what must it be like for them?' After a pause, he added: 'And it's not even music, it's just a noise.' I agreed, and shuddered to think of the shape of things to come, of this exquisite shore lined with big houses and reverberating with pop music. Daniel said: 'It's people like that who're going to destroy the Tuamotus. These big shots from Tahiti, they regard themselves as high class and take us for savages. They're going to make the Tuamotus like Tahiti, you'll see what it's like, all bars and noise and drunkenness. We don't want that, we want the Tuamotus to stay the way they are.' It was the only time I saw Daniel angry.

'When you've lived here for a while you'll see Polynesians don't like the French,' he said one night. 'It's in their heads from long ago. Do you know the story of the American shipwreck?

'Two years before I was born, an American four-masted ship carrying timber ran aground in the pass. The villagers rescued the sailors, and gave them food and shelter. The American captain was grateful and said the local people could have the cargo if they could salvage it. But the French officials said it belonged to their government, and in the end nobody got it. You know what happened? Another ship came from America to take home the crew, and on the way out of the pass the captain told them to stop and set fire to his old ship. They did, and it sank quickly. He was quite right, of course.'

Perceptions of justice vary from island to island in the Tuamotus. I cannot recall seeing a prison in Fakarava, and cannot imagine there being any need for one. It was not the kind of place where a locksmith could earn a living. The doors of some houses appeared to have old locks, but to the best of my knowledge nobody used them. When Daniel left his house in the village to accompany me to our thatched huts, he closed the front door to indicate he was not at home. The windows were naturally left open for ventilation.

Judicial authority was invested in a *mutai*, a kind of auxiliary policeman, whose duties were light to the point of being virtually non-existent. The current incumbent of this office was Temata Ganahoa, a big, strapping fellow whose usual uniform was casual shirt and shorts, and a red baseball cap bearing the legend *Big Red*. The only time I saw him wearing his official French uniform was on the day of the referendum, and he looked distinctly uncomfortable. This genial giant could have ended any argument by simply leaning on the disputants, but he was not very brave. On the rare occasions an incident required the intervention of the force of law and order, he would not dream of intruding without Daniel by his side. I liked Temata, and we became friends. When we met, I would say: 'Hi, Big Red.' He would laugh, and say: *'Salut, p'tit Écossais.'*

SOMETHING WAS PUZZLING ME. Stevenson referred to the archipelago as the Paumotus, but it was now known as the Tuamotus. Being in the company of a resident authority, I consulted him. 'Paumotus is the name of the people, it means "people of storm-cloud islands",' Daniel said. I looked at the sky, a clear, pale blue with only a wisp of cloud drifting in the trade winds. Daniel admitted that dark clouds were rare, but he said they were prophetic. 'Since olden times, a large black cloud in the middle of the pass means death,' he said. 'Once a young man from Kaueha was in Fakarava and he was very sick. His family came in a speedboat to take him home. They left at two in the afternoon, and two hours later a dark cloud came into the pass and stayed there. The people said the man must be dead, and we learned later that he had died on the boat. It may be just superstition, but it often happens like that. I may be a civilized man, but I respect the signs.'

There was no shortage of signs to guide Stevenson through the pantheon of Polynesian gods and their mythology. He was informed that a particular form of wedge-shaped cloud on the horizon would herald the arrival of a ship; a species of mermaid known as *mokurea* bathed in coastal pools; and *Mahuini*, the spirit of the sea, carried shipwrecked mariners ashore in the guise of a ray-fish.

On my last night in Fakarava, *Mahuini* came to Daniel's

birthday party. We were sitting in our usual place on the coral strand, celebrating the event with a bottle of wine. Nature had entered into the spirit of the occasion by producing a stunning crimson sunset, which transformed the lagoon into a sea of liquid gold. Suddenly the surface stirred, and a large manta ray flew out of the water and splashed back in, quickly followed by another. Barely turning round, Daniel said: '*Toerau.*'

'What does that mean?'

'A wind from the west. The people say when the rays leap from the water, the wind will change to the west and the sea will be calm and good for fishing.'

At the airport the next day, I asked the pilot which direction the wind was coming from. 'Funny you should ask,' he said. 'It changed during the night. It's coming from the west, which is quite unusual.'

EIGHT

Never retreat from a shark

IGNORANCE AND CURIOSITY are nature's ways of luring people into situations which logic and common sense dictate are best to avoid. There are times in the lives of even the most adventurous people when they reflect that they might not have taken a step into the unknown if they had fully appreciated the risks involved. From my own experience, the second time under fire in Beirut and a second parachute jump over the Namibian desert were harder to face than the first.

In years of scuba-diving, however, I had never observed big sharks at close quarters, and when an opportunity arose to do so, the attraction was irresistible. It was the equivalent of a mountaineer being invited to join an Everest expedition.

'Just two things to remember, Gavin. The ocean here is more than thirty thousand feet deep, so keep an eye on your depth gauge. The other thing is never retreat from a shark, or you could trigger an attack. If he gets too close, face up to him and punch him, but don't try to move away.' With these encouraging words, Yves Lefèvre checked my equipment and I stepped off an inflatable boat into the most terrifying experience of my life.

I would not have done it had it not been for Christian Petron. We had met briefly at Fakarava, where Christian and his assistant cameraman Cyril Isy-Schwart had been scouting locations for a documentary series on pelagic sharks — that is the big kind which prowl the ocean depths, as opposed to the smaller species more common in coastal waters. Christian was renowned in the diving fraternity for his underwater photography in the film *The Big Blue*, and as a fine cameraman who had dived all the oceans of the world in search of the awesome and the curious.

I had already decided to make a detour on my return to Tahiti to scuba-dive through the passes at Rangiroa Atoll, a site of almost mystical lure for French *cognoscenti*, which offered the thrill of being caught with all manner of exotic marine life in a six-knot current flowing into the lagoon. Fate intervened by placing Christian and me on the same flight from Fakarava, and in the same lodgings at Rangiroa.

While Christian planned his ocean dive, I went with a local instructor for an underwater sleigh-ride through one of the passes. The surface was as turbulent as that I had observed at Fakarava, but ten fathoms down we were in a peaceful twilight world where small fish were flitting around sparse coral on the sandy bottom. For a few minutes we drifted along with the current, rising gradually into the pass. There is a pleasant sensation of weightlessness and slow, dreamy motion in sports diving that induces a profound calm similar to transcendental meditation, and it was a shock when two large black shapes materialized from the gloom, heading directly towards us.

Manta rays are among the most fantastic creatures in Neptune's realm. They glide, or rather 'fly', through the density of water with seemingly effortless grace and power, like a cross between an albatross and a Vulcan bomber. In fact, they are related to the shark, being a kind of flattened cousin. Natives used to call them devilfish, but despite their fearsome appearance they are fairly harmless, having no tail-stingers and being by nature curious and playful rather than aggressive. At worst, they can be a nuisance to free-diving spear fishermen and pearlers, who can find themselves trapped beneath a flock of inquisitive rays and have to punch their way back to the surface.

The two specimens approaching us were flying in formation like skilled pilots, their black delta wings undulating in a measured rhythm. My companion tapped me on the shoulder, and I looked up to see another superb manta swooping down on us; at the last second he levelled off, his white belly flashing mere inches above our heads; then he banked, first to one side and then the other, sank to the ocean floor, and gradually faded from view. It was at once a heart-stopping moment and a virtuoso performance of aquanautics, and my companion and I accorded him an underwater standing ovation. I like to think it was *Mahuini* bidding us welcome to his domain.

A few minutes later we approached what appeared to be a shimmering silver curtain. On closer inspection it turned out to be a shoal of large barracuda, which we admired from a respectful distance. On surfacing, I was exhilarated by the dive, but felt a mixture of relief and disappointment at having seen no sharks. Christian was about to remedy this.

Over dinner that night, he said he had found a promising location about a mile off shore and intended filming there the next day; would I care to come along? It seemed like an ideal opportunity to satisfy my curiosity about sharks in the company of a man who knew a great deal about them, but it was not a decision to be taken lightly and I asked for more details. Basically the idea was that Yves Lefèvre, the owner of a local dive centre, would jump into the water with dead fish to lure the sharks from the deep, and Christian and Cyril would hover a few feet below him to film the sharks as they circled and devoured the bait. The plan seemed to me perfectly simple, effective, and absurd – like popping into a cage of lions with a lump of raw steak, saying: 'Here, kitty, nice kitty.' I was a bit concerned, but Christian was grinning at me, and all I could say was: '*Pourquoi pas?*'

We arranged to meet at Yves' house the next afternoon, but when I arrived the others were still preparing their equipment. While waiting, I browsed through a bookshelf and found an illustrated book on sharks by R. H. Johnson, an American biologist specializing in ichthyology and animal behaviour. The author argued that sharks were not as savage or dangerous to humans as sensational films and literature would suggest: fewer than fifty people a year were killed by shark attacks, while at least three hundred died from bee stings in the United States alone. This was good stuff, precisely what I wanted to read.

Sharks are pretty strong, however. Their jaws can exert eighteen tons of pressure per square inch, which I assumed would chomp my bones like spaghetti (the expression *al dente* came to mind). They are also pretty tough. It was reported that during the capture of a whale shark a blast of number two shot fired from a shotgun at a distance of two feet bounced off the hide, leaving only a circular depression. (Yves wanted me to *punch* one?)

Mr Johnson then discoursed on encounters between sharks and humans. If accepting the risk of deliberately entering the water with sharks, he strongly advised a preliminary observation from the safety of a boat or a stout cage (Christian, I knew, had no intention of doing either). It was possible to run the additional risk of baiting sharks, but it was unwise to do so where sharks exceeding six feet might be attracted (I knew Christian was after much bigger species). It was important to face a shark moving around in diminishing circles, and try to calmly remove oneself to safety (Christian, of course, would have no intention of removing himself). If a circling shark moved within six feet, the author suggested lashing out at a sensitive area such as the eyes, snout, or gills with a shark-billy, a knife, or as a last resort a fist; and if it actually turned towards a diver, the time had come to use a speargun, preferably with an explosive charge (I knew that none of our party was so equipped).

So I wondered if maybe I could just stay on the boat. '*Allez, Écossais. On y va?*' Christian was waiting for me, and he was grinning again. The man is insane, I thought.

Driving along the atoll, I inhaled the sweet scent of bougain-villaea, admired the graceful form of the palm trees, and watched locals pottering around their gardens and fishing nets – anything to avoid looking at the sea and thinking of our rendezvous with its most feared predators. We stopped at a hotel by the lagoon and walked along a jetty to where a young woman, one of Yves' diving instructors, was waiting for us in an inflatable dinghy with a powerful engine. We kitted up quickly and loaded the cameras in their bulky metal housings into the boat, under the curious eyes of tourists. My companions were in high spirits, looking forward to their adventure with the assurance of connois-seurs of danger; I sat quietly, checking my equipment and filling my mind with pre-dive procedures. We sped through the pass, waving to a lone fisherman on shore, and then the choppy waters of the channel gave way to the long, slow swells of the Pacific.

We had been moving away from land for only a few minutes when I caught sight of two dorsal fins slicing through the water. I froze, and before I knew what was happening Cyril had donned his mask and snorkel, seized his camera, and tumbled overboard without his scuba equipment. I looked enquiringly at Christian. 'Dolphins,' he said. 'Come on, let's see if we can herd them towards Cyril.' The girl gunned the engine and we began circling, but evidently the dolphins were not interested in film careers, because they sounded as soon as they approached Cyril paddling on the surface.

It was mid-afternoon when we stopped about a mile off shore, and Yves offered me his last-minute advice. I muttered a silent prayer to Neptune, and jumped overboard. It is a golden rule in diving always to remain close to your partner, or 'buddy' in the sub-aqua lexicon. During my initial training course, I had been so careless of this rule that my instructor once tied us together with a length of rope to instil the necessary discipline. On this occasion he would have been proud of me. As soon as I hit the water, I searched for Christian and Cyril as if my life depended on it, which in a sense it did. I spotted Cyril first, already several feet below me, having descended more quickly with the weight of his camera. I finned quickly down to him, pinching my nose to equalize with the rapidly increasing ambient pressure – at thirty feet it is already double the surface pressure. We settled at around sixty feet, where Christian glided down to join us. I looked up to see Yves above us, a dark silhouette dangling like a puppet against the brightness of the surface, releasing the first portion of the bait. Then I looked around me, and felt the first *frisson* of fear.

I felt like an insect in a vast preserving jar. In all my previous dives there had always been a coral formation, a reef wall, or the ocean floor to provide orientation and a measure of security. Here I was suspended in an immense blue void far from shore: the surface was tantalizingly close, but above several pressure layers which one could rise through quickly only at the risk of decompression sickness; beneath me yawned the blackness of an unimaginable abyss. There was no question that, in every sense of the word, I was out of my depth. I was the Incredible Shrinking Man in a world of monsters.

We were enveloped in an incredibly deep blue silent nothingness. It was an eerie sensation hanging there, watchful, waiting for sharks to detect our presence. Guess who's coming to dinner, I thought flippantly. As if in response to my musing, the first of our guests appeared, rising slowly from the depths. I regarded the sinuous motion of the creature, his asymmetrical tail fin lazily propelling his sleek bulk with immense power, with horrified fascination.

Under water, images are distorted by refraction so that everything appears a quarter closer and a third bigger. Even allowing for this phenomenon, our visitor was an impressive size. I learned later he was an eight-foot silky shark, so called because of the unusually smooth texture of his hide. I took up a strategic position behind and between the cameramen, turning slowly to keep my eyes fixed on the shark, which had begun circling us warily at a distance of about twenty-five yards. After a few rotations I had begun to relax when a grey reef shark that I had not seen sent my pulse racing by flashing past me towards the bait. Within a minute there were five sharks revolving around us on several levels. One by one they approached, snatched a morsel released by Yves, and then resumed their circling. I watched their gunmetal bodies and pectoral fins for any signs of twitching or exaggerated movements which would signal excitement or possible aggression, but they were cruising around placidly, taking the bait like well-trained dogs sitting up for scraps from a dinner table. Then it occurred to me that this was their dining-room, and we were intruders who might easily be mistaken for the main course.

It was impossible to keep track of all of the sharks simultaneously, and a big silver-tip startled me by coming up from beneath me at a rapid rate of knots. In turning to face this potential threat, one of my flippers brushed against Cyril's lower legs. I sensed rather than saw him spinning around sharply. He had the good grace to admit later without rancour that I had caused him to almost jump out of his wet-suit. Eventually the bait was gone, and Yves came down to join us; in the event, not a moment too soon.

Yves had the only defensive tool among us, an improvised shark-billy in the form of a thin metal tube. He had barely settled beside me when the silky approached, correctly identifying him as the waiter, possibly to enquire about second helpings. As he cruised by us, Yves prodded him gently in the gills. He slowed, considering this unexpected rebuke, and made to turn towards us when Yves prodded him more firmly in the flank. I felt the turbulence of the water as his tail fin flicked him out of range. Later I measured Yves' metal pole. It was four feet long.

By this time we had been in the water for twenty minutes and

I was reflecting on Mr Johnson's observation that time was essential: 'Remember that each passing minute permits the shark to realize that the diver represents relatively harmless and vulnerable prey.' I was beginning to feel that enough was enough and I signalled to Yves that I would quite like to go home fairly soon. In response to his signal 'Are you OK?' I gave a vague indication that under the circumstances I was as well as could be expected, but that I would rather like to be elsewhere. He motioned me to be patient, and drifted off to join Christian and Cyril who were a few yards away. It was then the monster appeared.

Rising swiftly from the depths, a thirteen-foot female silver-tip began circling, closer than the others. She was late for dinner, but she clearly wanted some and she was going to be very annoyed if she didn't get any. Without any preliminaries, her circling diminished rapidly; not for her good manners and waiting her turn to be served. From the first sight, I regarded this latecomer with fear and loathing. If there was going to be an attack, I sensed instinctively she would be the one who would precipitate it. The other sharks were still around us, but had moved further off as if giving precedence to their bigger relative.

As she prowled by about thirty feet away, she filled the limited vision through my face mask like a giant spaceship cruising across a cinema screen. Her lifeless eyes glinted dully in the marine twilight, and I could clearly see ugly mating scars on her flanks where she had been gripped by the teeth of her suitors. After a few circles she stopped, and slowly, but with massive deliberation, turned to face me.

The profile of a large shark changes dramatically with such a manoeuvre. Already awesome from the side view, it assumes in the head-on position the chilling form of a torpedo framed by pectoral and tail fins. A Russian helicopter gunship rising above an Afghan hillside has a similar menacing aspect; or consider standing on a runway in the path of a Jumbo jet to get a rough idea of the sensation: but here there was no noise, nor any sign of movement other than the shark's growing size to indicate it was drawing closer.

None of my companions was close at hand, and it suddenly occurred to me that I, alone of all of us, was defenceless. Yves had his metal shark-billy, and Christian and Cyril had sturdy cameras with which they could at least fend off a probing attack. All I had was an absurdly small cutting knife with no point (ironically to prevent accidental injury). I drew it slowly, but it flashed in the light remarkably like a small fish, and I quickly replaced it.

I stared stupidly at the approaching shark, transfixed by horror. To my enduring amazement, I did not panic. I believe I had lost the mental faculties for it. I was staring potential death in the face, but my mind was a total blank; the mesmerized dread of a rodent facing an adder about to strike. As she came in at waist height, Heaven knows where the instinct came from, I lashed out with my right fist in a karate-style punch; any wild swinging action would have sent me spinning momentarily out of control. Under the circumstances it was a pitiful gesture, and I failed to make contact; but it seemed to have some effect, because the shark stopped dead. For at least a second she stared at me balefully with those dreadful eyes, then moved slowly past, barely inches away, and resumed her circling.

Yves said later that sensing devices in her snout would have registered shock-waves from my punch as assuredly as if I had struck her. Was it a sizing-up of potential prey, or simply curiosity? I will never know, nor do I really wish to. Jacques Cousteau, who knows a thing or two about sharks, concluded an essay on their behaviour by saying that all that could be deduced with certainty was that they were unpredictable.

By now I was badly frightened, and it was an enormous relief when Yves signalled that Christian's film was finished and I should ascend with him. This was the tricky bit. We were at a depth of sixty feet; the maximum recommended ascent rate, to prevent the possible formation of nitrogen bubbles in the blood, is thirty feet per minute; we were surrounded by sharks who were said to consider retreat as an invitation to attack. It was a long two minutes. I edged slowly upwards, continually turning to observe two sharks showing interest in our departure. Christian seemed unconcerned, paying more attention to his wrist computer to monitor our ascent rate. When we broke the surface, the boat was heaving in a heavy swell and I had to wait patiently while the girl relieved Christian of his camera. Never have a diver's legs been drawn up more tightly against the underside of a boat. Normally the first item a surfacing diver hands to the skipper of an inflatable is his weight belt. I forgot all about it, and when my turn came I fairly flew into the boat, weight belt and all.

Christian was grinning at me again. 'I see Marguerite introduced herself to you; she's a dear old thing, isn't she?' (I learned later the silver-tip with the distinctive scars had been christened by Yves after a previous sighting.) Choosing my words carefully, I replied that I would have preferred a less intimate acquaintance, she had not endeared herself to me in the least, and furthermore I did not believe I had been so profoundly terrified in my life. Christian laughed. 'Is that so? Well, you didn't show it. You did very well, considering it was your first time.' I thanked him for the experience, but assured him it would be my last.

Back on shore, I consulted Mr Johnson's book to find out what we had been up against. 'The silver-tip (*Carcharhinus albimarginatus*) has been said to attack man, and its large size, strong dentition, and inquisitive and persistent nature make it a potentially dangerous species.' I am not sure I really wished to know that.

There was a festive mood at dinner that evening. Christian and Cyril had come back with good footage, and I had come back in one piece, so everybody was happy. As a memento of the occasion, Christian presented me with a golden shark lapel pin, which I assumed admitted me to the fraternity of very silly divers.

Just when I thought it was safe to go back in the water, another instructor told me of a deep dive site from which one could observe up to a hundred sharks milling around the reef wall. 'They're quite small, but it's a magnificent sight,' he assured me. They were not that small; some were almost five feet, but he was right about the view. From the relative safety of a shallow cave, I watched scores of reef sharks gliding before me in an underwater ballet wondrous to behold. I subsequently dived with sharks elsewhere in the Pacific, and my instinctive dread of them has subsided; but occasionally I have a vivid dream in which I am suspended alone in a deep blue void. No shark ever appears, but I awake in a cold sweat.

NINE

*I write to you from fairyland, where we are living in
a fairy story*

JIM HOSTETLER, the shipping agent who loved onward
tickets and loathed Papeete, was right. It looked as if I had
missed the boat for paradise by about two hundred years.

The evanescent charms of Tahiti which enchanted European
explorers had not survived their discovery. The scented isle of
vahine wearing flowers in their hair and little else had been
despoiled by generations of soldiers, sailors, and candlestick
makers. It had lost its virginity long ago.

When Gauguin arrived from France in 1891, he was bitterly
disappointed: 'It was Europe – the Europe I believed I had freed
myself of – made even worse by colonial snobbery, puerile and
grotesque imitation to the point of caricature. It was not what I
had come so far to seek.' With commendable candour, a French
judge at the time observed: 'This race is dancing gently into
oblivion. Our presence is killing them. So far we have found no
way of civilizing the natives other than to make them disappear.'

Stevenson hardly noticed Papeete. Arriving three years before
Gauguin, he was seriously ill with influenza contracted in Hiva-
Oa. He rarely stirred from a small house near the shore, met no
one of any interest, and soon grew tired of what was then an
ugly shantytown. His mother expressed their disenchantment in
a letter to her sister: 'I don't much like Tahiti. It seems to me a
sort of halfway house between savage life and civilization, with
the drawbacks of both and the advantage of neither.'

My first impressions were hardly more favourable. Papeete,
the metropolis of French Polynesia and gateway to an illusory
paradise, had become a grubby little town infested by impatient

traffic, expensive boutiques, and corrupt politicians. It was a mongrel society on a long leash, alternately licking and snarling at the French hands that fed it while straining for the dubious freedom of independence. Few Polynesians could afford the prices in the smart cafés, and the harbour was littered with broken dreams – yachts large and small put up for sale by owners whose funds and enthusiasm for roving the seven seas were exhausted. I shared Mrs Stevenson's dislike of the capital, but unlike her son I was well enough to stroll around and meet some interesting characters before following the Stevensons to a more agreeable part of the island.

Colin Stenhouse was polishing the brasswork on the after-deck of a hundred-and-thirty-foot luxury motor yacht when I paused on the quayside to admire its sleek lines. His French was fractured, so we reverted to English, and I was delighted to hear the familiar accents of the west of Scotland. Erstwhile cook, gamekeeper, and hotel manager, Colin had forsaken a career as a fire extinguisher salesman in Northern Ireland to cruise around the Pacific as a casual deckhand on a variety of vessels. He had no maritime papers, but he 'used to sail around the Clyde a lot'. Through Colin I learned about the vagabond life of sea gypsies like him who roam the world's ports in search of a boat to take them somewhere else. It seemed gloriously pointless, a perfect example of Stevenson's maxim about it being better to travel hopefully than to arrive. I sensed I had found a boon companion.

The next day he invited me to dinner on board a more modest sixty-five-foot ketch he had crewed from the Marquesas, which was anchored off a tourist hotel a few miles down the coast. The owners were dining ashore, so we would have the yacht to ourselves. I turned up at the hotel jetty at the appointed hour, but there was no sign of my host. An American approached me.

'Are you looking for Colin?'

'Yes.'

'He said to look out for a guy writing a book about Robert

Louis Stevenson and you look the part. Come on, I'll take you to him.'

I suppose I looked a bit lost.

Chugging out to the yacht in a rubber dinghy, I learned that the American was another sea rover meandering between Latin America and Polynesia with his wife and fourteen-year-old daughter. The girl had been eight when they left Los Angeles. I also discovered he had fond memories of the *Wellington Star*, which he had known as a ship's chandler. 'She was obsolete when she was built, but she has lovely lines,' he said. 'They don't make them like that any more.'

I suspect I would not like bouncing across huge oceans in the cramped quarters of a small yacht at the whims of winds and currents, but relaxing after dinner in a ketch bobbing gently at anchor between Tahiti and Moorea is another matter. As Colin poured me a glass of excellent Bourgogne, I gazed at the splendour of the sun setting over the craggy peaks of Moorea. Successive hues of gold and crimson gradually ebbed from the sky, leaving two brilliant stars, one high above the other; then I turned to watch the moon washing over the dark mass of Tahiti in rivulets of silver. Native drums throbbing over the water from a floor-show at the hotel completed a magnificent *son et lumière*.

Colin turned out to be an incurable romantic torn between his love of the sea and a wistful desire for the local beauties that seemed to be rarely reciprocated. He wore his heart on his sleeve and the *vahine* barely noticed; he should have sailed with Bougainville or Cook. In a post-prandial glow, I tried to put the loss of his latest *amour* in perspective by quoting Stevenson: 'We are all travellers in the wilderness of this world, and the best that we find in our travels is an honest friend.' Colin then recited a few lines in a similar but more lyrical vein. Neither of us knew who the author was, but I thought they were good and I noted them: 'Oh the comfort, the inexpressible comfort of feeling safe with a person; having neither to weigh thoughts nor measure words, but to pour them all out, chaff and grain together, where a faithful hand will take them and sift them, keep what is worth keeping and with a breath of kindness blow the rest away.'

I rowed myself back to shore in the yacht's dinghy, dipping the oars quietly in the still waters of the lagoon. It was good to have a buddy.

BENGT DANIELSSON was a man I had long wanted to meet. He was an anthropologist who had sailed on Thor Heyerdahl's *Kon-Tiki* expedition, an authority on Polynesian culture and history, and a prolific author of fascinating books on the islands. He settled in Tahiti in 1953 with his French wife Marie Thérèse, raised a family, and infuriated the French authorities with unremitting opposition to the nuclear testing programme. Greenpeace considered him a sound fellow and an important ally in the Pacific.

I found him in a bungalow on a small estate by the beach twelve miles down the west coast from Papeete, surrounded by thatched dwellings which served variously as living, sleeping, and eating quarters. The more modern building was his office and library, which contained more than seven thousand volumes. I noticed an entire shelf was devoted to works by and about Stevenson, and it became apparent that Danielsson had read them all. A tall, imposing figure with more hair in a straggly beard than on his scalp, he welcomed me with the distracted air of an academic and proceeded to deliver an eloquent, two-hour dissertation on the decline and fall of Tahitian society.

It may be useful to point out here that Polynesians were establishing thriving farming communities in the Pacific while Europeans were still living in caves and wondering where all the brontosaurus had gone. According to the Bishop Museum in Honolulu, which I visited later in my travels, their ancestral homeland was a triangular area around the Philippines, Indonesia, and Borneo. The first migration to Fiji, Tonga, and Samoa took place between 1500 and 1000 BC, which was around the time the Druids were putting Stonehenge together. Centuries before the likes of Wallis turned up and pronounced the islanders savages, they were ranging over the Pacific in great double canoes up to a hundred feet long on voyages equalling those of Columbus. More than a thousand years ago a Polynesian navigator recorded 'cold rocks growing out of the sea' – an early description of icebergs. By the time Tahiti was settled, between AD 650 and 850, the Polynesians were farming taro, breadfruit, pigs, and chickens, and cooking them in ornate pottery.

Not much happened for a while, until Europeans came along and instilled them with syphilis, smallpox, and the fear of God. It was pretty much downhill from then on. Pomare V, the last of the Tahitian kings, deprived Gauguin of a royal audience by inconsiderately drinking himself to death within a few days of the artist's arrival. His favourite cocktail was a mixture of champagne, beer, absinthe, whisky, red wine, and Benedictine. It was not until 1963 however that French Polynesia really entered the twentieth century, when de Gaulle decided to detonate atom bombs in the skies above the Tuamotus. An advance guard of twenty thousand troops was followed by tens of thousands of French civilians, causing enormous social and economic upheaval. A lot of people also began to die of cancer.

According to Danielsson, there was an abnormally high incidence of cancer among those working at the test site at Mururoa, many of whom were taken to military hospitals in France, and brought back in coffins. 'Scientists from New Zealand recorded radioactive fall-out throughout the Pacific after the atmospheric tests, but the French denied there was any in their islands,' he said. 'Are we to believe the particles acted in a patriotic manner and jumped over French Polynesia to other islands? The other possibility, of course, is that the French were lying.'

After being spied on and threatened with deportation by the French authorities, Danielsson found an unexpected ally in François Mitterrand. 'He used to come and see me. Once he was sitting where you are sitting now, and he told me that personally he was opposed to the testing programme and he would stop it if he could.' By the time I met Danielsson the tests had been suspended, but the old Tahitian way of life was gone for ever. 'Most Polynesians remain kind, hospitable, and generous by nature, but they have lost their land and many young people are unable to find work. Now we have slums, delinquency, and crime. There have been assaults on Frenchmen in Papeete. I advise you to be very careful and to speak English, and you will not be attacked.'

I thanked him for his advice, and left in a sombre mood. It was Sunday and there were few buses running, but a Tahitian schoolteacher stopped and gave me a lift to my hotel. She told me: 'Mr Danielsson is right. Life here is not what it used to be. Before people were smiling and generous, but now they're selfish and greedy. Money, money, money is all they want, and it's a vicious circle. When wages go up, prices increase even more. We're running faster just to stay still.' She had no particular affection for the French, but she had no illusions about independence improving matters. 'It's true some people want independence, but I think it's a bad idea. How will the country support itself, who will pay my wages if the French leave? Our dilemma is that we've been seduced by a consumer society and now we're trapped in it.'

That evening I went with Colin to a night-club frequented by young French servicemen. Beneath the flashing lights, sad-eyed Polynesian girls sat at the bar like puppets with broken strings, waiting for raucous youths to buy them expensive drinks and whirl them on to the dance floor. I had seen the same vacant expressions in the eyes of young girls in bars around American military bases in South-East Asia, and I found it infinitely depressing. The atmosphere was much better in another club where we found Tahitian couples waltzing to island melodies played by a local band. Evidently a kind of apartheid had developed in Papeete night life, as we were the only foreigners in the place; but we were careful to be polite and to talk in English. We knew we had been accepted when the barman gave us his repertoire of anti-French jokes.

'The problem is that nobody wants to read or write Tahitian any more,' John Martin said. I had come to see him because he had translated *Isle of Voices* and *The Bottle Imp*, another mystical Stevenson tale set in the South Seas, into Tahitian. We met in the offices of *L'Academie Tahitienne*, a cultural organization of which he was the director, at the end of a dusty corridor on the second floor of a nondescript commercial building in Papeete. 'We published a thousand copies of Stevenson's stories under the title *Na' A'Amurii*, which means "two little tales", but we sold only a few to local teachers. Tahitians read very little, and if they do, they read in French. The only Tahitian book most of them know is the Bible.'

Martin traced his ancestry to a Scotsman who married into the royal family of the Gilbert Islands at the beginning of the eighteenth century, but he regarded himself as much a Tahitian as anybody else and recalled being resentful that his native tongue was banned in schools during his youth. It only became the official second language of Tahiti in 1980, and began to be taught in schools two years later. Even then parents resisted the move, believing it would be more advantageous for their children to be educated in French. When the Academy was founded in 1978, it launched an annual competition for modern Tahitian writing; it lasted four years, then there were no more entries. It then began producing grammars and dictionaries of classical Tahitian, as opposed to the mongrel biblical version, and experimenting by 'launching' new words into Tahitian society, but Martin conceded they had made little progress. 'It will never replace French, we mustn't dream. As for independence, I am not convinced it will be the panacea for our ills. The prices of *vahine* and palm trees are not good on the world market.'

On a beach outside Papeete, I watched three magnificently tattooed Tahitians practising their art on French soldiers in the middle of a throng of tourists with video cameras. The spectacle of this ancient rite lost something through the natives' wearing gold jewellery and expensive wrist-watches. I also noticed they were using battery-operated tools instead of the traditional bone implements. One of them explained to me that this was quicker, less painful, and more hygenic. 'We can clean the needles each time and prevent the spread of AIDS,' he said.

Tahiti is littered with monuments to French navigators, administrators, and servicemen, but the only surviving memorial of any size to the old race of Polynesians is an ugly mausoleum of coral stones enshrining the remains of the drunken Pomare V a few miles from Papeete. It is adorned by a sculpture of what was supposed to be a Grecian urn, but most visitors regard it more appropriately as a liquor bottle. Gauguin, who attended the funeral, thought the monument formed 'a painful contrast with the beauty of the site'.

I thought I might have found a memorial at Mahaena, a small village on the east coast. It was here that almost a thousand Tahitian warriors rebelled in 1844 against the French annexation of their island. Assisted by a few British sailors and French Army deserters, they spent a month digging three parallel trenches more than a mile long, and then calmly waited for the enemy to appear. The French duly dispatched two warships, whose fire-power was decisive in routing the poorly armed Tahitians after a day of close-quarter fighting with French Marines. When the smoke cleared, more than a hundred Tahitians lay dead. The French casualties were fifteen dead and fifty-one wounded. A century before, the Jacobite clans of Scotland suffered a similar fate before the guns of an English army, but monuments were erected throughout the country to their cause. At Mahaena, the Culloden of the Tahitians, there is not even a simple cairn. The only national symbol is a French flag flying from the *mairie*.

ONE ASPECT OF TAHITI has not changed since the first Cook's tour of the island was conducted in 1769 by Lieutenant James of that ilk: the scenery remains magnificent and largely unspoiled, the interior being an uninhabited and trackless wilderness of jagged peaks and deep gorges carrying rivers and streams to the sea. However, it is difficult to admire when you are stuck in a traffic jam in Papeete, or crawling past supermarkets and advertisement hoardings along the heavily populated west coast.

It was with a sense of relief that I packed my belongings into a rented car, left the noisome bustle of Papeete, and drove leisurely down the quieter east coast to Never-Never Land.

'I write to you from fairyland, where we are living in a fairy story, the guests of a beautiful brown princess. We came to stay a week, five weeks have passed and we are still indefinite as to our time of leaving.'

Thus wrote Fanny in a letter to Colvin of the Stevensons' sojourn in Tautira, then as now the most remote village in Tahiti in terms of distance from the capital. The island comprises two roughly circular land masses connected by a narrow isthmus; paved roads reach halfway down either side of the smaller and less populated portion known as Tahiti-iti, gripping it like a claw, and Tautira lies at the end of the road along the northern shore. A few hamlets beyond it can be reached only by boat.

The *Casco* made heavy weather of the passage from Papeete, and was almost lost twice. Stevenson wrote of one incident to his brother:

In the southern bight of Tahiti we had a near squeak, the wind suddenly coming calm; the reefs were close in with, my eye! what a surf!

*The pilot thought we were gone, and the captain had a boat cleared,
when a lucky squall came to our rescue. My wife, hearing the order
given about the boats, remarked to my mother, 'Isn't that nice? We
shall soon be ashore.' Thus does the female mind unconsciously skirt
along the verge of eternity.*

I suspect Stevenson misjudged Fanny. Given her fear of the
sea she was probably well aware of the danger they were in, and
putting a brave face on it for the sake of the others. Fanny also
proved to be an accomplished horse-trader, succeeding where her
husband had failed in persuading a Chinese trader to loan them
a wagon and horses to convey them from Taravao on the isthmus
to Tautira twelve miles along the coast.

There Stevenson settled into one of the happiest periods of his
life as an exile, collecting songs and legends and resuming work
on *The Master of Ballantrae*. Perhaps it was weariness with his
South Seas travel book, perhaps it was the enchantment of his
surroundings, but he abandoned his journal and left no record of
the two months he stayed at Tautira other than a few pages of
correspondence. In one letter he described the village as 'the
Garden of the World, otherwise called Hans Christian Andersen-
ville', and in another 'the most beautiful spot, and its people the
most amiable, I have ever found'.

I found Tautira at the end of a road of flowers and smiles. Far
from the grimy, congested highways around Papeete, this
meandering coastal road was lined with shrubs and flowers in
shades of red, green, and yellow; bicycles were more common
than vehicles, and I noticed that pedestrians looked into passing
cars, ready to smile and wave at friends. There were no bars,
night-clubs, or restaurants to detract from the grandeur of green
hills rising steeply on one side and a calm lagoon on the other.
Commerce was limited to a few small stores, and the tallest
buildings were ornate churches and decaying colonial-style
houses with elaborately carved wooden verandas. I felt my car
was an intrusion in the quiet beauty of the place, and that

driving at any more than twenty m.p.h. would have been reckless haste.

The last curve in the road leads to a bridge over a broad, shallow river, and Tautira lies on a low promontory to the left. I understood at once Stevenson's delight. It was as lovely a spot as I had seen on Tahiti, framed by the lagoon and a range of mountains rising from a deep valley. The inland scene was reminiscent of the Scottish highlands; one peak in particular bore an uncanny resemblance to a distinctive mountain above Loch Long at Arrochar.

The Stevensons rented a house at an exorbitant rent, but the next day they were visited by Princess Moe, formerly Queen of the island of Raiatea, who took pity on the invalid – Stevenson was still suffering from congestion of the lungs and fever – and invited them to live with her in the home of Ori a Ori, the sub-chief of the village and one of her subjects. Thus began a close friendship with one of the most impressive characters Stevenson encountered in the South Seas. Fanny described their host as the finest native they had seen: 'He is several inches over six feet, of perfect though almost gigantic proportions, and looks more like a Roman Emperor in bronze than words can express.'

My host in Tautira did not look like Caesar, but he was a man of some influence as the district mayor and a former member of the French parliament. In this remote corner of Tahiti, Tutaha Salmon was a kind of Polynesian Godfather elected by due process of law. The nearest hotel was six miles away, and as I had expressed a wish to stay in the village he invited me to spend the first night at his home. It was dusk when we arrived, and we had to stop for a small religious procession led by a man bearing a cross, and assistants carrying statues and candles. I asked Salmon what they were celebrating, but he had no idea. 'They're Catholics,' he said with a shrug. With the exception of the Marquesas, French Polynesia remains predominantly faithful to Protestant doctrines introduced by the London Missionary Society in 1797.

The Tahitians were still having a pretty good time in those days, lying around in the sun and dancing and making babies. The righteous indignation of the LMS envoys in frock-coats and top hats soon put a stop to all that nonsense. Cover up thy nakedness, they commanded, and nubile bodies were enveloped in voluminous 'Mother Hubbard' print dresses; stop dancing and kneel in prayer to the one true God, they ordained, and so on. By the time the English writer Robert Keable arrived in the early twentieth century, he found the natives had been decimated by venereal disease, gunpowder, and alcohol. The half-breed residue were wearing European clothes, living in stuffy shacks with corrugated-iron roofs, and eating tinned meat. Although Keable had been a vicar in the Church of England, he was not impressed by the missionary zeal of William Ellis, a leading light of the LMS a century before. 'From the point of view of the average man today,' he observed, 'it is a thousand pities that the Tahitians did not convert Mr Ellis.'

After supper, Salmon accompanied me on a stroll to point out where Stevenson had stayed. A man who owned all the cinemas in French Polynesia restored the house of Ori a Ori in 1948, erected a sign to indicate that Stevenson had lived there, and used it as a weekend home until the 1960s. Unfortunately it disappeared, along with ninety per cent of the village, in a hurricane in April 1983. The site was now occupied by two ramshackle dwellings owned by elderly Chinese. The buildings were squalid, and the garden was overgrown with weeds. It was a far cry from the haven in which Stevenson wrote much of *The Master of Ballantrae*, while Fanny lay smoking native cigarettes with women plaiting hats and little girls came to amuse them with games of hopscotch. Salmon was apologetic. 'Look at that, it's disgusting. If our municipality had been operating at the time I would have acquired the site and kept it as a memorial.

But it's too late now. Hardly anybody remembers what Ori's old house looked like.'

The next day he introduced me to Temana Haro, the town clerk and a direct descendant of Ori, who had inherited his ancestor's imposing appearance. He told me that a silver communion service presented to the local church by Stevenson's mother was still in use, and he took me to see it.

'It's over there,' he said.

'Where?'

'In that cupboard,' he said, pointing to a corner of the church. The doors of the building were open, and the cupboard was not locked. I opened it, and withdrew a nineteenth-century goblet and two salvers. All of them were tarnished, but biblical inscriptions in Tahitian were still legible, as well as the legends: *Tautira 1889*, and *Gifted by Mrs Thomas Stevenson, Edinburgh*.

'We have a new service now,' Temana said. 'But the old people won't use it. They prefer this old one. They say it was a gift from a good heart.'

A few weeks later, I mentioned the discovery to a Hawaiian millionaire who had spent a fortune amassing a huge collection of Stevensonia. 'You mean they were just lying there, in a cupboard in a village church?' he asked. He seemed quite shocked.

NOT MUCH HAPPENS IN TAUTIRA. People harvest copra in the surrounding plantations, fish in the lagoon, and tend their gardens in a gentle rhythm which barely disturbs the profound peace of their surroundings. After leaving Temana to his midday siesta, I strolled along a path heading out of the village by the lagoon. I passed a few people gathering coconuts in a leisurely kind of way, and they waved a friendly greeting. A little girl cutting open a breadfruit turned at the sound of my approach and smiled. Just beyond her, a youth was lounging in a rowing boat while two friends were fishing in the shallows with masks and snorkels. Out by the reef, a small motor boat was trailing a fishing line. I sat on a rock by the shore with a *pain au chocolat* and a soft drink, and watched brightly coloured fish flitting around my bare feet. They were the most energetic forms of life in the place.

The liveliest events of the day were the arrival and departure of the school boat, ferrying about fifty children to and from remote hamlets along the coast. In the days before Britain disappeared beneath motorways and ring-roads, I used to enjoy cycling to school on a rusty old machine with a mind of its own – it was inclined to make diversions through parks when football games were in progress – but the Tautira municipal boat looked like even more fun. Salmon arranged for me to travel on it that afternoon, spend the night with the boatman and his wife, and return the next day.

Tu Faoa and his wife Josette were waiting for me by the stone jetty, a middle-aged couple surrounded by a gaggle of children trooping aboard the wooden fishing boat. Long John Silver should have been with us. The rugged coast dominated by wild green hills was a perfect setting for the *Hispaniola* to appear around a headland with young Jim Hawkins at the helm, her boom tearing at the blocks in the ocean swell. I entered into the spirit of the occasion by intoning the old shanty from *Treasure Island*: 'Fifteen men on the dead man's chest – yo-ho-ho, and a bottle of rum!' in my best baritone. The children laughed, and I felt RLS would have approved, but Tu regarded me doubtfully. I was thoroughly enjoying my self-appointed role looking out for pirates, but at each wooden jetty we lost members of our bold crew to smiling mothers and dogs with wagging tails. The voyage ended at Faravo, the last settlement on the island, where I stepped ashore to find half a dozen small houses nestling among luxuriant foliage.

This lonely spot had been the refuge of Frederic Pfeiffer, one of the 'nature men' inspired by Rousseau to turn their backs on Western civilization, take off all their clothes, and spread the gospels of vegetarianism and pacifism. Ernest Darling, the most famous of these hardy souls to settle on Tahiti, lived beyond the last hamlet on the other side of the peninsula. His favourite party trick was to beat his fists on his slight frame and declare: 'The gorilla in the African jungle pounds his chest until the noise of it can be heard a mile away.' When Jack London visited him in 1907, civilization was pursuing Darling in the form of a road being built along the shore. 'Never mind their pesky road,' the nature man told London. 'I'll get an air machine soon and fool them. I'm clearing a level space for a landing stage for the airships, and next time you come to Tahiti you will alight right at my door.'

Personally, I think Darling was on to something. Imagine a world without roads: no noise, no pollution, no traffic wardens, and no mangled bodies; just paths for pedestrians and cyclists, and the odd horse and cart, with airships drifting quietly above them. When you are sitting by a tranquil shore ten miles from the nearest road on Tahiti-iti, it is easy to become enthusiastic about airships.

Pfeiffer seems to have been an equally charming eccentric. Tu and Josette knew him well, because he was her stepfather. A former soldier, he spent his pension on building a small wooden house and a windmill to provide electricity, went about entirely naked, and lived off natural foods such as fruit and root vegetables. The locals liked him, and when he died they respected his wish not to be buried in a coffin. Since he had come from the earth and was destined to return to it, he reasoned there was no point in putting him in a wooden box. Josette painstakingly stitched a shroud around his body, and buried it in an unmarked grave on the hillside. 'He was a good man,' Josette said. 'He never harmed anyone.'

Unfortunately, the house that Fred built was wrecked in the

1983 hurricane. Tu and Josette vacated it when the sea began pouring in through the windows. They had replaced it with a concrete bungalow which was simply furnished, and decorated with turtle shells and seashell necklaces. As Josette prepared dinner, Tu sat with me on the doorstep and explained why they lived there.

'Here we have fish, fruit, and vegetables, what more do we need?'

'The problem is our children,' Josette called from inside. 'We push them to get degrees, but what for? There are no jobs. They should learn to be self-sufficient like our forefathers.'

'Yes, but young people today won't look back,' Tu said. 'Those days are gone.'

After dinner, Tu consulted me on an issue dividing the community. Half of it wanted the road extended to transport their produce to the markets, and the other half wanted to be left in peace. Sensing Pfeiffer turning in his grave, I said I assumed most people had chosen to live in Faravo for its tranquillity rather than commercial considerations, and I could not see the point in ruining it with cars and trucks.

'Yes, that's it,' Tu said. 'If they want trucks let them live beside a road.'

It rained heavily that night, and as I lay in bed reading by candlelight, with the rain drumming on the iron roof, I had a wonderful vision of a road construction gang fleeing from an angry ghost with no clothes on.

ON RETURNING TO TAUTIRA the next day, I found the mountains behind the village wreathed in clouds, creating a mystical effect. At such times Stevenson thought of Hans Christian Andersen. I was reminded more of Tolkien: the dark crags became the land of Mordor, and the wind carried the hoofbeats of the Riders of Rohan. To those of a fanciful turn of mind, this corner of Tahiti at least remains true to the title of Keable's book: *Isle of Dreams*.

Salmon had gone to Papeete on business, and arranged for me to spend that night at the home of the woman who cleaned his offices. But I was longing for a hot shower, and solitude to collect my thoughts and write up my notes, so I drove a few miles along the coast to a small hotel. It was a pleasant complex of cottages in gardens by the lagoon, and I was the only guest. It was still raining, and a blue and white fishing boat bobbing at the quayside provided the only colourful contrast in a scene that was uniformly grey. I donned an oilskin cape, and splashed along a path to the hotel terrace for lunch.

Across the bay, white flashes of surf rifling along the distant reef were the only distinction between sea and sky. The rain pattered a gentle rhythm on the trees and the flat, calm surface of the bay. I was not in the least depressed by the change in the weather; rather I found it refreshing. Sitting by the shore of the lagoon, I felt like a figure in a landscape painting.

The weather was no less bleak than in the Marquesas, but the mood was different. The scene was softer, gentler, and, above all, more open. I sensed, rather than saw, green rolling hills behind me and the gradual slopes of the main island in the distance. I was not trapped, as I had been in the Marquesas, by towering walls of dark rock with only treacherous muddy tracks leading to gloomy hamlets. Papeete, with its bars, cinemas, and night-clubs was little over an hour's drive away. I had no wish to visit them, but it was good to know they were there if I felt the need for them.

As I sat musing in my solitude, the opaque blur began to dissolve and take on shapes and colours. A cloud reappeared against the faint glimmer of a pale blue sky, and in the distance a canoe glided towards a lone fisherman on the reef. The rower paused, apparently exchanging a few words with the fisherman, then surged on with powerful strokes, his sleek craft slicing a silver ribbon across the lagoon.

I probably knew the rower by sight, having seen a few of the locals training for a forthcoming three-day canoe race in the Leeward Islands. In a community where canoe racing, inspired by the exploits of ancestral heroes, is regarded as the highest form of sporting endeavour, this annual marathon is the equivalent of an Olympic event. The competition for selection is fierce, and the rivalry between islands and villages is intense. The fame bestowed on the victors is well deserved, considering their race across the open Pacific requires a combination of immense strength and endurance and fine seamanship. One badly judged stroke in a head sea and the canoe founders. The lads I saw preparing for this event looked as if they had been born for it. With the deep chests of competitive swimmers and the leg muscles of track athletes, they epitomized the noble physique Stevenson admired in Ori a Ori. One youth in particular I saw jogging along the road barefoot, his long hair swept back from high cheekbones in a pony-tail, could have been an Olympian statue brought to life.

MICHEL TEVAARAUHARA did not look in the least like an Olympic athlete. He was a stout, jovial character more like a Polynesian Friar Tuck, which in a sense he was as the pastor of Tautira. Michel had a relatively simple philosophy on life. Essentially, four elements were required to sustain mankind – the sun, the sea, the earth, and God; one had only to plant and fish in accordance with the seasons determined by nature, and pay due reverence to the Creator, to nourish both body and soul. He had inherited the teachings of the early missionaries, but he was not what one would call a militant Christian. He was not into blessing soldiers going to war, and proclaiming God to be on their side, and so on. I like to think his attitude was closer to what Christ had in mind. This is it: 'Earth was made for living, not for killing.'

When I first met Michel and his wife Justine they were packing their bags for a transfer to another island, and they invited me to a farewell lunch, a ceremonial *Ahima'a*, offered by their neighbours, the Tiaahu family. Basically the idea is that people dig a pit in the earth, throw in smouldering firewood and stones and huge quantities of food, cover it up again, and then let the food bake until the next day when they come back and have the kind of feast that legends are made of.

The Stevensons attended a similar event in the village in 1888, during which a man presented Stevenson with two eggs, saying: 'Carry those to Scotland with you, let them hatch into cocks, and their song shall remind you of Tautira.' Fanny wrote to Colvin: 'By the time we had taken our respective places on the veranda in front of our door, an immense crowd had assembled . . . all were dressed in their gayest *pareus*, and many had wreaths of leaves or flowers on their heads . . . Louis made his oration (translated by the chief) to the accompaniment of the squealing of pigs, the cackling of hens, and the roar of the surf which beats man-high upon the reef. Somehow the whole effect of the scene was like a story out of the Bible, and I am not ashamed that Louis and I both shed tears when we saw the enchanting procession of schoolchildren.'

The Tiaahu family had laid on an equally sumptuous feast for their beloved pastor and his wife. About a mile out of the village, along the path by the lagoon, we found the preparations almost complete. Beneath an open shed, a long wooden table had been covered with banana leaves which had been passed lightly over the fire to make them pliable; the pillars of the shed were wrapped in palm fronds and flowers, and other exotic leaves were adorning the rafters. A gay crowd was scurrying around in a haze of woodsmoke, ferrying food to the table amid much squawking and yelping from a menagerie of dogs, hens, and pigs. It was like a South Seas version of 'Old McDonald's Farm'.

On our arrival, I was presented with a powerful fruit punch and graciously introduced as a writer retracing the travels of an illustrious fellow Scot. This created much interest, and Michel was called upon to translate anecdotes of Stevenson and Ori a Ori; Fanny's allusions to a fairyland ruled by a beautiful brown princess had the women rocking with laughter. At the appointed hour, men dug away the earth over the oven. Layers of oilskin covers, corrugated-iron sheeting, and banana leaves were removed to reveal a huge metal basket resting on heated stones and crammed with pork, chicken, and vegetables. The food was transferred to large wooden bowls for the final preparation of delicacies such as *poe*, a sweet paste of bananas and flour mixed with coconut milk. Soon the table was laden with all manner of traditional dishes – wild orange bananas, breadfruit, raw fish marinated in coconut milk and lime juice, curried river shrimps, sweet potato, fermented coconut, roast pork and chicken, and an assortment of tropical fruits.

About twenty members of the Tiaahu family spanning several generations took their places on wooden benches at the table. I have rarely seen such a handsome gathering. The patriarch was a lean, lively character, whose eyes sparkled with good humour; his wife was a fuller, more dignified figure who had attained a serene beauty with age; the sons, who ran a construction business, were all strong young men with fine features; and the girls were heart-stoppingly pretty. It felt good just to be among them.

Michel motioned to me to take the place of honour reserved for him at the head of the table. I protested, but he insisted, and everybody else seemed to consider this fitting, so I sat between Michel and Justine, and we bowed our heads. Michel said grace in Tahitian, and the sound of his voice over the murmur of the surf sounded like a real blessing. If God existed, I thought, he would look down on this assembly with a glad eye.

As we tucked into the food with our hands — by far the best way of enjoying such a banquet — Justine told me that a museum near Papeete had tried to acquire the silver communion service donated by Stevenson's mother.

'The people refused to let it go. You know, especially the older people are very attached to it. They think it must have made Mrs Stevenson very happy to give this gift with a good heart, and it would be a shame to her to give it away. I think it was a sign of love for the people of Tautira, and even if the giver is gone, the sign remains, like Jesus.'

I looked at Justine, and admired her sincerity. This was the essence of Christianity I had lost sight of long ago in the dreary pews of Scottish Presbyterian churches, and the killing fields of so-called 'Christian' militias in Lebanon. Maybe the missionaries had not been such a bad influence after all; it just took the inherent good nature of Polynesians to transform their austere Victorian tenets into a benign code of life.

When the feast was over, Michel stood up and made a speech. Despite the fact the occasion was in his honour, I gathered from the few words I understood that much of his discourse was devoted to my visit; Stevenson's name was mentioned repeatedly, along with Ori a Ori. When he had concluded, he suggested I might wish to say a few words which he would translate. As I rose to speak, I saw Stevenson's lean frame standing before a similar gathering a century before. Lacking the man's eloquence, I made a brief speech about being gratified to see that the passage of time had not altered the beauty of Tautira or the kindness of its people. This was warmly applauded, then the eldest son formally thanked me for my presence and for my stories of their ancestors. I spent the rest of the afternoon playing games with the children, and in idle contemplation of a happy scene. It was the kind of day that lingers long in the memory.

*

THE NEXT DAY I DECIDED to explore the highlands above Tautira, and discovered a narrow road leading to a plateau on the western shoulder of the mountains. Within minutes, I was startled to find I had left Polynesia behind. The palm trees gave way to green fields, with dairy cattle grazing around chestnut trees. There were buttercups and daisies in the meadows, and beyond hedgerows lining the road small farmsteads resounded with the squealing of pigs and barking of dogs. Rounding a corner, I paused to admire thoroughbred horses cantering around a grass paddock complete with a jumping course. The air was cool and fresh, and a fine mist obscured the rest of the island, enclosing me in an illusion of rural Britain.

At the end of the road, a muddy track led through the clouds to a grassy hillock. Donning my oilskin cape, I wandered around enjoying the freshness of soft rain, a welcome change from the languor of the tropics, and the sharp, clean smells of the grass and trees. I could hear rivers rushing on either side of the hill, but the valleys were too steep and deep to see them. I lay on the grass, letting the rainwater run between my lips; I bounded up, and skipped around singing snatches of Scottish songs with tuneless gusto. It occurred to me that friends at home in such weather might dream wistfully of palm-fringed beaches by sleepy lagoons, and here was I revelling in my escape from them. Had anyone chanced along the path, I imagine this noisy, yellow-caped apparition would have been taken for a 'nature man' gone mad; in fact I was blissfully happy.

The good news for Stevenson in Tautira was that his health recovered; the bad news was that both masts of the *Casco* were discovered to be consumed by dry-rot, and she had to return to Papeete for repairs, leaving the Stevensons virtually destitute in Tautira.

Fanny wrote to Colvin:

'We had used up all our stores, and had only a few dollars of money left in Tautira . . . I burst into tears, upon which the princess wept bitterly . . . and then Ori of Ori, the magnificent, who listened to the tale of the shipwrecked mariners with serious dignity, asked one or two questions and then spoke to this effect. "You are my brother; all that I have is yours. I know that your food is done, but I can give you plenty of fish and taro. We like you, and wish to have you here. Stay where you are till the *Casco* comes. Be happy – *et ne pleurez pas.*' Louis dropped his head into his hands and wept, and then we all went up to Rui and shook hands with him and accepted his offer.'

Ori later risked his life by sailing in a whaleboat to Papeete in bad weather to bring news of the *Casco*, along with money and provisions. The supplies sent by the captain included champagne, which was produced at a dinner to celebrate Ori's return. Fanny recalled: 'Ori drank his glass and announced it beyond excellence. "I shall drink it continually," he added, pouring out a fresh glass. "What is the cost of it by the bottle?" Louis told him, whereupon Ori solemnly replaced his full glass, saying, "It is not fit that even kings should drink a wine so expensive." It took him days to recover from the shock.'

I wondered what Ori would have made of the extravagance of another celebrated author who visited Tahiti-iti a few years later. Zane Grey, who made millions of dollars writing about cowboys, spent a lot of them indulging in his favourite hobby, which was killing big fish. In 1929 he established a luxurious base on the other side of the peninsula and assembled a task force of four powerful launches led by his flagship, a hundred-and-ninety-foot yacht equipped with all the latest gadgets. Not content with world-record catches of sailfish and dolphin, Grey was driven on like Captain Ahab after Moby Dick by local legends of a monster marlin. The following year he caught it. In the struggle, sharks removed about two hundred pounds of flesh from this magnificent creature, but it still weighed in at more than eight hundred pounds. I saw a photograph of Grey standing beside his prize, which had been strung up by the tail. His head barely reached the marlin's gills.

I visited the site of Grey's camp on a bluff overlooking the sea, and thought about the little man and the big fish. Here was this self-styled adventurer sitting in a luxurious yacht, with the most powerful and sophisticated fishing equipment that riches could buy, doing battle with a fish armed with a spiked snout. He probably had a beer while the sharks were closing in on his prey. This he called sport. It seemed to me about as sporting as hunting a rhinoceros in a helicopter gunship.

In Tautira I met a man called Teama, who had been three times the spearfishing champion of French Polynesia, and once of all the Pacific. Armed with only a speargun and a knife, he would descend to prodigious depths in pursuit of big fish and then fight off sharks attracted by the blood in the water. He had been doing this for years, and I was told he never boasted of his exploits or took photographs of his catches. It would not have occurred to him.

It was raining on the day I left Tautira, as it was on Christmas Day, 1888, when the villagers congregated on the shore to bid farewell to the Stevenson party. Rifles were fired and flags were dipped in salute as the *Casco* weighed anchor, and its passengers lined the rails waving handkerchiefs until they were beyond the reef. Stevenson observed:

The day of our parting was a sad one. We deduced from it a rule for travellers: not to stay two months in one place – which is to cultivate regrets.

Nobody was firing guns or dipping flags as I walked to my car, but Michel gave me a firm handshake and a blessing, and Justine gave me a big hug, which was just as good.

BEFORE LEAVING TAHITI, I decided to spend a few days on a quiet stretch of the southern coast of the main island, which had attracted Gauguin, Keable, Somerset Maugham, and Rupert Brooke. This was how I came to meet a shipwrecked sailor, find a wonderful library, and learn of the curse of the Rurutu tombstone.

Roger Gowan was a mild-mannered Englishman who had wandered around the world in a vague kind of way, suffered shipwreck with the equanimity one would expect of a Norfolk man, and discovered he could make a living from farming vegetables and rabbits in Tahiti. He now owned two of the most popular restaurants on the island and arguably the most beautiful house – the erstwhile home of Robert Keable. We met over lunch in one of his restaurants by the shore at Papeari, overlooking the highlands of Tahiti-iti, and he told me his story.

He had originally intended being a farmer, but somehow or other he became a policeman in Rhodesia. After a few festive New Year drinks in a Bulawayo bar, he and three colleagues decided it would be a good idea to sail around the world. Undeterred by the fact that only one of them knew anything about boats, they returned to England and bought a thirty-seven-foot gaff-rigged ketch in Ramsgate for £1,500. In 1959 they set sail from Torquay, traversed the Atlantic and the Pacific via the Panama Canal, stopped off at Tahiti, and then arrived at New Zealand with a vague feeling that maybe they ought to go back to Tahiti. Having done this, disaster struck shortly afterwards.

Roger had agreed to transport a tombstone to the burial of a friend's wife at Rurutu in the Austral Islands, south of Tahiti. At the funeral, a native told him his ship would be cursed for bringing the stone. A few minutes later, the proceedings were interrupted by a horseman galloping up from the coast with the news that Roger's ketch had snapped her anchor chain and was breaking up on the reef. Submitting to the whims of fate, Roger returned to Tahiti, fell in love with a beautiful Chinese–Tahitian girl, and proceeded to raise a family and prosper in the catering trade.

The house they lived in, and where they invited me to stay, had an equally romantic history. Robert Keable, like Stevenson, suffered from tuberculosis and settled in Polynesia for the sake of his health. He achieved brief literary fame with a religious novel, *Simon called Peter*, which sold four hundred thousand copies, and a sequel, *Recompense*, which passed the two hundred thousand mark; but he remains best known for the enduring charm of his Tahitian books, *Tahiti, Isle of Dreams* and *Numerous Treasure*. Like Stevenson, his period of exile was brief. Less than four years after arriving in Tahiti, he died in 1928 at the age of forty (RLS lived in Samoa for five years and died shortly after his forty-fourth birthday).

Keable's house is a handsome villa clad in white wood and set in landscaped gardens overlooking the lagoon a couple of miles from Roger's restaurant near the Gauguin Museum. Being a wealthy man, Keable furnished it sumptuously with oriental rugs, divans, a piano, and rows of bookshelves. I was pleased to see the shelves were still in place, and filled with old books including one of the finest collections of South Seas literature I had seen. It was here that Keable recorded a recollection of Stevenson:

'I have met but one native in Tahiti who remembered Stevenson. He is a very old man who held my hand long merely because I professed my admiration for the Master. And he said: "We shall never see his like again in Tahiti. He is dead, and we are dying. None of the Europeans are as he was, whose body, soul, and spirit were white as the moon and pure as the stars."'

I was installed in a white wooden cottage in the grounds. It was a cosy little place which smelled of wood and old books, and the windows and bed were draped in matching fabrics; I felt that if I looked out I should see English countryside, rather than the green volcanic peaks of Tahiti. Instead, I was drawn to shelves of books with titles like *The Corpse in the Crimson Slippers, Moon over Stamboul,* and *About the Murder of a Startled Lady*.

I have always enjoyed the elegant prose of old books, evoking images of authors penning mysteries and romances before log fires in Victorian studies. Here I had found a treasure trove, and I began reading a book at random: 'The truth about the case of the foundling bones should have been apparent at the start . . .' There was a knock at the door, and Roger's wife appeared with a pot of Earl Grey tea. A sudden squall rattled the window panes, and I looked out to see Tahiti-iti disappearing behind a curtain of rain. I closed the door, poured a cup of tea, and curled into an armchair to peruse the mystery of the foundling bones.

AN EQUALLY INTRIGUING true story, involving two celebrated English men of letters and a 'missing' painting, had enfolded in the nearby village of Mataiea years before. While the rest of the so-called civilized world was plunging itself into the collective insanity of World War I, Rupert Brooke wandered dreamily into Mataiea in the early months of 1914 to look for 'lost' Gauguins. The artist had lived there for eighteen months between 1891 and 1893, and Brooke believed a few masterpieces might still be lying around. He was right, but he never found them. This may have been due to his preoccupation with his landlady's lovely daughter Mamua, whom he immortalized in his poem 'Tiara Tahiti'.

Two years later, Somerset Maugham came to Mataiea to gather material for his novel *The Moon and Sixpence*, inspired by Gauguin's life. Being less susceptible than Brooke to female charms, Maugham discovered three glass-panelled doors painted by Gauguin at the wooden bungalow of the artist's Tahitian landlord. Children had picked out most of two of them, but the third was reasonably well preserved. The owner agreed to sell it, but he wanted a new door which would cost a hundred francs. Maugham gave him two hundred, took tools from his car and unscrewed the door, and had it installed in his villa on the

French Riviera. Shortly before Maugham died in 1965, the door painting was sold at auction to Mr P. I. Berman, an American banker, for £13,000.

I found the French staff at the nearby Gauguin Museum more interesting than the exhibits. The complex of low buildings in the Tahitian style by the shore at Papeari was more of a memorial than a museum; the only original Gauguins were a few woodcut prints, three carved wooden spoons, and a small vase. But it had an amusing curator in Giles Artur, who was assisted by an attractive young woman called Dominique, and an itinerant art student who played a decent game of tennis. Dominique showed me around the museum, and that evening I was invited to dinner in the living quarters, a pleasing jumble of old furniture, books, and paintings with a good selection of classical music and two friendly dogs.

Giles knew a great deal about art, as one might expect, but he was not snobbish about it. One wall was adorned by two paintings by Serge Poliakoff (1900–69), which were each worth a million francs. To me they were a confusion of colours and patterns which suggested nothing other than the artist amusing himself, and I asked Giles if he considered them worth the money.

'I don't think any painting is worth a million francs, but do you think footballers and pop stars deserve to be millionaires? It's true it's absurd. It's a money game played by rich people, like the stock market, and equally artificial.'

I said I preferred masters like Rembrandt to modern painters. Giles said: 'Personally, I think art reflects the societies we live in, and I don't think art is worth as much as it was before.'

Security was literally fearsome at the museum. Giles rarely bothered to lock the doors or gates, because he had supernatural guardians in the garden in the form of three stone *tikis* from Raivavae in the Austral Islands. The locals were terrified of them, apparently with good reason.

They had been brought to a museum in Papeete in 1933, despite warnings that they should be left undisturbed. Within two years, the schooner which had transported them was wrecked on a reef, and its captain was dead. When it was decided to transfer them to the grounds of the Gauguin Museum, no Tahitian would dare move them, and eventually the public works department employed Marquesans to do the job. That night the father of one of the workers was killed in a traffic accident, and on the day the new site was inaugurated the foreman collapsed and died. The museum gardener resigned, and the Tahitian assistant in the gift shop refused to work after dark. If the dogs don't get any intruders, it is confidently assumed by the locals that the *tikis* will. These are the same people who work at nuclear test sites, and watch American soap operas on satellite television.

It was Dominique who told me about a cottage in an adjoining botanical garden that was available for rent at a reasonable price. With a thatched roof and small garden by the lagoon, it looked like a perfect place to unwind and write up my notes before leaving for Hawaii. Not wishing to presume on Roger's hospitality, and swayed by the prospect of a week in such an agreeable spot with a pleasant companion, I moved in with Dominique. In the event, I achieved little work. The fragrant beauty of my surroundings and a spell of hot weather combined to wrap me in a profound tropical torpor. As the days passed, the desire to work ebbed away in languid contemplation of the sea, the exotic gardens, and the distant highlands of Tahiti-iti.

On my last night, we strolled barefoot on the grass by the lagoon and I was awed by the purity of the moonlight on a scene of inexpressible loveliness. As we stood watching the sea breaking on the reef, Dominique said: 'You know people come here looking for paradise, and they're disappointed. The truth is this *is* paradise, it's just that people don't know how to live in it. I'm not even sure they want to.'

A Qantas Jumbo jet was unloading hundreds of paradise seekers as I waited to board my Hawaiian Airlines flight for Honolulu. It was the middle of the night, but televisions in the terminal buildings were relentlessly projecting videos of *vahines* cavorting on golden beaches, and other contrived images of a Polynesian Utopia the tourists expected to find.

I opened Keable's book on Tahiti, *Isle of Dreams*, and I read the following passage:

'The old Tahiti is as dead as the Middle Ages. Its people have been exterminated, its beauty has been ravished, its very tradition seems almost obliterated. The tourist of the day or even of a month sees no more of the real Tahiti of the past than he would see at a well-conducted colonial exhibition . . . there is an utter certainty that total extinction awaits the race, at any rate in the eastern Pacific. The actual blood will run ever more thin and ever more mixed until it is gone, the veritable spirit will vanish away ever more swiftly before aeroplanes, wireless, and tourism.'

Keable wrote this in the 1920s. I felt like calling out to the new arrivals: 'Hey, never mind the videos. Read this.' Then I thought I was being a pompous ass, and walked to the departure gate.

TEN

I'm happy to share my treasures. I never turn a
Stevenson man away from my door

THE FIRST CHARACTER I SAW when I left the arrivals
hall at Honolulu airport was the Devil. I know it was the Devil,
because he had horns and a spiked tail and cloven hoofs. He was
pursuing a nun and lifting her habit with a pitchfork to reveal
singularly unchaste frilly underwear. Both of them seemed to be
enjoying the experience.

Driving along Ala Moana Boulevard towards Waikiki, I
noticed the sidewalks were crowded with oddballs: Einstein,
Superman, and an assortment of wizards and dinosaurs and so
on. It took a while for my jet-lagged brain to realize it was
October 31, and the citizens of Hawaii were gearing up for the
collective lunacy of Hallowe'en.

When I was a child, this event was regarded as an amusement
for youngsters, who would dress up as pirates and witches and
subject adults to excruciating song and dance routines in
exchange for sweets, nuts, and pennies. It was fun, and I still
remember my dismay at the age of thirteen when my mum
suggested I was too *old* to be the Lone Ranger. I hung up my
guns sadly; the age of innocence was dead.

Americans have no such inhibitions, having discovered that
Hallowe'en offers endless possibilities to dress up in outlandish
costumes and indulge in fantasies; it is more fun to be Genghis
Khan than an insurance salesman. In the evening Kalakaua
Avenue, the beachfront boulevard in Waikiki, was swept up in
a kind of *Mardi Gras* for witches and space invaders. I stumbled
in a daze into the Rose and Crown, which billed itself as an
authentic English pub, and ordered a bottle of British beer. The

barman had four arms, but this did not strike me as unusual at the time. Next to me a giant lizard was messing around with a mermaid, and in the corner John the Baptist was murdering 'If you knew Susie like I knew Susie' on a honky-tonk piano.

Less than twenty-four hours before I had been contemplating a Tahitian lagoon by moonlight. Travel is said to broaden the mind; in this case it had hurled mine through a cultural time-warp. I slept fitfully that night, my brain whirling with bizarre images including one which, in the local vernacular, zonked me out. I had never seen a topless unicorn before.

The passengers of the *Casco* were accorded a more dignified welcome to Honolulu. Fanny's daughter Isobel had been living there for more than six years with her husband Joe Strong, an artist who had come to Hawaii to paint for the royal court. Thus after a family reunion, Stevenson was presented to David Kalakaua, the last of the Hawaiian kings.

By all accounts, Kalakaua was a colourful character. Dubbed the 'Merry Monarch', he was a Hawaiian revivalist who tried to ensure a measure of autonomy for native Hawaiians, by then a minority in their own land; he composed the national anthem which became the state song; and he revived the *hula* after decades of suppression by missionaries who regarded it as a heathen dance. Having acquired a taste for pageantry, he proceeded to build a splendid palace for what was then considered the extravagant sum of $360,000. His reign was distinguished by lavish spending, big parties, and general incompetence which incurred the wrath of powerful sugar barons who forced him under threat of armed rebellion to accept a new constitution strictly limiting his powers.

Lloyd Osbourne recalled Kalakaua as a much maligned man:

'From the stories told of him one would picture a grotesque savage, who was constantly drunk; a sort of Sambo in ridiculous uniforms, whose antics and vices became so intolerable that finally a long-suffering community had to sweep him away. He was, on the contrary, a highly educated man, with an air of extreme distinction and a most winning graciousness and charm, who would have been at ease in any court in Europe . . . he was the greatest gentleman I have ever known.'

This splendid figure was a frequent guest at a house which the Stevensons rented at the eastern end of Waikiki Beach, in those days a quiet settlement of twenty or thirty residences set in shady gardens three miles from Honolulu. The city already had more than twenty thousand inhabitants, a telephone system, and two daily newspapers, and electric street lights had been installed the year before. But Waikiki was still a rural village by a narrow coral sand beach and surrounded by rice paddies. It was typical of Stevenson that instead of choosing the best room in the house, he installed himself in a dilapidated shack, papered with mildewed newspapers, with his cot and ink-bottle, and set himself to completing *The Master of Ballantrae*. 'It is a grim little wooden shanty,' he wrote to a friend. 'Cobwebs bedeck it; friendly mice inhabit its recesses; the mailed cockroach walks upon the wall; so also, I regret to say, the scorpion . . .'

Here the royal equipage would draw up and deposit Kalakaua immaculate in white flannels, with his chamberlain bearing books, to spend afternoons with Stevenson discussing Polynesian lore and antiquity. Osbourne noted that the king was a mine of information on these subjects:

'It was his hobby to record the fast-fading history of his race . . . Together they would pore for hours over the king's notebooks, in which in his fine, slanting hand he had transcribed the legends of his dying people . . . this grave, earnest, rather careworn man . . .'

Kalakaua's gravity was compromised on several of these occasions by his fondness for wine. After one session in which five bottles of champagne were consumed in little more than three hours, Stevenson noted that the sovereign was 'quite presentable, although perceptibly more dignified at the end . . .'

A few bottles of champagne might have softened my perception of modern Waikiki, but I doubt it. The aim of its architects seems to have been to cram as many hideous buildings as possible into the smallest space, and to hell with the beautiful scenery around it. There is so much building going on, the locals have adopted the construction crane as the state bird. On any given day, Waikiki has twenty-four thousand permanent residents and sixty-five thousand visitors. At the last count it had thirty-four thousand hotel and condominium rooms, four hundred and fifty restaurants, three hundred and fifty bars and clubs, and mazes of shopping malls lining six-lane highways – all this in an area roughly one and a half miles long by half a mile wide.

The important thing is not to look up. At street level you are diverted by the bright lights and the bustle of the vacation crowd; look up, and you are lost in a nightmare of concrete boxes blotting out the sky. Emerging from this urban mess at the seafront, the first thing you notice about Waikiki Beach is that there is hardly any beach. There is a succession of thin sandy coves separated by stone breakwaters, erected by landowners to delineate their territory. Unfortunately, these barriers have also disturbed wave patterns and currents to such an extent that the beach has been all but swept away. A government project to enlarge it with a hundred and forty-six thousand cubic yards of sand, at a cost of £10 million, had been stalled by squabbles over where the property lines should be drawn. Meanwhile the sea, not having been consulted in the matter, was clawing back what remained of the beach.

Here are two interesting facts about Hawaii: (a) the state comprises eight inhabited islands and a hundred and twenty-four smaller ones strung out across the northern Pacific for more than fifteen hundred miles; (b) they are all drifting away from the rest of America at the rate of about three inches a year, and they are slowly but surely sinking. It will take some time of course, but I like the idea of this geological conveyor belt dumping thousands of garish hotels and fast-food joints into the sea.

The skies were overcast on the day I wandered down to the beach, but it was packed with bodies. I was hungry, and joined a crowd of tourists queuing for assembly-line junk food in a Jack in the Box restaurant on the beachfront. A paper liner on my tray assured me that, in accordance with company policy to improve the quality of the environment, my utensils were made of recycled materials. I also learned that the table bases were manufactured from melted-down automobile engine blocks. By refusing to buy beef from rainforest countries, and by diverting more than a million pounds of materials from 'the waste stream' every year, more than one thousand Jacks in the Box across America were resolved to make the world a cleaner and healthier place to live in. I looked at my burger and chips, and then out at the boulevard choked with traffic, and was deeply gratified for living on such a clean and healthy planet.

THERE WERE TOO MANY whites and not enough natives in Honolulu for Stevenson's liking, and he ignored Oahu, the island on which it lies, in his South Seas travel book; but he left detailed descriptions of his beachfront abode in various letters, so I went to look for it. At the end of Waikiki Beach, the concrete jungle gives way to a large park which extends to the slopes of Diamond Head. This imposing volcanic cone does not look like, nor did it ever contain, a diamond. It was christened by deluded British sailors who found calcite crystals sparkling in the sun there in 1825 and thought they had struck it rich.

As far as I could make out, the dwellings occupied by the Stevensons had stood on what was now a picnic spot by the beach which seemed to be popular with the local gay community. I stood for a while trying to imagine Stevenson toiling in his musty hut at *The Master of Ballantrae* in between drinking sessions with Kalakaua, but I was distracted by joggers and whizzing Frisbees.

I was beginning to despair of finding any trace of Stevenson in this tourist playground when I tracked down a millionaire who had known Fanny's daughter and had acquired a large collection of Stevensonia. Robert Van Dyke sounded enthusiastic on the telephone. 'You're writing about Stevenson? Meet me outside your hotel in half an hour and I'll show you some of my treasures.' It was a curious meeting. Van Dyke appeared as a big, untidy man with silver hair in a big, untidy car loaded with memorabilia. It was as if he had just driven from a garage sale at Stevenson's house. Instead of taking me to his home, he drove to a quiet corner of Kapiolani Park, near where the Stevensons had stayed. It was dusk, and he switched on the interior light of the car and began rummaging through piles of books, photograph albums, and jewellery in the back seat. Passers-by regarded us curiously. Maybe they thought we were drug dealers.

'This might interest you,' he said, passing me a gold ring. It was set with a topaz, and inside it was inscribed *F B Sydney, Feb 1892*. I knew that topaz was Stevenson's birthstone, that he had bought rings for himself and Fanny in Sydney early in 1892, and that F would stand for Fanny and B for Belle, the name by which her daughter Isobel was usually known. Van Dyke said Stevenson had been wearing the ring when he died. I had no idea whether it was authentic, but I had no reason to doubt him. I had never actually touched anything that had belonged to Stevenson, and I felt strangely moved. In a glass showcase, it would have been just a ring, but in the palm of my hand, it seemed almost alive.

'Hold it right there,' Van Dyke commanded. I was browsing through a scrapbook of photos and mementoes compiled by Belle, and he pointed at a picture of her. 'Those are the necklaces Fanny wore on her wedding day, and I have them here somewhere.' He searched through a thick folding wallet and produced the necklaces. Van Dyke's favourite expression was: 'I also have . . .' He would mention an item, and out it would come – rings galore, buttons from the coat Fanny was wearing on the day she married Stevenson, toy soldiers with which Stevenson and Lloyd Osbourne staged mock battles, a gold locket containing strands of Stevenson's baby hair on one side and death hair on the other, a ruby and pearl brooch of Fanny's, and so on. This is a snatch of his conversation: 'I also have a couple of very nice sketches done by Fanny during this period. I also have two letters that Oscar Wilde wrote to Belle, and I have this little idol and all this stuff.' He had difficulty opening a reading glass encrusted with diamonds, and said: 'My mother knows how to do this. I never look at the stuff.'

I was still dazed as we drove back to Waikiki and stopped outside an apartment building behind a grocery store. Van Dyke disappeared up a narrow staircase with his treasures, and returned with a large oil painting of Fanny. He showed it to me, standing on the pavement, as tourists passed in and out of the shop with packs of beer and funny hats.

'I also have the dress and the earrings she's wearing here,' he said. Somehow I knew he would. 'OK, I'll put it back in the closet and I'll be right back.' *In the closet? Above a grocery store?*

Over dinner in a noisy restaurant, Van Dyke explained that his grandmother had known Fanny in California, and his mother had been a friend of Belle. He recalled meeting Belle for the first time in Santa Barbara in 1946 when he was nine years old: 'She was a very charming woman. Every finger had rings on it, everything was done with a fluttering gesture. She normally didn't care having little kids around, but we got on famously.' Shortly before Belle died in 1952, she invited Van Dyke's mother to take what she wanted from the Stevenson heirlooms. 'We took a few items, but we should have called a moving company. There was so much stuff. Boxes and boxes of papers, clothes . . .' Most of the jewellery, including Stevenson's topaz ring, had been in a case which Belle gave to Van Dyke's mother for a nominal sum to evade tax. The sum was five dollars.

I never got a satisfactory answer to why Van Dyke had subsequently spent hundreds of thousands of dollars of his family fortune in acquiring such a vague mish-mash of relics of an author whose books he frankly confessed he did not find 'all that exciting'. It seems to have been the family connection, fuelled by an insatiable desire to accumulate Stevensonia for its own sake. 'I am constantly in pursuit of anything I don't have of Stevenson,' he told me. 'One never has a sense of completeness. Acquisition, say of a book you've been after for years, is the ultimate in life. But now I have so much stuff, often I wished I really hated somebody so I could leave everything to him to sort out.' Yet there was a disarming candour about the man. 'Maybe it's sick to keep all this stuff,' he admitted. 'Some of the world's greatest art collections are hidden away, by guys looking at stolen paintings and saying "mine". But I'm not like that. I'm more of a curator than a possessor. I'm happy to share my treasures. I never turn a Stevenson man away from my door, I feel it's a moral obligation.'

A couple of years before, Van Dyke had written to the RLS Society in Edinburgh, offering to travel to Scotland at his own expense and host a dinner to give a lecture and exhibit some of his collection. He said: 'I thought it would be kinda nice, you know, to share some of these wonderful things with people who would appreciate them.' He received no reply, which did not surprise me.

In the event of untimely death, he said much of his collection would go to a Hawaiian high school where he and his mother had been pupils. 'It's a kinda toss-up what to do with the jewellery,' he said. 'Who wants this stuff?' I thought of the topaz ring and choked on my food.

*

STEVENSON DID NOT CARE MUCH for Honolulu, but he cared deeply for a thirteen-year-old princess destined to become a tragic figure in the overthrow of the Hawaiian monarchy. Princess Kaiulani was the daughter of Archibald Cleghorn, a former Edinburgh merchant, and a sister of Kalakaua, who had died the year before Stevenson arrived in Hawaii. The two Scots became friends, and Stevenson was a frequent visitor to Cleghorn's estate on the outskirts of Waikiki, where he would spend hours sitting with the half-caste princess beneath a banyan tree telling her stories of Scotland and the South Seas.

When the girl sailed to England for a boarding-school education, she found a poem in her autograph album penned by Stevenson:

> *Forth from her land to mine she goes,*
> *The island maid, the island rose,*
> *Light of heart and bright of face:*
> *The daughter of a double race.*
> *Her islands here, in Southern sun*
> *Shall mourn their Kaiulani gone,*
> *And I, in her dear banyan shade,*
> *Look vainly for my little maid.*
>
> *But our Scots islands far away*
> *Shall glitter with unwonted day,*
> *And cast for once their tempests by*
> *To smile in Kaiulani's eye.*

The poet and the princess never saw one another again. Kaiulani blossomed into a beautiful woman, but she never met her Prince Charming. Instead of living happily ever after, she died young, unmarried, and dispossessed of her throne. Within five years Kalakaua and Stevenson were dead and the monarchy was overthrown, and five years later Kaiulani died of pneumonia at her father's estate at the age of twenty-three.

At a bookshop in Honolulu I found a booklet entitled *R. L. Stevenson Poet in Paradise*. It had photographs of Kaiulani which showed her as a delicate child, and as a young woman with fine features wearing an ornate Victorian dress and feathered hat. She had long black hair and big dark eyes, one of which was slightly squinted. The effect was a blend of beauty, intelligence, and vulnerability, and I understood why Stevenson had adored her.

The site of Cleghorn's estate was only a few yards from my hotel, where a map showed two parallel streets named Cleghorn and Tusitala. I set off hopefully, but Kaiulani's playground had been swallowed by haphazard urban development. I walked along nondescript backstreets of ugly buildings and vacant lots, searching in vain for mementoes of the leafy estate. The magic had gone, and so had the banyan tree. Cleghorn willed his estate to the territory for use as a park, but the politicians decided the community would be better served by subdividing it into lots and pocketing the cash. As the district expanded, the branches of the banyan in Tusitala Street were considered a danger to buildings in high winds; neglected, the tree became infested by rats and termites, and it was cut down in 1949.

When Stevenson visited Kalakaua in his palace, they could see the sea from the upper balconies. That view is now obscured by landfill development, the carriageway has become a car park, and the palace is dwarfed by the soaring skyline of downtown Honolulu. But it is still a magnificent structure set in spacious lawns. At the time of its construction, its architecture was described as 'American Florentine', whatever that means. Actually its ornate façade, with fluted columns supporting open balconies, is more like a cross between a French château and a Victorian railway station. The overall impression is of an imperial relic resisting the march of graceless modern monoliths.

I presented myself at an office in the palace barracks, a whimsical white building like a toy fort, and was issued with a ticket for a guided tour. My party included Bill, a middle-aged man who was visiting from California with his boyfriend. Bill was thrilled at the prospect of seeing a real royal palace, and he had dressed for the occasion in a powder-blue outfit with gold earrings, bracelets, and anklets. When he removed his sunglasses, I was startled to see that his eyes were a fashion accessory, perfectly matching the colour of his attire. He was an amusing companion, and provided an interesting contrast to prim ladies in floral gowns who shadowed us like ghosts wherever we went. The first one I saw in the entrance was standing so perfectly still I thought she was an exhibit, and I was taken aback when she smiled. One sensed that if ever the monarchy was restored, these women would form a redoubtable praetorian guard.

There is not much to see in the palace, most of the rooms being sparsely furnished, but I was impressed by the gloomy atmosphere of an upstairs chamber which was shuttered and dimly lit. This was where Queen Liliuokalani, a sister of Kalakaua who succeeded him to the throne, was imprisoned after an abortive royalist rebellion in 1895 against republicans who had deposed her two years earlier. To humiliate her, the white businessmen who staged the *coup* tried her in her own palace, and sentenced her to five years' hard labour, which was later reduced to nine months of house arrest in the upstairs room. She spent the rest of her life in a private residence near the palace, and died in 1917. I imagined the dusky queen pacing this dark room, her only contact with the outside world a lady-in-waiting, as soldiers patrolled outside. Even Bill was subdued by the melancholy of the room, and we were glad to step outside into the sunshine.

Stevenson made a return visit to Hawaii from Samoa in 1893, a few months after the republican *coup*. On leaving, he gripped Cleghorn by the hand and said: 'Now, Cleghorn, if I can be of any service to the royalist cause in Hawaii, just drop me a line, and I will come right back here.' By then of course, it was a lost cause – and Stevenson had little more than a year to live.

While I was there, Hawaii was preparing to commemorate the centenary of the overthrow of the monarchy. The occasion had become the focus for discontent among native Hawaiians, who were demanding compensation for lost lands and restoration of sovereignty. A columnist in the *Honolulu Advertiser* argued that Hawaiians were legally and morally entitled to more than $100 million in damages, and that sovereignty was not as crazy as it might sound. Similar sentiments were expressed on T-shirts I saw on Molokai, the most rural and traditional of the main islands, which declared: 'Keep Hawaiian lands in Hawaiian hands.'

There is no doubt the descendants of the original Polynesian settlers have become a kind of lost tribe in their ancestral homeland. In social terms they are at the bottom of the pile, being the poorest, sickest, and least educated people in the state. Not surprisingly, a lot of them kill themselves. That is the only category they come first in – the suicide rate. A 'Home Lands' scheme which was allocated two hundred thousand acres of land in 1920 for homesteading by native Hawaiians (a fraction of the 1.75 million acres of land seized by America when it annexed the islands in 1898) had become a sick joke. Most of the land had been leased to big business, ostensibly to pay for the administration of the programme – a single ranch was reported to be leasing more of the 'Home Lands' than the total occupied by native Hawaiians. Meanwhile almost twenty thousand homestead applicants were on waiting lists. It seemed crazy to me, but when I checked the figures with a local reporter he assured me they were correct.

So I had a lot of sympathy with the natives, but I had a problem working out who they were. The basic difficulty is that there are hardly any left. At the last count, the population of more than a million included barely eight thousand full-blooded Hawaiians. To qualify for homesteads, applicants have to be of at least 50 per cent Hawaiian ancestry, which is fine as far as it goes. But what happens if a homesteader on the genetic borderline marries, say, a Korean? Are their offspring thrown off the land because their blood-count falls below the Polynesian Plimsoll line? It all seemed hopelessly complicated to me, and I stopped reading about it.

THE BIG ATTRACTION on Oahu is the ocean. Or to be more precise, its enormous rollers which batter the north shore in the winter months. The surf breaks here have names like 'Himalayas', and 'Avalanche'. It is not a place to send your children out paddling; or maybe it is, depending on your view of children.

I drove across the island, passing a bleak succession of military bases (the armed forces control one-quarter of Oahu) to Haleiwa, the gateway to the north shore. The town caters for a rainbow of humanity, ranging from day-trippers to surfers, artists, and 'New Age' folks, the successors of beatniks and hippies. The Celestial Natural Foods store is sandwiched between a McDonald's and a Pizza Hut, and the Kaala art gallery is a short walk from the Banzai bowling alley.

I headed along the north shore to Waimea Bay, which was reputed to have the biggest surfable waves (up to thirty-five feet) and the meanest riptides in Hawaii. It held the record for the highest waves ridden in international competition. At first sight the sea was deceptively calm, although I noticed the curved beach shelved sharply down into the surf, and hardly anyone was bathing. Only three muscular youths with the close-cropped hair of the military were splashing about in the shallows, and everybody else was sitting up on the beach watching them with an air of expectancy. In the distance, I could see surfers floating on their boards off a point, waiting for the swell to build up.

I had been sitting on the beach for a few minutes when a metallic voice from a loudhailer on a lifeguard platform intoned:

'You people down on the beach, we got some big waves coming in, best move up the beach.' After a momentary pause, it added: 'Best move now.'

As I stood up, a barely perceptible movement in the sea took the form of a wave. With massive deliberation it grew until it became a towering wall of water at least twenty-five feet high, spray flying from its crest like a blizzard of snow as it gathered speed and raced towards the shore. One of the bathers was swept up from the preceding trough, and for a fleeting instant his profile was frozen inside the massive wave, like an insect seen through the green glass of a preserving jar, then the image disappeared in a thunderous roar as the wave curled and collapsed in a tumult of surf and foam. I had been standing at least twenty yards from the shore, but before I could move I was knee-deep in turbulent water, and felt its enormous power as it surged back into the trough of the next wave.

The bathers repeated their insect-in-a-jar trick twice, each time bobbing to the surface with yells of exhilaration, but with the fourth and final wave towering even higher, they wisely scrambled to the safety of higher ground. I asked the lifeguard, a hairless gorilla in designer sunglasses, how he managed to get in and out of the surf in an emergency.

'Timing,' he said.

'Do you have many accidents here?'

'Sometimes.'

'Thank you. Nice talking with you.'

'Yup.'

He was clearly saving his breath for an emergency.

I WATCHED this awesome spectacle for almost an hour, thrilled by the roaring and crashing and hissing, and then I drove a couple of miles along the coast to watch people apparently trying to kill themselves.

Ekuhai Beach has a natural off-shore phenomenon known to the surfing *cognoscenti* as the Banzai Pipeline. It is an expanse of water which produces phenomenal waves which curl before breaking to such an extent that they form a moving tunnel. Riding inside these waves is a death-defying feat, as they have an unfortunate tendency to break with considerable force over a shallow and extremely hard and sharp coral reef. It is a bit like skiing on an avalanche that is careering towards a barricade of granite boulders. Some people do this for fame and fortune, but most of them do it for fun.

When I arrived an international championship was in progress, and a large and enthusiastic crowd of deeply tanned bodies in colourful shorts and skimpy bikinis was quaffing beer and yelling its appreciation of hair-raising exploits being performed about half a mile off shore.

'Here comes Bill, he's uuuup an' runnin', an' he's innnsiiide, folks,' a megaphone blared from a platform, and a roar of encouragement rose from the beach. I saw a tiny figure flashing across the face of a huge wave and disappearing into the tunnel of water. A hush fell on the crowd. The wave seemed to go on for ever, then there were whoops of delight as the figure popped out of the Pipeline, briefly rode the collapsing wave, then flipped nonchalantly backwards, and began paddling back to the starting point.

Not all of the competitors were as successful. Some simply disappeared in the maelstroms of tumbling water. It seemed highly problematic that they would return to the surface, but evidently they were used to this kind of thing and nobody was posted missing.

I had optimistically brought a pair of swimming trunks to this stronghold of Banzai warriors. I put them in the car, and drove back to the gentler surf of Waikiki.

*

STEVENSON'S NEXT PORT of call was a more tranquil island, where he wrote of riding up the flanks of a volcano through mists and forests to a place of gods and goblins. This was Hawaii. To avoid confusion with the name of the state, it is known locally, and with good reason, as the Big Island. It is seven times bigger than Oahu, with seven times less people. I liked its sense of proportion and was eager to get there, but surprisingly there were no ferry services from Oahu.

At Honolulu's fisherman's wharf, I asked a large lady squeezed into a small kiosk advertising fishing charters if she could help. 'Nope, unless you got a thousand dollars to spare.' A woman red-eyed with Martinis at the Waikiki Yacht Club was equally discouraging. 'Unless you're experienced crew, you got no chance. This is a bad time of year anyway. It's pretty rough out there around the Big Island, winds of twenty knots and seas of fifteen feet, regular.'

Hawaiian Airlines was pleased to see me. A girl at the reservations counter said: 'Yes, sir, may I have your charge card please? Thank you, sir. Just sign here and you're all set. Have a nice day.' America is like that. Money commands courtesy and efficiency. The injunction to have a nice day can become tiresome, but a lone traveller still appreciates the sentiment.

Fanny and Louis Stevenson with Gilbertese friends on Butaritari.

Above: Rush-hour in Fakarava: Daniel Snow, head man and storyteller, pedals to work along the coral road.

Left: Temana Haro, descendant of a Tahitian chief, with a silver communion service gifted by Stevenson's mother in 1889.

Opposite, top: Teataake, the good shepherd of Butaritari, with his flock on the island of laughter.

Opposite, bottom: The brass band of Butaritari: sweet music from battered instruments and hand-written scores.

Overleaf: Japanese airmen committed ritual suicide on this bomber in 1943; now it is a playground for Gilbertese children.

Brian Ormes: an adventurer from the past ill at ease in the present, outside the ruins of his RLS Hotel on Abemama.

Paul Bauro, the last 'king' of Abemama, with a portrait of his fearsome ancestor Tem Binoka at the latter's tomb.

Pomp and circumstance at the daily flag-raising ceremony outside the Prime Minister's offices in Western Samoa.

Maintaining a proud Samoan tradition: the High Talking Chief of Aunu'u island displays his regalia.

'Home is the sailor, home from the sea ...'; Stevenson's tomb in a place he called
'beautiful beyond dreams'.

ELEVEN

It was a blessing to get among Polynesians again

THE BIG ISLAND lives up to its name. It is twice the size of all the other Hawaiian islands combined, it boasts the world's tallest mountain (when measured from its base on the ocean floor), its most active volcano, the finest astronomical observatories in the universe (as far as we know), and also the biggest privately owned cattle ranch in the United States. In terms of climates and landscapes, it is a miniature continent with rainforests and glaciers and just about everything in between.

It has cowboy country, fishing villages, neat little towns unscarred by tourism, farming valleys with wild horses, and funky 'New Age' folk living off the land. Despite periodic raids by helicopter-borne troops who destroy acres of foliage and arrest entire families at gunpoint, it also consistently produces the biggest marijuana crop in the US. I liked it immediately.

At Keahole Airport on the west coast of the island there was a queue for hired cars, but once I had driven across an expanse of black lava deposited by a restless volcano in 1801, the road became quiet and I was able to relax and sense the leisurely pace of the island. Highway 11 ascends the Kona coast gradually to an elevation of 1,500 feet, with massive green volcanic slopes on one side and the sea on the other. The road passes above the main coastal town of Kailua, and then becomes a narrow ribbon through hamlets of old wooden homesteads in varying states of decay and renovation, and antique stores and craft shops surrounded by lush vegetation. There is a frontier feel to the place which rekindles a spirit of adventure in the weary traveller. When I spotted a second-hand book store and stopped to have a look around, a passer-by looked me straight in the eye and said: 'Howdy.' After the anonymous crowds of Waikiki, it was like somebody saying welcome back to the planet Earth.

Kona means 'leeward' in Hawaiian. Sheltered from prevailing easterly winds and rain-bearing clouds by the stupendous bulks of Mauna Kea (the biggest mountain) and Mauna Loa (a massive volcano), the Kona coast has one of the most agreeable climates in the world. It is warm without the oppressive heat of the tropics, the air is clean and fresh, and breezes carry the scents of the sea and the earth. It is the kind of place where you want to get out of your car and admire the views and breathe deeply because it feels good.

My destination was Captain Cook, a nondescript little community straddling the road above a bay where the English navigator met an untimely end in 1779 after being mistaken for a Polynesian harvest god. More importantly to me, it was near the village of Hookena, where Stevenson landed from a tourist steamer in the spring of 1889.

I have just been a week away alone on the lee coast of Hawaii, the only white creature in many miles. A lovely week among God's best – at least God's sweetest – works: Polynesians. It has bettered me greatly . . . after so long a dose of whites, it was a blessing to get among Polynesians again.

There are few hotels in America these days with any character, but the Manago Hotel in Captain Cook is one of them. It is a rambling old wooden building painted in brown and cream with corrugated-iron roofs, which was opened in 1917 by Japanese immigrants who served bowls of *udon* and charged $1 for a futon on *tatami* mats. It has been in the hands of the same family ever since, and it still has the feel of a travellers' rest rather than a tourist hotel. It has ceiling fans and sash windows, rickety furniture and old photographs, a maze of corridors through which several generations of the Manago family bustle with mops and brushes and huge plates of food, and a dining salon where Gary Cooper could have played Wyatt Earp in between gunfights. I was given a room behind the original building, overlooking fruit orchards a mile above the ocean. From my veranda, the panorama to the south was dominated by Mauna Loa rising from the coast in a magnificent sweep of forests into a train of clouds.

Most of this view was obscured by rain on the morning of the 27th of April, 1889, when the steamer *W. G. Hall* entered the bay at Hookena and discharged a party of tourists heading for the volcanic craters. From one of the whale boats which took them ashore, Stevenson saw about twenty houses with verandas, painted green and white and set in narrow gardens. The natives had assembled on the shore to observe the weekly arrival of the steamer, and they were treated to an amusing spectacle.

The boat was run in upon a breaker, and we passengers ejected on a flat rock where the next wave submerged us to the knees. There we continued to stand, the rain drenching us from above, the sea from below, like people mesmerized; and as we were all (being travellers) tricked out with the green garlands of departure, we must have offered somewhat the same appearance as a shipwrecked picnic.

A guidebook published a year later described Hookena as probably the last purely Hawaiian community in the islands, but Stevenson found all of the houses were built in the European style; and his host D. H. Nahinu, a former judge to whom he bore a letter of introduction, 'was dressed in pearl-grey tweed like any self-respecting Englishman'. With the exception of the Hawaiian language and exotic dishes on the table, there was nothing in Nahinu's house which would have been unfamiliar in Europe, and Stevenson felt at home.

I walked that night beside the sea. The steamer with its lights and crowd of tourists was gone by; it had left me alone among these aliens, and I felt no touch of strangeness. The trim, lamplit houses shining quietly, like villas, each in its narrow garden; the gentle sound of speech from within; the room that awaited my return, with the lamp, and the books, and the spectacled householder studying his Bible:— there was nothing changed; it was in such conditions I had myself grown up, and played, a child, beside the borders of another sea.

The museum of the Kona Historical Society near Captain Cook had no record of Stevenson's visit, but it had photographs of Hookena at around the time he was there. They showed low wooden houses amid palm trees clustered around a small bay, with outrigger canoes drawn up on the beach. The women running the museum suggested I should get in touch with Roland Crisafi, who had married a woman from the village, and had been the last white man to have lived there before the community died in the 1950s.

Cris was an amiable big man with grey hair and an enduring affection for the community of fishermen which had accepted him as the *haole* (white) suitor of a local beauty. As a young Army sergeant, he had been heading for the Philippines in 1945 when an outbreak of measles caused his troopship to be diverted to Honolulu. Instead of invading Japan (Hiroshima made that unnecessary) his battalion was put to work removing barbed wire entanglements and other military installations along the Kona coast.

'I saw Hookena and I just fell in love with it, it was so beautiful,' he told me. 'Then I met my wife and I fell in love with her too, so when I was discharged I came to her mother's door and said I wanted to marry her, and her mother said OK.'

Cris learned to fish, and to adapt to a Polynesian lifestyle destined to disappear within a few years. For a while he worked as a local policeman, then he became a wildlife warden until he retired. He knew the names of all the old families in the area, and the Hawaiian names of the fish in the coastal waters, and the traditional methods of catching them. He was a good guide.

Hookena lies at the end of a narrow road which winds down a hillside through pastures of wild grass. It is a lovely spot, with lush vegetation crowding around a shore of lava rocks and a small sandy beach, but it is no longer the community of trim villas admired by Stevenson. Life began to ebb out of it in the 1950s, when fish prices dropped and the cost of living soared. One by one, the residents abandoned their canoes and left to work on ranches and coffee plantations, and in hotels being built further up the coast. The last person to leave in 1959 was Cris's father-in-law, who came to live with him in the hills above Captain Cook. Most of the houses were demolished, the old well where women washed clothes on flat stones was filled in, and the site was designated a beach park.

A drab shelter with dirty toilets and a ramshackle snack bar (open only at weekends) faced the breakwater where Stevenson had waded ashore. The only remnant of those days was a rusting carbide lamppost, which had been converted into a shower. A sign beside it said showers cost 25 cents a minute. A new community of weekend homes was rising behind the old dry-stone walls, and a few people had taken up permanent residence, but the place still had an abandoned air. I was reminded of old mining villages in Scotland, and felt a familiar sadness at the death of a community.

We sat on a stone wall by the sea. Cris said that after the war, there were sixteen families living in wooden shacks and they went fishing in outrigger canoes all day. In the morning they caught tuna, in the afternoon mackerel, and in the evening squirrel fish and small barracuda. They had little money, no electricity, and not the slightest inclination to work any more than was absolutely necessary. This lifestyle was much as Stevenson had observed it.

Their courage and goodwill to labour seem now confined to the sea, where they are active sailors and fearless boatmen, pursue the shark in his own element, and make a pastime of their incomparable surf. On shore they flee equally from toil and peril . . .

Cris said: 'Hawaiians are not naturally lazy, it's us who have made them lazy with all the modern stuff we brought here.

When I lived in Hookena, the whole village used to go up to five thousand feet to chop down mahogany trees and hollow out the trunks, then they'd drag them down to the village and carve them into canoes. But it was a happy-go-lucky community. All someone had to do was bring down a quart of wine and everything would stop. They'd sit on the shore drinking and talking, then they'd call for more wine, and the women would bring fish snacks, and this could go on for two or three days. Every so often there would be an empty space where a guy had passed out, then he would come and join in again. It was quite comical. That's just the way they were, they enjoyed life.'

They also liked practical jokes. When Cris returned from a fishing trip with his first *ahi* (tuna), a monster ninety-two pounder, his friend Kaupu announced gravely that it was the custom on such an occasion to swallow one of its eyes. In this case, the eyes were the size of human fists. Cris regarded them dubiously, but he could not spurn an ancient ritual with the village watching. He was given a glass of wine, and inserted one of the eyes into his gullet, where it remained for a disconcertingly long time. When eventually it went down, Cris noticed the locals were gazing at him in amazement. Kaupu said to him: '*Haole*, you are the first man in history of Hawaii who has eaten the eye of an *ahi*.'

In 1845, a resident of the Kona coast had a similar experience, but he did not live to tell the tale. It was recorded on his behalf by the Reverend Cochran Forbes, a missionary: 'I have just learned of the distressing death of a schoolteacher a few miles distant. He went to the beach near where he lived to fish, and having caught one about six inches long and flat, armed with sharp spines on the back, he attempted to crush its head between his teeth to put it to death. The fish at the same instant, by one spasmodic effort, darted forward into his throat. It was too large to get down, for he with great presence of mind took a stick and endeavoured to thrust it into his stomach, but failed. His wife then endeavoured the same but failed. She then seized it by the tail with her teeth to extract it if possible, but the sharp spines immediately fixed in his throat and prevented the extraction. In a short time the poor man died in great agony. Truly in the vigour of health he was at the door of death and knew it not.'

Cris told me that native superstitions noted by Stevenson had survived well into the twentieth century. There were, for example, several things that the people of Hookena never did after dark. They never hammered, because that was to hasten death by hammering nails in an imaginary coffin; they never swept their houses, because that was to sweep out good fortune; and they never whistled at night, because that was to summon evil spirits.

What they did after dark was fish. Cris's recollections of Hookena by moonlight in the late 1940s painted a picture that would have been familiar to Stevenson. As he was speaking, we were joined by a Hawaiian working for the county in clearing the bush. He sat beside us, without speaking. When Cris had finished, he said: 'Yeah, man, that's just the way it was when I was a kid. These are good stories. You like dried fish? Have some.' He offered me a piece of dried mackerel, and it was delicious.

I returned to Hookena the next day to wander alone around some of the sites Cris had pointed out to me, with a copy of a map drawn in the late nineteenth century. A few people were lazing on the shore and two girls were snorkelling in the shallows as I walked along a dirt road through the village to the old Nahinu property near the shore where Stevenson had stayed. A simple wooden house, obviously more modern, but similar to the one described by Stevenson, stood in a trim lawn surrounded by dry-stone walls. Inside, I heard a television droning out a quiz programme.

During his sojourn in Hookena, Stevenson admired the rugged features of Hawaiians which distinguished them from other Polynesians:

I know of no race that carries years more handsomely, or whose people, in the midst of life, retain more charm. I recall faces, both of men and women, with a certain leonine stamp, trusty, sagacious, brave, beautiful in plainness: faces that take the heart captive.

The descendant of Stevenson's host who emerged from the house still had a trace of dark good looks, but the bravery and leonine stamp had been knocked out of him by two years in Vietnam. John Nahinu shuffled into the sunlight, wearing combat fatigue trousers on his lean frame and a troubled look in his eyes. He listened with an abstracted air as I spoke of Stevenson and his own ancestor, former Judge Nahinu, but he had heard of neither. He said he had built his house on the family land in 1984 because he had 'nowhere else for to go', and he lived on a state pension because the trauma of Vietnam had left him incapable of work. 'If I work I get pressured,' he said in a soft voice. 'I get crazy.' I thanked him for his time, and left him to his can of Coke and TV quiz programme.

There were times in my travels when I was discouraged, and this was one of them. I was trying to span a century in which the world had been convulsed by wars, automobiles, air travel, and the insidious cult of television. How could I hope to relive Stevenson's adventures in islands where fishermen had abandoned their villages to build highways and nuclear bombs?

Even the old Hookena court-house had gone. It had stood near the Nahinu property, and it had been the scene of eloquent debate. Stevenson was impressed by the proceedings in a case concerning stray cattle, and in particular by the address of the young Hawaiian defendant:

I understood but a few dozen words, yet I heard the man with delight . . . there was no haste, no heat, no prejudice; with a hinted gesture, with a semitone of intonation, the speaker lightly set forth and

underlined the processes of reason; he could not shift a foot nor touch his
spectacles, but what persuasion radiated in the court – it is impossible to
conceive a style of oratory more rational or civilized.

Stevenson was flattered to be consulted on a point of law, and
satisfied with the verdict in favour of the defendant. He
concluded:

No court could have been more equally and decently conducted; judge,
parties, lawyers, and police were all decorous and competent; and but
for the (Portuguese) plaintiff, the business was entirely native.

The court had been demolished years ago, and in its place was
a compound of thatched buildings in the Polynesian style built
by Americans. The only court-room dramas being played out
there now were on a television screen.

The most poignant remnant of old Hookena lies beyond a
ruined church on the seafront. It is a circle of black lava stones
around a small palm tree in a clearing in the bush. On my map,
it was marked 'collecting point'. As Stevenson walked by the
spot, he heard a high-pitched lament and saw the crouched
figure of a girl, swathed in a black shawl, surrounded by grieving
relatives. She was about to be collected for shipment to the leper
colony on the island of Molokai, and in those days it was a
voyage of no return. Stevenson was deeply affected.

The thought of the girl so early separated from her fellows – the look
of her lying there covered from eyesight, like an untimely birth – perhaps
more than all, the penetrating note of the lament – subdued my courage
utterly.

The next day, he watched lepers boarding the whale boat of a
schooner lying off-shore. The girl was wearing a red dress and
had a red feather in her hat. He saw her face. It had not yet been
ravaged by the disease, but 'had a haunting look of an unfinished
wooden doll'. Stevenson stood among a small crowd of weeping
friends and relatives, and later recalled:

At the time, I was too deeply moved to criticize; a mere sympathy
oppressed my spirit. It had always been a point with me to visit this

station, if I could: on the rocks of Hookena the design was fixed. I had seen the departure of lepers for the place of exile; I must see their arrival, and that place itself.

I sat for a while by the circle of stones, watching the surf bursting on the lava foreshore. Brightly coloured birds were bathing in rock pools, and the air was filled with their gay chatter. Then I was startled by the harsh, plaintive call of a larger bird behind me. It had a piercing note like a cry of despair, and in my mind's eye I saw a girl in a red dress stepping into a whale boat.

Before sailing to Molokai, Stevenson made an excursion on horseback with Nahinu and a local schoolteacher along an old coastal trail from Hookena to Puuhonua O Honaunau, the Place of Refuge of Honaunau. This was a place with an interesting history.

For centuries, Hawaiian life had been regulated by a system of *kapus*, or sacred laws. Some of them were pretty hard to live with. For example, it was forbidden for a commoner to be close to a chief, to walk in a chief's footsteps, or to allow his shadow to fall on the chief's palace grounds. Seasons for fishing, hunting, and gathering timber were strictly defined, and woe betide anybody caught with a fresh mackerel at the wrong time. The penalty was always the same – death. To break a *kapu* was to offend the gods, who were likely to express their displeasure by destroying entire villages with volcanic eruptions, tidal waves, and earthquakes, and so on; obviously the only way of averting such catastrophes was to hunt down and kill the offenders as quickly as possible.

There was no right of appeal: 'Terribly sorry, my lord, I was just standing there admiring your palace from a respectful distance when the sun moved, and oops, my shadow fell on it. This is my first offence, and I—' At this point one assumes the outraged chief would interrupt him with something like: 'Off with his head.'

The only way for offenders to save their lives was to reach the sacred ground of a *puuhonua*, or place of refuge, where a priest would perform a ceremony of absolution to appease the gods and send the pardoned ones on their merry way. There was, of course, a catch. The sanctuaries were surrounded by chiefs and warriors with big clubs, who regarded bashing *kapu*-breakers as a divine mission.

In the case of Honaunau, would-be refugees were confronted by an early version of the Berlin Wall. Imagine the haven as a low coastal headland, enclosed on the landward side by a high wall with only one narrow gap in it. Outside these ramparts were encamped the aforementioned warriors. Off shore, sharks prowled heavy seas. It seems most fugitives elected to swim for it, but history does not tell us how many perished in the attempt.

I began the walk to Honaunau from Hookena in good spirits, looking forward to an interesting day. Within a few minutes, I came to a sign attached to a rusting metal post. It said: *McCandless Ranch. No trespassing. Turn around here.* I have always been prepared to respect other people's property, in the forlorn hope that they will respect mine, but I admit to an ingrained hostility towards signs which order me peremptorily to remove myself from areas of natural beauty just because somebody claims to own them. Once I was prevented at gunpoint from rambling over a Scottish mountain by a man whose sole purpose in owning it was to get a few buddies together and kill lots of deer. How can anybody with a brief lifespan on the planet *own* a mountain that has been standing for millions of years? It's absurd.

I looked ahead. There was no sign of cultivated land or livestock on either side of the dirt track, so I walked on and muttered: 'Come on, McCandless, make my day.'

Maybe Mr McCandless was trying to conceal the fact that his ranch-hands had turned the shore into a rubbish dump. The tangled vegetation was littered with the rusting hulks of derelict cars and pick-up trucks, and unpleasant odours emanated from ramshackle wooden buildings. Further on, I came to a clearing from which unmarked paths led to homesteads with more signs saying *Private, Keep Out*, and *Beware of Dog*. Fortunately at this point a young woman in a swimsuit appeared and directed me to the correct path heading north, a narrow defile through prickly bush with wild grasses sprouting waist high in the middle.

After a few steps, I became aware of a sticky substance brushing my face and arms. Looking more closely, I saw patterns of silver threads which in places spanned the width of the path. I should have paid more attention to Stevenson's account of his excursion:

I observed a spider plant, its abhorred St Andrew's cross against the sea and sky, certainly fifty yards from where I rode, and five feet at least from either tree: so wide was its death-gossamer spread, so huge the ugly vermin.

I have no phobia about spiders, but I have no particular fondness for them either, and it was distasteful to blunder through a web and find a black and yellow arthropod the size of my fist scurrying up my forearm. I furnished myself with a stout stick and walked on, beating the air in front of me and happily cutting a swath of destruction through death-gossamer spreads. Despite this precaution, a large spider got tangled in my hair and dropped down the front of my shirt. After a bit of hopping about, I managed to remove my shirt and we parted company to our mutual relief.

By now the sun was high, and with the enclosing brush stifling breezes from the sea it became uncomfortably hot. I was sweating freely, and walking with difficulty on broken slabs of lava. I envied Stevenson his horse. Descending a slight incline, I stumbled and fell and the straps of my knapsack broke. I cursed, quite loudly, tied the straps as best I could, and pressed on.

The path became an indistinct trail meandering through dense bush, and after about an hour I lost it completely. Faced with an impenetrable wall of vegetation, I searched half-heartedly for a way through and then gave up and turned back. The glare of the sun was now fierce, and it was at this point I discovered I had lost my sunglasses. I emerged from the bush a bedraggled figure, sweaty and disgruntled, my arms and legs covered with scratches and insect bites, and my clothing festooned with prickly burrs. Happily there was nobody around and I stripped off and waded into the sea, and lay for a long time in the shallows, reflecting that Mr McCandless's injunction to turn around had been sound advice. Then I walked back to my car and drove via the highway to Honaunau.

The Place of Refuge is now a historical site administered by the National Park Service. It costs a dollar to wander around ruins and temples and grinning idols, restored and reconstructed in accordance with the designs of the original builders, and it is good value for the money. There were few people around, and I was able to stroll along a circuitous path around lawns and a small sandy cove in peace. A few Hawaiians in native dress were seated in open huts, demonstrating traditional thatching, weaving and canoe carving, and they seemed unconcerned that hardly any tourists were there to watch them. The careful restoration, the splendid natural setting, and the absence of crowds combined to evoke images of the past.

The most impressive structure is the Great Wall, a massive barrier of mildewed lava blocks stretching for more than three hundred yards around the sacred ground. It is a masterpiece of dry-stone masonry which has withstood earth tremors, tidal waves, and tempests for more than four centuries, and for the most part it was as Stevenson observed it in 1889:

The ruin made a massive figure, rising from the flat lava in ramparts twelve to fifteen feet high, of an equal thickness, and enclosing an area

of several acres. The unmortared stones were justly set; in places, the
bulwark was still true to the plummet, in places ruinous from the shock
of earthquakes.

By the shore, the path led to a thatched hut enclosed by a rough wooden fence and guarded by a phalanx of wooden idols which warned off intruders with a variety of fearsome expressions. They were far more creative and effective than Mr McCandless's sign. This was the Hale o Keawe Heiau, the temple of Keawe, a high chief whose sacred bones protected the sanctuary. Early Hawaiians believed that such dignitaries had *mana*, a spiritual power which extended to their possessions, the ground they walked on, and their bones after death. By the time the refuge system was abolished by royal decree in 1819, Keawe's temple contained the earthly remains of at least twenty-three chiefs, thereby investing it with a lot of *mana*.

The English missionary William Ellis, who passed by four years later, was not impressed by the 'indigent nakedness' of the graven images which scowled at his presence: 'The horrid stare of these idols, the tattered garments upon some of them, and the heaps of rotting offerings before them, seemed to us no improper emblems of the system they were designed to support; distinguished alike by its cruelty, folly, and wretchedness.'

Nor did he care a toss for local sensibilities regarding the sanctity of the site. Ignoring natives who implored him not to enter the temple, he pushed aside a board across the doorway and peered inside. For the first time, Western eyes beheld in Keawe's sanctum the images of dead Polynesian chiefs grinning with rows of sharks' teeth and staring with eyes of pearl shells. He also saw several bundles of human bones, cleaned and carefully tied with sinnet made from coconut fibre, along with rich shawls and other valuable articles which he assumed had been worn by the deceased. Stevenson, who recorded the missionary's account, observed drily:

Thus the careless eyes of Ellis viewed and passed over the bones of sacrosanct Keawe, in his house which he had builded.

Stevenson's impression of the remains of this ancient civilization was somewhat different:

These rude monumental ruins, and the thought of that life and faith of which they stood memorial, threw me into a muse. There are times and places where the past becomes more vivid than the present, and the memory dominates the ear and the eye. I have found it so in the presence of the vestiges of Rome; I found it so again in the City of Refuge at Honaunau; and the strange, busy, and perilous existence of the old Hawaiian, the grinning idols of the Heiau, the priestly murderers and the fleeing victim, rose before and mastered my imagination.

His reference to homicidal clerics was drawn from the Hawaiian custom of offering human sacrifices to various gods. What happened was this: on the eve of a full moon, drums were beaten to summon all males to the local temple, where a priest would select a few unfortunates as the dish of the day for divinities such as Ku, the god of war. Amid a lot of chanting and rituals, the victims were brought to a platform where they were strangled, and their bodies later burned.

Resistance was futile, but occasionally relatives appealed successfully to more benign gods. One legend which I liked tells of a man who lost nine of his ten sons to sacrifice on the island of Molokai. Before the next full moon appeared, he went with his remaining son to a valley which was the home of Kauhuhu, the shark god, and related his sorry tale. Kauhuhu was furious with the priests, and promised to punish them. The next day the island was lashed by a terrible storm, whose flood waters wrecked the temple and swept the priests out to sea — where they were devoured by sharks.

It was late afternoon when I left the Place of Refuge, and the sun was casting long shadows over the palace grounds. I looked at the shadows, and realized one of them was mine — a capital offence in the old days. Then I looked at the escape route, the narrow gap in the wall fifty yards away, and imagined the place swarming with warriors. A vision of running that dreadful gauntlet was playing around in my mind when a sudden thump made me whirl around. I had forgotten about a warning in the park brochure. It said: 'If you leave the trail, watch out for falling coconuts.'

THERE WERE NO BROCHURES to warn Captain James Cook of local hazards when he sailed into Kealakekua Bay, a few miles up the coast, with his ships *Discovery* and *Resolution* on the 17th of January, 1779. As fate would have it, he arrived during an annual festival in honour of Lono, the god of harvest, who had sailed off years before in a big canoe and promised to return on a floating island covered with trees. The tall masts of Cook's ships, and the way he had sailed clockwise around the island, accorded with the prophecy of how Lono would reappear on the scene. The English navigator was thus assured a reverential reception, and for a couple of weeks his men enjoyed the usual favours bestowed by Polynesian women on the acolytes of gods.

When eventually they set sail from the Big Island, fate intervened again with a storm in which the *Resolution* broke her foremast. Cook decided to return to Kealakekua Bay to make repairs, which proved a fatal mistake. This time the festival was over, and his divine status was compromised by his approaching from the wrong direction and with a broken mast. The visitors became fair game for thievery, and Cook responded by attempting to take the high chief hostage for the return of a stolen cutter. Unknown to him, a lesser chief had been killed in a skirmish with his sailors, and he found himself being surrounded by an angry mob. Cook promptly released the high chief and began walking to his boat, but he was pelted with stones. Sailors in boats close to the shore fired into the rabble, but before they could reload, Cook was struck on the head. He staggered and fell into the shallows, where he was clubbed and stabbed to death.

His men went on the rampage, burning a village and beheading two natives, and rowed across the bay with the heads on poles. The chief sued for peace, and returned those parts of Cook's dismembered body he was able to find. They included the skull, although it had been stripped of skin in accordance with a practice bestowed on great chiefs. Cook's remains were buried at sea, and the repentant natives placed a *kapu* on the bay.

Stevenson was aware of his proximity to the site of Cook's last stand, but he did not visit it, perhaps because it was virtually inaccessible by land. My guidebook to Hawaii (in the *Lonely Planet* series which produces consistently excellent travel guides) told me the bay was enclosed by steep cliffs, but it could be approached by a rough trail which began near my hotel:

'To get to the trailhead, turn off Highway 11 on to Napoopoo Road and go down about two hundred yards to the dirt road on the right after the second telegraph pole . . . just before reaching a metal gate marked *Private Property*, there's a parting through tall grasses on the left. Don't expect a well-beaten path. Also, it's not a good hike to do in sandals.'

These are the kind of directions I like in travel guides. Heeding the writer's advice to take a supply of drinking water and snorkelling gear, I set off and found the track without difficulty. It wound down the hillside through shoulder-high elephant grass, but it was less arduous than the coastal path to the Place of Refuge, and I was pleased to see it was frequented by butterflies rather than spiders.

After about an hour, the trail veered across a broad ledge above the sea and then down through thick woodland, and I emerged on a volcanic shore dominated by a tall white obelisk. The monument was a few yards from the sea, enclosed by a heavy metal chain suspended between iron pillars which resembled upright cannons. A simple plaque intimated that the memorial to Cook had been erected in 1874 by 'some of his countrymen'. Commemorative plaques had been embedded in concrete in front of it by visiting ships from various countries, but evidently theft was as much a local problem as it was in Cook's day. At least half of them had been dug up and stolen. I found this sad and offensive, and solemnly invoked the wrath of the shark god on the perpetrators.

The narrow beach was flanked by cliffs rising sheer from the sea and pitted with caves reputed to have been the tombs of Hawaiian royal chiefs. It has been speculated that some of Cook's remains were concealed there. I was alone, and contemplating the deserted beach it was easy to imagine the tumult of enraged natives, the sharp report of muskets, and the flashing of daggers as a doomed figure in the uniform of a British naval officer stumbled and fell in the shallows. I looked into the clear water, alive with brightly coloured tropical fish, and thought of it being suffused with the blood of Cook.

For once I was disappointed by Stevenson in his brief reference to this infamous bay as the place where 'the far voyager Cook ended a noble career not very nobly'. The remark seemed to me flippant. Cook was not only an illustrious navigator, he was a humane man concerned about the impact of Europeans on the Pacific islanders. On leaving Tahiti, he wrote: 'I cannot avoid expressing it as my real opinion that it would have been far better for these poor people never to have known our superiority in the accommodations and arts that make life comfortable, than after once knowing it, to be abandoned in their original incapacity of improvement.'

Cook's senseless death oppressed me. To shrug off a vague melancholy, I dived into the sea from a stone jetty, and drifted for a while among shoals of trumpet and clown fish. It was like swimming through a rainbow. On leaving, my spirits were restored by a host of butterflies.

TWELVE

I have seen Vesuvius since, but it was a mere toy,

a soup kettle, compared to this

THEN I WENT TO WATCH two goddesses hurling molten rocks and stormy seas at each other, in a domestic dispute which moved mountains and destroyed islands. A word of explanation may be required here.

According to ancient legends, the south-eastern Puna district of the Big Island is the domain of Pele, a daughter of Haumea the Earth Mother and Wakea the Sky Father. She is the goddess of fire, the maker of mountains, melter of rocks, eater of forests, and burner of lands – in short, the goddess of volcanoes. This fiery character came to Hawaii pursued by a cruel older sister, Na Maka o Kaha'i, the goddess of the sea. First she dug a crater on the island of Niihau, but Na Maka broke into it and she fled to a neighbouring island, with the same result. She sought refuge in a succession of islands and each time she was driven out, until at last she built her biggest fortress on the Big Island, where she remains under siege by her vindictive sister. Geologists say the legends accord with the process by which the Hawaiian islands were successively formed by the creation of volcanoes, and destroyed by the forces of erosion as they moved away from a 'hot spot' on the Earth's crust.

At the time Stevenson was in Hookena, Pele was blowing her top forty miles away in a spectacular eruption which lasted for a century. Mark Twain had viewed the lava crater twenty-three years before in 1866 and reported: '. . . circles and serpents and streaks of lightning twined and wreathed and tied together . . . I have seen Vesuvius since, but it was a mere toy, a soup kettle, compared to this.'

Curiously, Stevenson gave the volcanoes a miss in favour of quiet contemplation and writing in his fishing village.

I found it hard to justify my choice of a week in an unheard-of hamlet, rather than a visit to one of the admitted marvels of the world. I do not know that I can justify it now to a larger audience. I should prefer, indeed, to have seen both; but I was at the time embarrassed with arrears of work; it was imperative that I should choose . . . For there are some so constituted as to find a man or a society more curious than the highest mountain.

I assume Stevenson preferred to spend his time on the Big Island in the company of its natives, rather than with tourists, which is understandable; but Pele was fuming at her big sister again, and I wanted to witness the event.

The scene of this titanic struggle is a national park like no other, with two active volcanoes and terrain ranging from tropical black sand beaches to the sub-arctic summit of Mauna Loa, a volcano that is reckoned to be the largest mountain on Earth when measured from its base on the ocean floor at a depth of ten thousand feet. The coastal road that skirts this monster is a kind of geological roller-coaster, passing from tortured black landscapes of ancient lava flows to pastoral scenes reminiscent of the west of Ireland, with green slopes running gently to the sea. It then climbs into wild highlands, where the massive rounded bulk of Mauna Loa broods over a patchwork of brush and volcanic deserts. On entering the park, visitors are issued with brochures listing such attractions as 'Sulphur Banks', 'Steaming Bluff', and 'Devastation Trail'.

By the time I arrived, lava had been flowing from a vent in the east rift zone for six weeks, and the visitor centre was crowded. A park ranger was explaining that so far the lava had travelled six miles and destroyed an important archaeological site, six camp grounds, and sections of a coastal road. It had also increased the size of the island by eighteen acres.

I strolled across trim lawns and through a small wood to the

Volcano House Hotel, a low wooden building perched on the rim of the caldera of Kilauea, classified the most active volcano on Earth. Within this enormous pit, measuring two miles across and four hundred feet deep, the crater of Halemaumau – Pele's living-room, so to speak – had erupted seventeen times and collapsed four times since 1924. This may seem an odd place to build a hotel. In fact, scientists regard Hawaii's volcanoes as relatively gentle. Violent outbursts, involving tremendous explosions, earthquakes, clouds of poisonous gases, and showers of hot mud and rocks and so on have occurred only twice in recorded history. Both, however, happened at Kilauea, one around 1790 and the other in 1924. The only direct fatality this century occurred during the later eruption when a boulder fell on the leg of a photographer, who bled to death.

Nobody in the hotel appeared unduly concerned that Pele might blow them all to kingdom come at any moment. They were more interested in an American football game on a giant television screen. A few yards from where they sat, panoramic windows offered a vista of one of the great natural wonders of the world, but the Miami Dolphins had just lost six yards on a third down. Not for the first time, I wondered at this electronic umbilical cord to which so many of us seem attached, and what would happen if ever it were severed. I assume life would cease to exist as we know it. This might not be a bad thing, of course.

I strolled over to the window and gazed out. At first sight, the caldera was disappointing. There was no fire, no boiling lakes of magma, no torrents of molten rock. Everything looked dead. It was how I imagined the surface of the Moon would appear to an astronaut. Below lay a vast, roughly circular depression in a barren landscape, grey and flat, enclosed by dark cliffs. It was like a gigantic excavation site. The only signs of volcanic activity were thin wisps of smoke rising from the caldera floor and walls.

I was not disheartened, as the scene of the current eruption was several miles away and I would go there later. In the mean time, I went for a drive around the caldera. A surfaced road runs for eleven miles around the rim, with parking places at the best viewing sites and helpful signboards pointing out the various attractions. It had not been disfigured by fast-food outlets and souvenir shops, for which the Parks Service should be commended. My first stop was a museum and observatory, perched on a bluff with a magnificent view over the caldera. This had been the site of a hut where sorcerers used to amuse themselves by luring people inside and then watching them fall through a false floor into the fiery pit below. At least the victims did not suffer for long. When scientists lowered their first thermometer into the lava lake in 1911, it measured 1,832°F before melting.

A display in the museum said that vents on Kilauea's flanks emit hundreds of tons of sulphur dioxide every day. It also said this was nothing compared with the variety and quantity of poisonous gases swirling around most urban and industrial areas elsewhere in the world. I mused for a while on the conclusion that it is healthier to live on a live volcano than in Los Angeles or Mexico City.

Driving on around the western rim of the caldera, I parked my car and walked a couple of hundred yards to a viewpoint above Pele's lair, in the crater of Halemaumau, and peered in. It was a deceptively quiet, horribly menacing, dark pit about two hundred and fifty feet deep, with fumes curling from cracks in the walls. In 1982, with only three hours' warning, fissures appeared in the caldera floor and lava began pouring from the walls of the crater. An image of the earth trembling, cracking, and spewing out rivers of fire seared through my brain with a rush of adrenalin. To appreciate the cataclysmic forces stirring beneath this hellish place, it is sufficient to gaze around the crater floor. The first impression is of a World War I battlefield; but the desolation of the ashen grey landscape is so total and the scale so vast that it conjures up a more appalling vision. One senses this is what London or New York would look like after being incinerated by a thermonuclear blast.

From this apocalyptic scene, it is less than five miles around the caldera to a little Garden of Eden. Clinging improbably to the eastern slopes of Kilauea is a miniature rainforest, alive with the red and silver flashes of honeycreeper birds flitting among ferns twenty feet high and the yellow and red blossoms of *mamane* and *ohia* trees. The principal attraction of the forest is a lava tube, a cold, dank subterranean passage about the size of a railway tunnel. Dim electric light and a handrail have been provided to allow visitors to walk through it, and apparently idiots are catered for. A sign at the entrance says: *Reduced light. Remove dark glasses.*

It was now well past midday, and time to drive down the aptly named Chain of Craters road to the coast and the scene of Pele's latest eruption. I had briefly considered taking a helicopter tour, but an event the next day confirmed the wisdom of staying on the ground. Flying over the scene, a helicopter crashed into a live vent. The pilot, who had remained with his wrecked aircraft, was rescued by another helicopter, but two passengers who had tried to climb out became trapped and spent a night roasting in Pele's noxious oven. They emerged well cooked but alive, and one of them said later he had seen Pele, which did not surprise me.

Hundreds of cars were parked along the coast, and I had to walk for more than a mile with a throng of sightseers before reaching a traffic sign you don't see very often. It said: *Danger. Hazardous fumes. Steep cliffs. Rough surface. Hot lava.* The road ahead had been cut by a lava flow, and park rangers directed us to a narrow path meandering over scrubland towards the sea. The site was screened at first by a grove of tall palm trees around a cluster of wooden huts, and partly obscured by huge clouds of smoke. A military helicopter throbbing above the trees completed a vivid illusion of a scene from the Vietnam War.

Then I saw it: a dark grey mass of solidifying lava creeping towards the shore, hissing, smoking, and cracking to reveal flashes of intense red beneath its thin crust. At the edge of a low cliff, great chunks were breaking off and lava was oozing lugubriously into the sea like the blood of a loathsome creature in its death throes. In other places where the momentum of the flow was greater, the lava reached out like monstrous tongues and fingers, licking and clawing at land and sea. The clash between the goddesses was a heated, tempestuous affair. You could tell Pele's big sister was seriously angry. A heavy swell was running, and great rollers repeatedly lashed at the lava, sending enormous white clouds billowing into the sky and drifting over the sea as if it was on fire, which, in a sense, it was.

Behind me, another lava flow was reducing a camp site to its constituent elements, so I joined a crowd gathered around its leading edge. It was possible to approach within a few yards of the seething mass, and some people were conducting interesting experiments by throwing rocks on to it. The results were not spectacular. The viscosity of the cooling lava was so great that the rocks just made a dull plunk as they hit the surface, before melting into the flow. Gazing into this fiery ooze, I reflected that I was looking back in time to the dawn of creation; this was the process by which islands and entire continents were formed aeons before man turned up. I was startled by a splintering sound, and turned round to see a sign falling into a morass of molten rock. I caught a glimpse of it before it disappeared. It said: *No swimming. High surf and dangerous currents*.

The other big attraction was the sight of two approach roads being devoured by separate lava flows. Tongues of flame were actually licking at the tarmac, and occasionally methane gas trapped underground ignited with muffled explosions like mortar bombs. It was a surreal scene, like watching a science-fiction film, and a man standing near me said: 'Wow, isn't that cool?' Cool was not perhaps the *mot juste*, but I took his point. Behind us, the main flow from the erupting vent scarred the wooded flanks of Kilauea in the late afternoon like a 'black' ski run through an Alpine forest. When night fell, it was transformed into a 'red' run glowing in the dark, a glittering cascade of fire flowing down the mountain. It was kinda cool.

THERE ARE FEW EXPERIENCES more memorable than witnessing the eruption of primeval forces which created the Earth. One of them, at the top end of the mind-blowing scale, is observing a galaxy of stars twelve billion light-years away. On the summit of Mauna Kea, some people get paid for doing this.

I have always been fascinated by stars, but the closest I got to them in my travels was in the garden of a house in England where a friend had mounted a small astronomical telescope. Peering unsteadily into the eyepiece after a few beers in the local pub, I beheld for the first time the surface of the Moon. It was a dark, cloudless winter night and my senses swam with a brilliantly clear vision of craters and plains on that cold, distant planet where American astronauts had walked around picking up rocks and planting flags a few years before. I found the concept of men flying around the universe hard to deal with; on the snow-clad summit of Mauna Kea, I found men peering into reaches of space and time utterly beyond my comprehension.

Stevenson did not venture into the zone of gods and goblins high above Hookena, but I reasoned that if its present collection of astronomical observatories had been in existence then, he would have done. Driven more by my own curiosity than this flimsy excuse, I arranged to visit one of them. I chose the United Kingdom Infrared Telescope (UKIRT), because at the time it was the biggest of its kind in the world, and had recently identified the most distant galaxy yet discovered. Also it had a

Scottish connection – it was operated by the Royal Observatory in Edinburgh.

The aptly named Saddle Road snakes across the Big Island between the rounded hulks of Mauna Kea and Mauna Loa, rising from coastal moors through ranch pastures to a wilderness of coarse grassland as far as the eye can see. It is the most remote road in Hawaii, having no gas stations or any other facilities along its fifty miles, and car rental companies discourage clients from using it. It has an army airfield, and signs warning of troops and tanks traversing the area, and not much else. At its highest point, an unmarked spur road climbs steeply for six miles up the flanks of Mauna Kea to a small stone building which is a visitor centre. When I got there, it was closed. A leaflet taped to the door warned of heart and circulatory problems at high altitude, and advised visitors to abstain from smoking for forty-eight hours before venturing to the summit. I stubbed out a cigarette, vowed for the zillionth time to give it up, and drove on to a complex of low buildings which serve as a mid-level accommodation centre for astronomers and technicians.

My car had laboured up the last section in the thin atmosphere, and I was not in much better shape. Having ascended more than nine thousand feet in less than an hour, I felt chilled and slightly breathless and I was glad to relax for a while in the warmth of the scientists' mountain retreat. Apart from a library of astronomical reference books and photographs of galaxies adorning the walls, it was like a cosy hotel in a ski resort. Over lunch, I was introduced to the wonders of star-gazing by Kevin Krisciunas, an affable young American astronomer in jeans who contrived to explain the principles of a complex science in terms I could understand.

Essentially, infrared telescopes are time machines stuck in reverse. They span unimaginable distances to observe star systems as they were aeons before our own planet existed – while it was still a twinkle in the Creator's eye, so to speak.

Astronomers call this 'cosmic look-back time'. Kevin said they could look back to within 1.5 billion years of the 'Big Bang', give or take half a billion years.

'That's somewhere between 9.5 and 18 billion years ago,' he added helpfully.

About all I remembered from science classes at school was that light travelled at 186,000 miles per second. Bearing this in mind, I had a problem comprehending UKIRT's discovery of a galaxy 12 billion light-years away. Kevin was honest enough to admit he found it pretty mind-boggling:

'Imagine, those photons travelled for twelve billion years and found their destiny in my eyeball. Isn't that amazing?'

Then he lost me with talk of inverse hyperbolic signs and decaying neutrons, so we climbed into his four-wheel-drive vehicle for the eight-mile drive to the summit.

It was cold and misty, and the mountain was streaked with snow. We scrunched along a narrow dirt road winding up through bleak terrain, and Kevin pointed out a valley of cinder and rocks where the Apollo astronauts had tested their Lunar rover before rocketing to the Moon. We were now in the realm of another of Pele's sisters – Poliahu, the Snow Goddess. They were a tempestuous family: legends tell of monumental rows in which Pele would erupt from Mauna Kea, and Poliahu would bury her with ice and snow. Again, the mythology is geologically correct. Scientists have determined there were eruptions through glacial ice caps here as recently as ten thousand years ago.

I may have mentioned that the summit is high. In fact it is 13,800 feet above sea level, which is almost twice as high as any other major observatory site in the world. The good news for astronomers is that this places it above 40 per cent of the Earth's atmosphere and 90 per cent of its water vapour, and beyond the reach of most dust and smog. The bad news is that it can experience rain, sleet, snow, hail, and freezing fog in the course of a summer's day, and winter storms packing winds of over 120 m.p.h. Also there is not much oxygen around, which makes people feel weird.

Kevin told me altitude sickness was a common problem, but scientists had found that by the third or fourth day, provided they remained no more than twelve hours at the summit at a time, they could function almost normally. Having whizzed up from the coast in a couple of hours, I was feeling distinctly light-headed.

The first recorded ascent by a white man was in 1823, when the Reverend Joseph Goodrich hiked to the summit alone by moonlight, equipped with a coat, a blanket, some food, and fire-making implements. On a subsequent ascent, he noted: 'A severe headache, affecting the natives as well as myself, with sickness at the stomach and vomiting of bilious matter, usually attends me in these lofty regions.' The Scottish botanist David Douglas (after whom the Douglas fir is named) turned up in 1834 and wrote: 'While on the summit I experienced violent headache, and my eyes became bloodshot, accompanied by stiffness in their lids. Were the traveller to express the emotions he feels when placed on such an astonishing part of the Earth's surface, he would feel himself as nothing, as if standing on the verge of another world.' His words were prophetic. Douglas duly passed into another world six months later in mysterious circumstances, when his gored body was found a few miles away at the bottom of a pit for wild cattle, in the company of an angry bull. The coincidence of Douglas and a bull falling into the same trap was regarded as highly suspicious, and fingers were pointed at an escaped convict who had been hiding out in the area and who had been the last person to see Douglas alive.

The summit was enveloped in freezing mist when Kevin and I stepped from his vehicle to perceive a curious sight. Strung out along a high ridge in the gloom was a succession of white and silver domes which looked for all the world like golf balls. It was an absurd illusion of a golf-driving range for giants. When I mentioned this to Kevin, he looked at me closely and suggested I sit down for a while.

Strange things happen here. Kevin recalled that one of his colleagues heard a knock at the door of the observatory one day and opened it to find a young couple who asked if they could be shown around. When they were inside, the woman removed her coat to reveal a shapely, naked figure. It transpired she was a member of the oldest profession, who wished to offer her services to an astronomer in the world's highest observatory for the fun of it. Kevin said: 'He was a bit discombobulated for a while.'

The telescope was a bit disappointing. It was like a big navigational buoy pointing at the roof, with wires all over the place – and no eyepiece. I had hoped to gaze at the heavens, but instead I was taken into a control room to look at images of galaxies on computer screens. This inner sanctum of astrophysical research was also equipped with a game of Trivial Pursuits, and a recording of Holst's 'Planet Suite'.

After looking at a red whirlpool which Kevin said was Galaxy M51, I asked him about life on other planets. He said:

'Well, this galaxy has about two hundred billion stars, and we reckon several billion of them probably have temperatures similar to ours. Personally I think there's got to be a lot of stars with life. Intellectually, I just can't accept we're the only life in the universe.'

So why had there been no contact with other beings?

'Who knows, maybe they think we're ugly because we've only got one head.'

Kevin grappled with a computer for almost an hour before it flashed an image from a recent observation. It looked like the bar code on the back of a packet of breakfast cereals which a child had coloured with crayons.

'Now I don't know what the heck that is,' he said. 'It's some source of infrared light, could be a quasar.'

I said thank you. I was beginning to feel drowsy, and when Kevin began talking about pixels (picture elements) I had to make an effort to suppress a giggle. I asked him how he was feeling.

'Just normally weird,' he said.

When we stepped back outside, the wind was gaining in strength and whipping ghostly fingers of mist around the summit. I was concerned that we might be hit by a storm, but Kevin put a new perspective on my fear of high winds. A few years ago, he said UKIRT had registered a cosmic wind in the centre of our galaxy blowing at 700 kilometres per second. I worked this out at 1,565,000 miles per hour.

Back in the accommodation centre, I asked what the point of it all was. Kevin admitted that astronomical research was fairly esoteric and had few practical applications, but he said it was all related to the origin of life and the eternal question 'Where do we come from?'

'We're looking for a better understanding of interstellar chemistry and the way stars are formed. We're also looking for fame and fortune, of course. But in some ways it's almost like a performing art. It's the creative process at the most advanced levels of the human mind, and sometimes it's very exciting.

'Also,' he added, 'it's better than making bombs.'

Driving back down the Saddle Road, I stopped to admire a stunning sunset. For reasons only people like Kevin could explain, the sun was distorted into an enormously swollen, glowing globe of intense orange. I got out of the car and walked a few paces over an old lava field. A light drizzle was falling, and the only sound was the wind moaning over the plateau. Behind me, the sky around the mountains was a brilliant lilac, and as I watched, a rainbow formed a perfect arch a few hundred yards away. I looked back at the misshapen sun, a solitary figure in a bleak landscape contemplating the grandeur of the universe, with its seemingly infinite galaxies and winds of inconceivable velocity. I stood there for a long time, and I felt very small.

THIRTEEN

No stranger time have I ever had, nor any so moving

IN THE HAWAII STATE ARCHIVES there is a photograph of a pretty girl in a white dress with her hands folded across her chest. She is looking slightly away from the camera with a curiously lifeless expression, as if something within her had just died. The hand of an unseen person is holding a board beside her head, which says *Kalihi Hospital Oct 19 1934*, followed by the number *3306*.

It is like a mugshot of a convicted criminal. In a sense it was, because eighteen-year-old Olivia Robello was about to be condemned to a life of exile among the 'living dead' in a remote place from which there could be no escape. Her crime: she had contracted an infectious disease which the natives called *mai hookaawale*, the 'separating sickness'. It was more widely known as leprosy.

Kalaupapa, the settlement to which Olivia was banished, had been in existence for seventy years. It was created after King Kamehameha V approved 'An Act to Prevent the Spread of Leprosy' in 1865, and it was well situated for the purpose – on a flat lava plain extending from the northern shore of the island of Molokai, bounded by tempestuous seas and the tallest sea cliffs in the world. For thousands of hapless victims of the disease, it was a one-way trip.

The first of them – nine men and three women – were unceremoniously dumped on this forbidding shore on the 6th of January, 1866. There were no doctors, nurses, helpers, medicines, or adequate shelter, and little was done for the boatloads which followed them. By all accounts the conditions in which they lived were unspeakable, and the place became infamous for drunkenness and debauchery. Above all, it was pervaded by a sense of despair. In 1873 a young Belgium priest arrived in this hell-hole and set to work cleaning it up. Throughout history, there have been acts of selfless devotion which almost defy belief. The life and work of Father Damien De Veuster on Molokai falls into this category. Before falling victim to the disease, Father Damien transformed the settlement into an orderly community and restored a measure of dignity among its inhabitants. By caring for them, he encouraged them to care for each other.

This is the place to which Stevenson followed the little girl in the red dress from Hookena on the 21st of May, 1889, three weeks after Father Damien had died at the age of forty-nine. On the deck of the steamship *Kilauea Hau*, Stevenson felt a mixture of fear and loathing at what awaited him beneath the cliffs in the grey half-light of dawn. Approaching the settlement in a whale boat, only the company of a small group of Franciscan sisters maintained his courage. In a dispatch to the *New York Sun*, he wrote:

In the chronicle of man, there is perhaps no more melancholy landing than this of the leper immigrants among the ruined houses and dead harvests of Molokai . . . when we drew near the landing-stairs and saw them thronged with the dishonoured images of God, horror and cowardice worked in the marrow of my bones.

It took Stevenson less than an hour of wandering around the settlement to regain his composure:

All horror was quite gone from me: to see these dread creatures smile and look happy was beautiful. On my way through Kalaupapa I was exchanging cheerful alohas with the patients coming galloping over on their horses; I was stopping to gossip at house-doors; I was happy, only ashamed of myself that I was here for no good.

I flew into Molokai on a wing and a prayer. In a scene reminiscent of the Marquesas, the propeller plane of Hawaiian Airlines which brought me from Honolulu droned into dense cloud enshrouding the island. Descending through the gloom, we were rocked by a strong cross-wind, and our. first view of Molokai was an expanse of uneven turf rising to meet us with startling rapidity. The aircraft banked sharply, the tip of its starboard wing trailing only a few feet above the ground, then we clattered on to the runway of Hoolehua Airport with, speaking for myself, a sense of relief.

There are a few places in the world, most of them off the beaten track, which have enchanted me at first sight. Molokai is one of them. Emerging from the little airport, I found myself in a quiet rural landscape, cool, green, and fresh beneath a blanket of cloud. I noticed people were moving slowly, exchanging greetings and collecting baggage in a calm, unhurried manner. I was reminded of a maxim I had come across years ago: 'Don't hurry, don't worry, and don't forget to smell the flowers.' This seemed like a good place to practise this philosophy.

Molokai is the least developed of the main Hawaiian islands, due to a monumental run of bad luck. Its economic calamities began in the mid-1800s when the introduction of cattle and sheep devastated native vegetation, causing upland soils to wash down into coastal fishponds and destroy a centuries-old system of aquaculture. In 1898, the American Sugar Company tried to establish a big plantation. It built a railroad to transport the cane, developed harbour facilities, and installed a sophisticated irrigation system. Within two years, the well-water became so saline the entire crop failed. Next the company tried honey. For a brief period Molokai was the world's biggest honey exporter, until an epidemic wiped out the hives in the 1930s. Pineapple production flourished for a few years before collapsing in the face of overseas competition, resulting in the highest unemployment in Hawaii. At least the cattle ranches survived – until 1985, that is, when state officials detected bovine tuberculosis and ordered the slaughter of every head of cattle on the island.

The result is a largely uncultivated island, in the shape of a basking shark almost forty miles long and ten wide, with one town, three roads, and a laid-back population of about seven thousand of whom almost half are of native Hawaiian ancestry. There are no traffic lights, no parking meters, and no shopping malls. The tallest structure is still the steeple of the old church in Kaunakakai, the main town on the south coast. There is no local newspaper, and the prime source of news and announcements is bulletin boards outside the stores. Take away the palm trees and the pick-up trucks, and Kaunakakai looks like Dodge City in the days before the railroad arrived.

I checked into a motel on the outskirts of town and began preparing for my excursion to Kalaupapa. Tours were available, but they were strictly controlled and visitors were not permitted to leave the old school bus which drove them around, or to meet any of the inhabitants. Like Stevenson, however, I had been granted special permission by the health authorities to spend a week in guest accommodation in the settlement. I passed the eve of my departure reading historical accounts of the place Hawaiians used to call 'the living tomb'.

In all, more than eight thousand people were taken from their families and sent to the wind-swept peninsula to die. At the time of Stevenson's visit, the disease (afflicting nerves, skin, and eyes) was still regarded as highly contagious, and segregation laws had swelled the population of the settlement to an all-time high of almost one thousand two hundred. It was not until the mid-1940s that sulfone drugs were developed which arrested and cured the condition. It is now known that leprosy is among the least communicable of infectious diseases – only about five per cent of the world's population is even susceptible to it – and most new cases are treated on an out-patient basis.

The new drugs and the eventual abolition of isolation laws in 1969 came too late for the surviving residents of Kalaupapa. They were cured and free to leave, but most remained partially crippled and scarred by the disease and chose to remain in the only community they had known. I was told there were still more than seventy elderly residents, who were assured of free medical care and welfare support as long as they lived. I was also warned that the terms 'leprosy' and 'leper' were banned at Kalaupapa; the condition was known officially as Hansen's Disease, and residents were referred to as patients.

In the shark profile of Molokai, the Kalaupapa peninsula is the dorsal fin jutting from its northern shore. The seas around it are generally too rough to permit boat landings except on calm summer days. This leaves only two ways of reaching it – by light aircraft or by a narrow, precipitous path down the face of a sixteen-hundred-foot cliff. Mules were available for hire, which my *Lonely Planet* guidebook suggested was an interesting excursion: 'There's a certain thrill in trusting your life to a mule while descending sixteen hundred feet on twenty-six narrow cliffside switchbacks.' I decided to walk.

I had been told that provisions at Kalaupapa were limited, and advised to bring along some basic supplies. My small rucksack was thus weighed down with tinned food, in addition to books and clothes, when I hitched a lift to the trail-head high above the northern shore of Molokai. At the top of the cliff there is a magnificent view. Far below, the lava plain extends from the base of the cliffs within a white ring of surf. A village is apparent on the western shore, with parks and churches, and a few houses clustered around sheltered bays. Diminished by distance, it is like a toytown in a children's story-book, a green and pleasant land inhabited by little people. I felt like Gulliver surveying Lilliput.

The path begins easily enough through a copse of trees and past an uneven field, reminding one of English country lanes. Then it turns a corner, there is a strong gust of wind, and suddenly one is on the exposed rock face, gazing from a dizzying height at an almost perpendicular coastline plunging down into heavy seas. It is the only occasion on which I can remember looking down at a rainbow. A light drizzle was sweeping across the cliffs. The path was rocky, treacherous with mud, and in places no more than two feet wide as it snaked around dozens of hairpin bends. For most of the way it is bounded on the seaward side by vegetation which provides an illusion of safety, but frequently only flimsy wooden spars separate the traveller from sheer drops of more than a thousand feet. It is not a place for those who suffer from vertigo.

The trail became easier near the bottom, but there the noise of the surf became a savage, heart-stopping roar. At the base of the cliff, I squelched along a muddy path a few feet from where huge grey waves were breaking and hissing on a narrow beach of black sand. The first sign of habitation beyond a dilapidated wooden fence was two ancient trucks rusting quietly in a field. They looked like relics from a museum. Like Stevenson, I entered the village with trepidation. I had never seen a victim of Hansen's Disease, and I wondered how I would react. Most of us tend to shrink from unpleasant sights, and fear of the unknown runs deep. I had nothing to fear here except my own ignorance, but I was tense and nervous and I wished I was not alone.

At first the village seemed deserted. I had passed a few wooden bungalows set in neat lawns and seen no sign of life when a truck stopped beside me, and the driver politely offered me a lift. His face and arms were badly disfigured, but I was prepared for it and there was no sense of shock. I had seen worse in Angola and other countries ravaged by war. I declined his offer, preferring to take in the atmosphere of the place in a stroll to the administration buildings. The administrator was absent, but I was expected, and one of his assistants showed me to my quarters.

It was as if I had entered a time-warp and emerged in a model American village of the 1940s. Cottages with wooden verandas, and lace curtains in the windows, stood within gardens by the side of quiet roads. We passed a church, a post office, a store, and a petrol station. Occasionally an old car or truck would crawl by, and I would see a figure in the distance, but otherwise the scene was like a still-life painting. An impression of walking through a living museum was one that would grow on me. Surrounded by the dull roar of the surf and the awesome bulwark of the cliffs, the village was a haven of tranquillity. There was an air of timelessness, and of profound peace. It occurred to me with satisfaction, as I walked through Kalaupapa, that I had forgotten to bring my watch.

The visitors' quarters were in a low wooden building by the shore, like a school dormitory, painted cream and white with red window frames and filled with the scents of the sea and old wood. It had individual bedrooms, communal bathrooms, and cooking facilities in an adjacent bungalow. I was the only occupant, and I had been allocated the best room at the end of an L-shaped corridor, with an enclosed porch overlooking the sea. My room had two single beds, a chest of drawers, and a chair. It also had a mirror, and I found that when I lay on one of the beds it reflected a profusion of elephant grass outside my window. Apart from the rushing of the sea and the sigh of the wind, it was perfectly quiet. I could have wished for nothing better.

After unpacking my few clothes and books, I heated some soup and coffee I had brought with me and sat on a cane chair in the porch to read a leaflet of rules and regulations for visitors. It was mostly about what was not permitted: no hunting, no camping, no diving tanks, no surfboards, no net fishing, no pets, and no children under sixteen. Photographs of patients could be taken only with their written permission. Violation of any of the rules were grounds for immediate expulsion from the settlement and revocation of the host's guest privileges. Fair enough. I had come to observe, not to amuse myself, and I didn't fancy surfing into two-thousand-foot cliffs anyway.

I passed a while in idle contemplation of the stark beauty of

my surroundings, mesmerized by the magnificent crashing of
the Pacific against the cliffs, and it was late afternoon before I
decided to stroll to a lighthouse at the point of the peninsula.
Apart from a few workers of the Health Board and the Parks
Service, which jointly administer Kalaupapa, I was the only
pedestrian and I was alone with my thoughts as I passed out of
the village on a straight road bounded by open countryside and
a succession of graveyards. I reflected that the remains of more
than eight thousand people were buried here, but there was no
sense of the anguish and despair of the past. There was not even
sadness. It was as if an infamous era had been interred with its
victims, and its scars had been healed by Father Damien and his
successors.

The land was windswept and barren beyond a hut beside a
grass runway which served as the local airport, and the sound of
the waves breaking on the shore was a steady, thunderous roar. I
walked over sparse grass to a point where the waves were
exploding into plumes of spray more than fifty feet high, and
was reminded of the Outer Hebrides of Scotland when the
westerly gales come. On a slight rise, the lighthouse seemed
frail and vulnerable in this swirling vista of huge seas and cliffs,
as if it could be swept away at any moment by a wall of water.
Walking back over the low headland, the crashing and hissing
of the sea was occasionally so loud that I instinctively turned
around with a tremor of fear.

It was now dusk, and in the east the sky was glowing in
brilliant shades of gold, lilac, and aquamarine. But to the west
night was closing in, bringing a shower of rain, and I hurried
my steps as I passed the darkening cemeteries. The wind was
moaning among the ancient tombstones, and I was deep in
thought about ghosts of the past, when I heard a disembodied
voice with a high-pitched tone saying quite clearly: 'Where are
you going?' I did the next best thing to jumping out of my skin,
which was to hop and turn in midair and say: 'Ha!' I stared

speechlessly at the mangled face of a little old lady, framed by a straw bonnet with a pink ribbon, in the cab of a flat-bed truck. I had not heard her approaching, due to the tumult of the weather. She was regarding me with concern. 'I'm sorry, did we startle you? Would you like a lift?' Once my pulse had stopped hammering like a crazed woodpecker, I climbed on the back of the truck and the lady wiped a corner dry for me to sit on. She apologized for not having an umbrella, and said she hoped I would not get too wet. At the entrance to the guests' quarters, she and her husband enquired whether I needed any coffee or warm clothes, and then they wished me good night. I walked along the dark corridor, put an extra blanket on my bed, and lit a candle to read Stevenson's account of his first night in the settlement.

He had been allocated a vacant house on the eastern side of the peninsula, near a hospital and an old store.

Singular indeed is the isolation of the visitor in the lazaretto . . . he returns at night to solitary walls . . . he returns and sits by his lamp and the crowding experiences besiege his memory; sights of pain in a land of disease and disfigurement, bright examples of fortitude and kindness, moral beauty, physical horror, intimately knit. He must be a man very little impressionable if he recall not these hours with an especial poignancy; he must be a man either very virtuous or very dull, if they were not hours of self-review and vain aspirations after good.

The flame of the candle was flickering in a draught as I read this passage, and outside the elephant grass was rustling in the wind. I was quite alone, and yet I did not feel in the least lonely. In this wild place I felt warm, safe, and peaceful. I also felt closer to the spirit of *Tusitala* than I had ever been.

'LIFE IS PRETTY MELLOW down here,' the administrator said. 'We have our problems, but mostly we find a way round them.' Bernard Schwind, a lean, soft-spoken man with a far-away look in his eyes, was explaining why he had come to Kalaupapa. We were sitting in his office, near the post office, as rain pattered on the windows. 'The first time I came here it was a sort of awesome feeling, the cliffs, the history, it fascinated and attracted me. To the outsider, it seems very tranquil, but at times life here is challenging and difficult. Not everyone could adjust to living and working in a place like this.'

Bernard told me the seventy-five surviving patients were entitled by law to remain as long as they lived, and to receive state pensions, rations, clothing, and medical care. Some were paid small amounts for part-time jobs, such as running the library and the petrol station. 'It's kinda to make up for what they faced here at first,' Bernard said. Most of the patients were in their seventies, and he reckoned the settlement would close in about twenty years. Then the health authorities would leave, and it would become a national park.

Life in Kalaupapa was not all sweetness and light. Some of the residents still resented their initial treatment, and at first relations with outside workers were strained. But a community spirit was emerging, and friendships were being formed. In the hospital, a nurse told me of a severely crippled old woman who had impressed the staff with her unfailing good humour. 'She never complained. On her last night I was holding her hand, and feeling pretty miserable. You know what she said to me? She said, "Don't worry, dear, soon I'll be beautiful again."'

Stevenson's lodgings lay on the eastern shore near the village of Kalawao, which is now abandoned, and often he would ride a couple of miles across the peninsula to the Bishop Home for Girls at Kalaupapa, then supervised by Franciscan sisters.

As for the girls of the Bishop Home, of the many beautiful things I have been privileged to see in life, they, and what has been done for them, are not the least beautiful . . . the general impression of the house was one of cheerfulness, cleanliness, and comfort . . . plays of their own

*arrangement were a favourite evening pastime. They had a croquet set;
and it was my single useful employment during my stay in the lazaretto
to help them with that game.*

Stevenson was advised by the sisters to wear gloves while
playing croquet with the children, but he refused, believing that
it would remind them of their condition. On his return to
Honolulu, he bought a grand piano and had it shipped to the
girls' home.

There were only elderly nuns living in the rambling old
building when I strolled over the lawn where Stevenson had
played croquet. But near by I found a woman who remembered
playing on his piano. Lucy Kaona was fourteen years old when
she was taken from her family on the Kona coast in 1942 and
landed at Kalaupapa. I found her in the library, where she had a
part-time job.

'Sure, I used to pound on that old piano. It was fun, but I
can't say what happened to it. Haven't seen it for years.'

By the time Lucy arrived at the settlement, conditions had
improved. She had spent her entire adult life as an outcast, but
she said: 'I liked being in the Bishop Home because the nuns
were good to us. I've had a good life. God's been good to me.
I've had a few ups and downs, but my family has been very
supportive. You can't hold bitterness for ever.'

Lucy married another patient and they had three children, but
they were born in Honolulu because she did not want the stigma
of Kalaupapa on their birth certificates.

'I knew what would happen if I had children. We were not
allowed to keep them, and I actually wanted them to be taken
away from here. I knew they would come and visit and I accepted
that, but it was hard in the beginning.' She paused, thinking
about the past. 'Listen, we were the lucky ones. We got the new
drugs and now the state is taking care of us. I'd say in our time
we've had the best of it. Why should I complain? I have a roof
over my head. A lot of people in the world don't.'

It was only as I was walking away from the library that I realized I had barely noticed Lucy's deformities.

Before the lepers arrived, there was a small community of farmers and fishermen on the peninsula. In 1853 they built a church of lava stones, cemented by lime melted from coral rocks. It is the only structure which remains from those days. Over the years it served as a jail, a repair shop, and a warehouse. Now it is a fire station, with a splendid red truck gleaming with chrome which was shipped from Chicago in 1936. This is where I learned from residents tending the station how to say *ahoeho*, which means 'till we meet again', and *malamapono*, which means 'take care'.

Walking back to my quarters, I was struck by the absence of children. It gave the village a curiously lifeless air. I was surrounded by graveyards – of people, buildings, vehicles, and machinery. It was always quiet, and sometimes I felt as if I was sleep-walking, as if the characters I met were unreal. Yesterday the place was a nightmare, today, it is a slow-motion dream, and tomorrow it will be gone.

'IT WAS LIKE a graveyard opened and we walked out. I guess we were like the living dead . . .'

The speaker weighed his words carefully, his voice coming from the television in a tone of sadness, but without bitterness. I was listening to him in Rea's Bar, which is where residents go out for a drink in Kalaupapa. It is a simple wooden shack, with a few scruffy chairs around a bare table, a jumble of old photographs on the walls, and an enclosed porch with similar furnishings popular with the regulars, who are mostly men. There were about a dozen of us, watching a documentary about Kalaupapa by a German director, who had brought her film to the settlement for its first screening. I have been to cinema premières before and since, but none affected me as much as the haunting images of this extraordinary community on a windy night in Ray's Bar. The speaker's voice went on: 'Before Damien it was the law of the jungle, the survival of the fittest . . . what some people fail to appreciate is that even in a diseased body you still live, you think, you can love people.'

The film ended and the speaker, who had been sitting beside me, rose and said: 'Well, Christa, you've made a good film. It tells it like it is.' The spokesman was Bernard Punikaia, one of the few patients to have left Kalaupapa and lived 'topside', as the outside world is known. From his home in Honolulu, Bernard has relentlessly harried the authorities to improve conditions for victims of Hansen's Disease. He is not only a cultivated and eloquent man, he is an accomplished musician with a lively sense of humour and he makes very good pasta. A few of us were invited to his beach house after the film show, and as far as I can remember we had a good time. My recollections are vague and my notes indecipherable due to large quantities of beer which accompanied the meal, but I remember being impressed by Bernard's arguments in favour of socialism and pacifism, in which he quoted Bertrand Russell and Gandhi. He also told a lot of funny stories, but unfortunately my memory banks lost them somewhere. I walked home happily in the rain, declining the offer of the loan of an old truck, and returned to my room with the sound of the surf beating outside my window.

In the third book of Moses (Leviticus) in the Old Testament, there are extensive instructions to priests on how to diagnose leprosy. The correct way to deal with people afflicted with the disease was as follows: 'And the leper in whom the plague is, his clothes shall be rent, and his head bare, and he shall put a covering upon his upper lip, and shall cry, Unclean, unclean. All the days wherein the plague shall be in him he shall be defiled; he is unclean: he shall dwell alone; without the camp shall his habitation be.'

In medieval Europe, the Catholic Church carried out these

instructions to the letter. A symbolic funeral was staged, in which the sufferer was laid on a bier and covered with a black cloth. When the service was over, pallbearers carried the victim to a hovel where he or she would remain in isolation until death. The practice was pretty much unchanged when the first patients were dispatched to Kalaupapa in 1866. Seven years later, as tales of horror began to emerge from the settlement, the editor of the Hawaiian newspaper *Nuhou* penned an emotional appeal for help: 'If a noble Christian priest, preacher, or sister should be inspired to go and sacrifice a life to console these poor wretches, that would be a royal soul to shine for ever on a throne reared by human love.' Father Damien arrived three weeks later.

He was thirty-three years old, a sturdy and energetic son of peasant farmers from the Flemish region of Belgium. A photograph taken at the time shows a handsome young man, square jawed with high cheekbones and penetrating dark eyes. He has a wilful, determined look about him. There were more than seven hundred lepers in the settlement when he arrived, living in appalling squalor. Most of them were emaciated through lack of proper food, fresh water was scarce, and their threadbare clothes were rarely cleaned. They passed their time in crude thatched huts playing cards, dancing, and drinking home-made beer. The melancholy refrain which rose from this community of outcasts was *A'ole kanawai ma keia wahi* (In this place there is no law). Damien later reported: 'The smell of their filth mixed with exhalation of their sores was simply disgusting and unbearable to a newcomer. Many a time in fulfilling my priestly duty at their domiciles, I have been obliged, not only to close my nostrils, but to run outside, to breathe fresh air.' He resolved the problem by taking up pipe-smoking.

An able carpenter, he set about building decent dwellings for his parishioners, dressed their sores as best he could, organized games and sports, and formed a choir. But it was a grim task. After a few months, he wrote to his brother: 'Sometimes, indeed,

I still feel some repugnance when I have to hear the confessions of those near their end, whose wounds are full of maggots. Often, also, I scarce know how to administer Extreme Unction, when both hands and feet are nothing but raw wounds.'

Damien's talents did not include tact. By all accounts he was a stubborn man who could be taciturn, and he repeatedly fell foul of the authorities in pestering them to provide cement, lumber, clothing, and better food. His uneasy relations with the state and Church authorities were not improved by the local media hailing him as a hero, and ultimately as a martyr. After three years at Kalaupapa, Damien developed skin lesions that did not show perspiration, a common early symptom of leprosy. The disease lay dormant until 1889 when it progressed rapidly. He coughed a great deal, his voice was reduced to a rough whisper, and painful sores broke out all over his hands. He lingered between life and death for almost two weeks, lost consciousness on the 13th of April, and died two days later, apparently from bronchial pneumonia. The next day he was buried beneath a pandanus tree at Kalawao, where he had slept during his first few nights at the settlement. At the request of the Belgium government, his remains were exhumed in 1936 and returned to his home town, where they now lie in a crypt at St Joseph Chapel in Louvain, a national shrine. The Catholic Church initiated beatification proceedings, a step towards saint-hood, two years later. Mahatma Gandhi called him a hero.

It was a source of regret to Stevenson that he never met Damien, who died five weeks before he visited Kalaupapa, but he penned a compelling eulogy of the man:

We must take folks' virtues as we find them, and love the better part. Of old Damien, whose weaknesses and worse perhaps I heard fully, I think only the more. It was a European peasant: dirty, bigoted, untruthful, unwise, tricky, but superb with generosity, residual candour, and fundamental good humour . . . a man, with all the grime and paltriness of mankind, but a saint and hero all the more for that.

A few months later, a congregationalist minister wrote a damning indictment of Damien's character. According to the Reverend Dr Charles M. Hyde, the priest had been 'a coarse, dirty man' who had no hand in the improvements at Kalaupapa, he had had 'impure' relations with women at the settlement (a charge Damien categorically denied during his lifetime), and his disease and death should be attributed to his vices and carelessness. Stevenson was beside himself with fury, and wrote a scathing 'open letter' to Hyde which is still regarded as a masterpiece of invective. It began:

If I have at all learned the trade of using words to convey truth and to arouse emotion, you have at last furnished me with a subject . . . with you at last, I rejoice to feel the button off the foil and to plunge home.

Wielding his pen in accordance with the metaphor, Stevenson cut Hyde to ribbons. The minister was lampooned as growing fat in his mansion, while the priest toiled amid unspeakable horrors at the lazaretto:

You, who were so refined, why were you not there, to cheer them with the lights of culture? Damien was dirty. He was. Think of the poor lepers annoyed with this dirty comrade! But the clean Dr Hyde was at his food in a fine house.

And so on.

Hyde was unrepentant. In a reply in the *Congregationalist*, he claimed the lepers had been no worse off than the average Hawaiian, of whom he wrote: 'Accustomed as I was to the purity of a New England home, there yawned before me, in Hawaiian social and family life, an abysmal depth of heathen degradation, unutterable in its loathsomeness . . . Hawaiian home life is abominably filthy.' And as for Stevenson: 'His invective may be brilliant, but it is like a glass coin, not golden, shivered into fragments of worthless glitter when brought to the test of truthfulness.'

Clearly there was a problem of communication between a

cleric who regarded Polynesians as depraved heathens, and a writer who considered them God's sweetest creatures. There is no evidence that Stevenson ever read Hyde's reply, although he wrote later to a friend:

I regret my letter to Dr Hyde. Yes, I do; I think it was barbarously harsh: if I did it now, I would defend Damien no less well and give less pain to those that are alive . . . on the whole, it was virtuous to defend Damien; but it was harsh to strike so hard at Dr Hyde.

My mind was full of conflicting images of the pugnacious priest who sparked such controversy as I stood where the pandanus tree had been, looking at his grave. It is a simple black stone monument, which declares he died 'a martyr to the charity for afflicted lepers'. A bunch of orange flowers was growing beside it. I wondered: saint or sinner? Being human, he was probably a mixture of the two, but invested with a great deal more of the former than most of us. 'I am going gently to my grave,' he wrote to his brother. 'It is the will of God, and I thank Him very much for letting me die of the same disease and in the same way as my lepers. I am very satisfied and very happy.'

Recalling those lines, I wondered whether he would have consented to the removal of his earthly remains from his chosen resting place. Given his temperament, I would not have been surprised if he had risen from his grave in 1936 and told the clergy exhuming him to leave him be. The graveyard around his church in Kalawao, on the wilder side of the peninsula, seemed a more appropriate place for him to contemplate eternity than a gloomy crypt in a church on the other side of the world.

The community on this side died years ago, but the bleak grandeur of the scenery is unchanged. Winds gust over the promontory and through deserted buildings in the shadows of a massive hill scarred by erosion; to the east, the indented coastline unfolds in a succession of spectacular sea cliffs rising sheer to three thousand feet, the tallest in the world; the sea seethes in and out of shallow coves with a noise like jet aircraft; and a singular stack of dark rock rises from the bay in the form of a dorsal fin, the home of a legendary shark god. This, I thought, is where Damien should have been allowed to remain.

Before coming to Molokai, I had been fascinated by old photographs of a little Protestant church a few yards down the road from Damien's grave. Framed by dark mountains, it seemed to epitomize the wild frontier ethos of the place. I found it, a modest white wooden building with a single door and a small steeple perched on the roof. Inside, there is a seriously bad oil painting of the church. Of more interest, on one side of the altar there is a bronze plaque listing the names of the founding congregation of 1871, and the following inscription:

> Thrust out by mankind
> these 12 women and 23 men
> crying aloud to God
> Their only refuge
> formed a church
> The first in the desolation
> that was Kalawao

The name of the church is *Siloama*, which is the Hawaiian pronunciation of a healing pool in Jerusalem mentioned in the Bible.

I wandered alone over the nearby foreshore, looking for the site of the guest house where Stevenson stayed. But all that remained of the old visitors' quarters, and a nearby hospital and dispensary, were obscure jumbles of rocks half-buried in the undergrowth. But the road from Kalawao has hardly changed since Stevenson rode along it to the Bishop Home. It is a broad track beneath a wall of mountains fractured by deep valleys at the southern end of the peninsula, running almost straight across rough moorland which is a habitat for rare flora and fauna.

Scattered in the undergrowth are the remnants of stone walls, agricultural terraces, and shrines dating back to the descendants of the first settlers from the Marquesas.

The most imposing feature along the road is the crater of Kauhako, a small shield volcano whose lava flows created the peninsula. A narrow path ascends to the rim at an elevation of four hundred feet, where a large white cross and a few ancient tombstones command a magnificent view over the entire plain. In the crater, a dense deciduous forest drops down to a murky lake far below which is thought to be connected to the sea, giving rise to a legend that it is bottomless. I followed an indistinct path down through the forest for a few yards, but soon found the vegetation closing in on me and began to feel claustrophobic. The way was steep, and the atmosphere was airless and vaguely sinister. It occurred to me I was alone, and there were better ways of leaving the planet than falling into a bottomless lake, so I cravenly retraced my steps and walked with pleasure back to my home in Kalaupapa.

There I found another monument to Damien. It is an old Celtic cross on a patch of grass by the roadside, made of red granite and adorned with a circular marble relief. It was donated by 'the people of England' through a committee headed by the Prince of Wales, later Edward VII, and erected in 1893. The inscription is from John, 15:13: *Greater love hath no man than that a man lay down his life for his friends*. It is framed by a profusion of bougainvillaea, and two painted stones lie before it. One has the image of a smiling sun, and the other says: *Smile — it no broke your face.*

By a curious coincidence, the latest successor to Damien was also a Belgian priest, with a similar name: Father Daenen. We met on the porch of his cottage in the church grounds, where we discussed Damien over a cup of tea. He told me beatification ceremonies were due to take place in Belgium in May 1994, and he had a list of sixteen patients and nurses who were planning to attend the event. Not being familiar with Catholic practices, I asked what it meant.

'Not much, really, His name will appear on the Church calendar and he'll have a special day.'

Did he consider Damien a saint?

'Well, strictly speaking sainthood requires two miracles and so far I think we have only one, which is still being debated.'

It seemed to me that Damien had performed dozens of miracles every day simply by bringing smiles to the faces of poor wretches who had been deemed unfit for human society, but evidently this doesn't count at the Vatican. In any case, Father Daenen was not convinced sainthood was such a good idea.

'I can't see Damien as a statue in a church,' he said. 'Also, Saint Damien doesn't sound right. He's always been known as Father Damien.'

On leaving, I asked Father Daenen whether he expected to remain long in Kalaupapa.

'Yes, I hope so,' he said. 'I would like to be the one to blow out the candles.'

I hope he gets his wish. I like the historical symmetry of it.

On his return to Honolulu, Stevenson wrote to Colvin:

I can only say that the sight of so much courage, cheerfulness, and devotion stung me too high to mind the infinite pity and horror of the sights . . . I have seen sights that cannot be told, and heard stories that cannot be repeated: yet I never admired my poor race so much, nor (strange as it may seem) loved life more than in the settlement.

After a few days, I understood. I had entered the settlement with apprehension, and I knew I would leave it with regret. My days had passed in hazy contentment, thrilled by the wild beauty of my surroundings and cheered by the friendship of kind people. Of course these were superficial impressions. Some residents told me the old community spirit had gone, the ties that had bound them in common misfortune had unravelled, and households were becoming isolated. I never saw the private angst behind the lace curtains. Yet for a few days in this extraordinary community, after months of wandering alone around the Pacific, I felt singularly at peace with myself and my neighbours. I can only assure the reader it was a deeply satisfying experience.

There was one other person I wanted to meet before leaving – the pretty girl in a white dress whose photograph in the Hawaii state archives of 1934 had been drifting around in my mind since I arrived. Olivia Robello was living alone in a cosy cottage on the edge of the village. She was a sprightly, good-natured woman whose disabilities failed to mask natural good looks and strength of character. I felt as if I was meeting an ageing film star I had admired as a youth.

'Hello, Gavin, nice of you to call,' she said. Over tea and home-made cakes, we talked about the photograph. I said that at first her expression had appeared lifeless, but on reflection I thought I saw a mixture of despair and defiance. 'You're dead right,' she said. 'They told me to hold up that sign with my number on it, but I refused. That's why my arms are crossed over my chest. The photographer said "Smile." Think about it. I had just got engaged to a nice young man, and they were sending me to a terrible place with an incurable disease. "Smile," he said. I was dying inside.'

How had she felt when she came to Kalaupapa? 'The fear lasted longer than anger. When I saw the people here I thought, Oh God, I'm going to look like that. Actually it was more than fear. It was total panic. I used to cry an awful lot. I figured it was the end of the world.' It wasn't. Within a few years she met and married a patient called John Breitha, who had been a horse-trainer. She recalls him as a sensitive, soft-spoken man who made life worthwhile. They built a farm and raised chickens and produced fruit until he died in 1973.

Olivia knew little about Stevenson, and listened with interest when I sketched his life and quoted his impressions of Kalaupapa. As I was leaving, she said: 'I wish I had met Stevenson. He seems to have been a really good, sensitive guy. I'm sure when he passed away God gave him a little pat on the back.' This image stayed with me for some time. It was the best tribute to RLS I had ever heard.

On my last night, Bernard the superintendent and his friend Fe, a nurse at the settlement, invited me to dinner. The conversation turned to ghosts, and Bernard said they were rarely troubled by them. However, there was a red lady who had been seen outside one of the rooms in the guest quarters. I was reminded of the little girl in the red dress whom Stevenson had seen departing from Hookena. That night I lingered by candlelight in the haunted corridor, but all that happened was a draught of wind blew out the candle. Maybe she was just wishing me farewell.

Stevenson experienced a moment of truth on the day of his departure. He had been issued with a pass to enter the settlement – but not to leave it. At first the captain of the steamer refused to take him. In spite of his admiration and affection for the community, he was desperate to get away. It may have been a heightened awareness of his own chronic illness that induced panic at the thought of remaining among the sick and dying of Kalaupapa, but this is how he described the incident:

My heart panted for deliverance . . . I had not known till then the eagerness of my impatience to be gone; it gave me persuasion; the Captain relented, and it was not long before I was tossing at sea, eating untainted food, drinking clear sea air, and beholding the headland of the lazaretto slip behind upon the starboard quarter.

My own departure was less dramatic. I walked alone out of the village, stopping briefly to say goodbye to Olivia, and hiked back up the cliff trail. An overnight storm had loosened some rocks, and a worker descending at dawn had been slightly injured. The rain had abated, but the track was muddy and strewn with boulders, and I stepped warily around the hairpin bends. Several times I had to stand aside, my back over dizzying drops, to make way for a party of tourists coming down by mule, but I was barely aware of the danger. My mind was full of impressions and memories of the past week. In the words of Stevenson: 'No stranger time have I ever had, nor any so moving.'

FOURTEEN

The whole extent of the South Seas is desert of ships;
more especially that part where we were now to sail

MY FIRST PRIORITY on returning to Oahu was to get away from it again as quickly as possible. It was early December, and Waikiki was bursting at the seams with vacation crowds jetting in for Christmas. After the haunting beauty of Kalaupapa, the crescendo of contrived gaiety and relentless commercialism was hard to take. When they began wrapping palm trees in silver paper and red ribbons I knew it was time to leave.

My destination was the Republic of Kiribati, formerly the Gilbert Islands, a group of thirty-three atolls lying astride the Equator and scattered over two million square miles of the central Pacific. In that vast expanse of sea and sky there were roughly three hundred square miles of coral islands barely breaking the surface of the ocean, with a population of less than seventy thousand. It is about as far from the madding crowd as it is possible to get with the exception of the polar ice caps. One of the few travel guides which mentions Kiribati says: 'There is no place here for the demanding tourist or for those in a hurry. Kiribati is a fragile destination, intent on retaining its culture, and it's best suited to travellers who care about wonderful, underdeveloped places off the beaten track.'

Unfortunately it was so far off the beaten track that hardly any travel agents in Hawaii had heard of it. Part of the problem dates from its independence from Britain in 1979, when the government decided, for reasons best known to itself, to transform its name into the vernacular. As there are only thirteen letters in the language, and *s* is not one of them, Kiribati is the closest they could get phonetically to the Gilberts. (A *t* followed by an *i* becomes *s*, thus it is pronounced Kiribas.) To confuse matters further, one of its three constituent groups of islands is still called the Gilberts.

Eventually I tracked down two men who knew where the islands were, and how I might get there. Tom Colson of the Island Maritime shipping company said he had a small freighter coming up from Kiribati, and he could arrange passage for me on the return trip in a couple of weeks. Even better, I would have an adventurous fellow traveller, in a detached kind of way.

The ship would be accompanied by a man who was sailing around the world in a twenty-four-foot inflatable boat powered by soybean oil. He was doing this to demonstrate the viability of renewable, non-polluting sources of energy. A magazine article on the preceding leg of his voyage, from Oregon to Honolulu, said that instead of noxious fumes, his craft was enveloped in an aroma of Chinese cooking. He also used the fuel as suntan oil. His only problem was carrying enough soybean to traverse the Pacific, which is where Tom's ship would come in as a floating filling station. 'My husband,' the man's wife was quoted as saying, 'is not like a normal human being.'

I looked forward to meeting this intrepid navigator, but Tom's ship was making heavy weather in its trip up from Kiribati. As the days passed, he reported that the heavy weather had become rough weather and it was anybody's guess when the ship would arrive. 'It's kinda strange,' he said. 'Typhoons are appearing where we've never seen them before.' I must have paled at the mention of typhoons, because he reassured me: 'It shouldn't be so rough on the way back down, because you'll have following seas instead of pounding seas.'

While waiting for further news of the freighter, I went to see Bill Paupe, a former US overseas aid worker who served as the Consul of Kiribati and ticketing agent for its national airline, Air Tungaru. Bill told me Air Tungaru no longer had any aircraft capable of reaching Hawaii, but he could offer me a ticket on a weekly flight on Air Nauru (of the neighbouring island republic) which went to Tarawa, the Kiribati capital, via Kiritimati (Christmas Island) in the Northern Line Islands. As insurance for getting out of Hawaii, I bought one for a few days hence. That afternoon, Bill called to say the flight had been cancelled and there was no guarantee it would turn up the following week. I never did find out why. The handling agents claimed there was a shortage of aviation fuel in Kiribati, but a reliable source told me later the wife of the president of Nauru had a penchant for borrowing the aircraft for shopping trips to the Marshall Islands.

Stevenson had encountered similar difficulties. The charter of the *Casco* had ended at Hawaii, and then as now there were few vessels heading in the direction of the Gilberts. He wrote:

The whole extent of the South Seas is desert of ships; more especially that part where we were now to sail. Where you may have designed to go is one thing, where you shall be able to arrive another.

He negotiated passage on the *Morning Star*, an American missionary ship, through the Gilberts and the Marshalls to the Carolines, where he hoped to return to Europe via Manila and China. However, the prospect of spending months at sea in the company of missionaries was daunting to a man of intemperate language and habits, and he was pleased to find an alternative in the *Equator*, a sixty-two-ton trading schooner. Its itinerary after the Gilberts was vague, and Stevenson's charter for a four months' cruise contained peculiar provisions: the captain agreed for a fixed daily extra price to land anywhere on its route at Stevenson's demand; and wherever it stopped for its own business, if Stevenson wished it would remain there for three days at no extra charge. Thus when the *Equator* sailed from Honolulu on 24th of June, 1889, the Stevenson party did not have the faintest idea where it would end up. A news item in the *Honolulu Pacific Advertiser* that day said: 'It is to be hoped that Mr Stevenson will not fall victim to native spears; but in his present state of bodily health, perhaps the temptation to kill him may not be very strong.'

In fact, the Stevensons had a narrow escape even before the ship weighed anchor, when they turned away two Belgians who had sought passage as deck hands. Fanny, who took a dislike to them, called them 'importunate'. Actually they turned out to be murderous pirates, who made a habit of taking over ships at sea, shooting and poisoning everybody on board, and selling the vessels at their next ports of call. (Leonce Degrave eventually died of dysentery in the penal colony in French Guiana, and his younger brother Eugene ended his days in a Colombian prison where he had been committed for stealing amethysts.) Fanny later recalled their encounter with the brothers 'with some qualms'.

While waiting for the first boat or plane that came along, I moved to quieter lodgings at the far end of Waikiki near Diamond Head. I was drawn by the promotional leaflet of the Kaimana Beach Hotel, which said: 'Dine in the shady arbor that sheltered author Robert Louis Stevenson a century ago. You'll know why he recommended this spot as one of the best in the islands for enjoying good food, good company, and beautiful scenery.' This was fairly close to the truth, being extrapolated from comments written by Stevenson in the register of a nearby inn where he stayed on a return visit to Hawaii from Samoa in late 1893.

The hotel manager gave me a luxurious suite of rooms overlooking Kapiolani Park and Diamond Head for the price of a single room, for which I was grateful. But I was impatient to be gone, and days passed with no news of either Tom's ship or the Air Nauru plane. It seemed as if they had disappeared in a Pacific version of the Bermuda Triangle.

It was Rasa who rescued me from Waikiki and took me to a vestige of old Polynesia surprisingly close at hand. Rasa was a free spirit from the Canary Islands who liked to swim naked by moonlight. This was prohibited, which made it all the more fun. One day she took me to the upper Manoa valley, a short drive from downtown Honolulu, where a small rainforest survives in a bowl of mountains thanks to the efforts of conservationists at the University of Hawaii. Beyond a fine arboretum, a trail follows a rocky stream through a sylvan wonderland alive with bird song and the sound of rushing water. For anyone who likes trees, it is a paradise of exotic species. At the head of the trail, there is a waterfall which plunges a hundred feet into a shallow pool, forming as idyllic an image of rural Polynesia as one could wish. Provided nobody else is around, swimming costumes are not required.

It was a pleasant farewell to Hawaii. That evening Bill rang to say Air Nauru's Boeing 737 had materialized at Honolulu, and would be departing the next day. Tom's ship was still ploughing through heavy seas somewhere in the far reaches of the Pacific, so I decided to fly.

FIFTEEN

Don't worry, in Kiribati there is plenty of time

THE PASSENGERS for the Air Nauru flight from Honolulu International Airport were easy to spot. They were the ones squatting on the floor of the departure terminal amid a jumble of cheap luggage and cardboard boxes. It was my first encounter with Micronesians, and I liked what I saw: a relaxed, friendly bunch chatting and playing cards in family groups, oblivious to the hustle and bustle around them. They had waited long enough for the plane, and now that it had arrived they reasoned it wasn't going to leave without them.

Time is a relative concept in Kiribati. It is the only country in the world where some of its people live perpetually in the past – or in the future, depending on their geographical location and point of view. The determining factor is the international date line, which runs between its three principal groups of atolls. When it is Sunday in the Line and Phoenix islands, it is Monday in the Gilberts. This can be confusing for an airborne visitor. The first leg of my flight due south to Christmas Island presented no difficulties. It was on the two-thousand-mile run west to Tarawa, the capital, that we gained two hours and lost a day, or rather we lost twenty-two hours. I asked a flight attendant for help in figuring it out.

'We left Honolulu on Tuesday, right?'

'Yes, sir.'

'What day is it now?'

'Tuesday.' I looked blank.

'But soon it will be Wednesday. In about half an hour.'

'Thank you.'

A fellow passenger, returrning to his village for Christmas, assured me: 'Don't worry, in Kiribati there is plenty of time.' I was to discover he was right.

Most of the passengers had disembarked at Christmas Island, which is the world's largest atoll, with a circumference of about a hundred miles. It was uninhabited when Cook discovered it on Christmas Eve, 1777, and a century later its big claim to fame was the amount of bird droppings on it, which kept a guano industry going for a while. From the air it looks like a battlefield, a low land mass pock-marked by more than a hundred lakes and ponds like bomb craters. The simile is apposite – Britain used the island as a base for atomic experiments in the 1950s, and the United States did the same in 1962. The main settlements are called London, Poland, and Banana.

The airport comprises two wooden huts, outside one of which a fireman rolled me a cigarette with pungent tobacco imported from Papua New Guinea and asked me why I had come to Kiribati. He told me he had read *Treasure Island*, and did I know where it was? I confessed I did not, but then neither did Stevenson. When asked the same question by an Australian journalist, he said:

Treasure Island is not in the Pacific. In fact, I only wish myself that I knew where it was. When I wrote the book I was careful to give no indication as to its whereabouts for fear there might be an undue rush towards it. However, it is generally supposed to be in the West Indies.

The fireman seemed disappointed, but pleased at the same time he had inside information to share with his children.

I then flew around the middle of the globe, one degree above the Equator, for four hours in a virtually empty aircraft until it shuddered through clouds obscuring Tarawa and slammed on to a rain-soaked runway. Given the difficulties of getting here, I had not the least idea of when and how I might depart, so I did not have the required onward ticket. This was a new experience for the immigration officer, but after some hesitation he accepted a letter of introduction from Bill Paupe, and I stepped out of the little airport into a world of sea and sky and thatched huts.

The island of Tarawa is not really an island at all. It is a disjointed series of low-lying islets connected by causeways, enclosing an enormous lagoon like the skeletal fragments of a crooked elbow. Strung along this narrow ribbon of land are hamlets of open-sided native huts among the palm trees, and a few wooden bungalows in the European style. It was by far the most primitive and traditional Pacific island community I had seen in my travels. A young mechanic gave me a lift to my hotel in a pick-up truck, and as we swished along the wet road, half-naked urchins stood beside puddles and squealed with delight when we drenched them.

Kiribati is not exactly overrun with tourists. It attracts about two thousand foreign visitors a year, most of them businessmen. The only other foreigners on my flight were an American fisherman and two Japanese scuba divers, who got off at Christmas Island. At the last count, the resident foreign population was two hundred and sixty-four. The entire nation has seventy hotel rooms, about half of them in a collection of motel-style buildings by the shore of the lagoon at Tarawa, which is where I made some new friends after dinner.

On the terrace of the Otintaai Hotel I was invited to join a sociable bunch of New Zealanders which included their acting High Commissioner, an amusing young man who looked like Oscar Wilde and rejoiced in the wonderful name of Perena Quinlivan. In the days to come, they became agreeable companions and valuable sources of information about life in the islands. I slept soundly that night, lulled by the patter of rain and the rhythmic throbbing of a ceiling fan. In the morning I was wakened by the refrain of children singing in English outside my window: 'Listen to the rain, oh listen to the rain . . .'

Again my priority was to leave this port of call, and to head for the outer islands of Butaritari and Abemama where Stevenson had fetched up in the *Equator*. I had just missed a ferry taking schoolchildren home to Butaritari for Christmas, and decided to wait until after the festivities were over and take the first available flight on Air Tungaru. An invitation to a traditional English Christmas lunch played a part in delaying my departure.

My host, Bill Rowstron, the chief instructor at a marine training college, was the epitome of an English sea dog – a tubby man with a splendid beard, a lively sense of humour, and a fund of amusing stories. Supplies of virtually everything other than fish and coconuts are limited in Kiribati, but Bill's wife Sandy performed a minor miracle by obtaining a turkey, sausages wrapped in bacon, and the ingredients for a Christmas pudding with brandy sauce. We tucked into this feast, put on silly paper hats, and blew up balloons as a squall loomed over the lagoon and lashed the palm trees with an opaque curtain of rain. The wind howled in impotent rage as we sang carols about snow and reindeers.

Tropical storms are rare in Kiribati, the islands being in the doldrums between the north-east and south-east trade winds. But this was the season of rain and westerly gales, which made navigation of any kind a hazardous business. One day I was invited by a few expatriates to join a scuba-diving trip to the reef wall outside the lagoon. The weather was calm as we piled into the motor launch of the Australian High Commission, but as we were heading for the open sea a storm loomed on the horizon. The sky darkened remarkably quickly, until half of the world became an ominous dark grey wall advancing towards us. Light-hearted banter on the boat died as we began bouncing in choppy water, and eventually one of us asked the native boatman his opinion.

'I think it is not good,' he said.

That was good enough for us, and by common consent we turned tail and fled back towards the lagoon. It was not a moment too soon. Stevenson once described a squall falling on the *Casco* like an armed man. In our case it was more like a ghostly army battering our little craft with gusts of wind, sheets of rain, and confused seas. All this in a shroud of almost total darkness. For an experienced sailor, a tropical squall may be of no more concern than a passing shower to a hill-walker, but for a landlubber in a small boat on a big ocean, it is scary. One feels barely more secure back on land, driving over exposed causeways in poor visibility between scraps of low-lying land, with the sea and the lagoon heaving on either side. On Pacific atolls in such weather one has the uneasy feeling there is not nearly enough land and far too much sea. Yet it is a time of extravagant natural beauty and special effects. By some curious phenomenon, the lagoon appeared to lighten in colour as the skies darkened. Thus when the winds abated I found myself in a gloomy twilight world enclosing a shimmering, almost luminescent, body of water of the palest green.

The Australian motor launch sank a few days later. One of the survivors told me what had happened. A big surf had been running, and the boatman stood off the reef, waiting for the right moment to run into the lagoon. Choosing a wave, he gunned the engine – and it spluttered and died. Powerless in the surging sea, the boat flipped backwards and turned turtle, trapping an Australian administration officer and a police training official under the hull. They managed to struggle free and swim more than a hundred yards to the shore, where they were joined by the boatman, who had been thrown clear with a head wound, but the boat was flung on to the reef and smashed beyond repair.

The next day, High Commission personnel were examining the wreckage when they saw a small fleet of outrigger canoes heading out of the lagoon. There was a heavy swell, and when the fishermen saw the size of the waves all but one of the canoes turned back. Within minutes, the craft which carried on was overwhelmed by a wave and its four occupants were swept overboard. One man simply disappeared, and another was sucked under by clashing currents only a few yards from where the Australians stood on the reef, powerless to help. The deaths of the two fishermen coincided with reports of Fiji, more than a thousand miles to the south, being battered by the worst typhoon in its history.

An Englishman working on a fisheries project told me the islanders were renowned seamen, but it was not uncommon for them to be swept out of sight of land and lost at sea. He knew of one man who had survived on fish and rainwater for six months before being rescued near Samoa. The most remarkable part of his ordeal was that he had managed to keep his canoe afloat. According to the fisheries expert, a drifting boat becomes a fish-aggregating device – that is it develops its own eco-system, with plankton becoming attached to the hull and attracting small fish, which in turn draw larger fish which can be caught and eaten. The drawback is that attendant wood-worms, small crabs, and fish feeding on the hull eventually weaken and destroy it, and the boat sinks.

While waiting for the next flight to Butaritari, I hired a car and explored the further reaches of Tarawa. The tourist information office near the hotel had no tourists and hardly any information. It had no maps either, but a woman gave me a typewritten brochure on the culture of I-Kiribati (Kiribati people) which she thought might be useful. It said: 'Many things that were I-Kiribati eighty years ago seem to have changed today, and what is I-Kiribati today may not look I-Kiribati in fifty years' time, still they are I-Kiribati. Even though there have been many changes since the coming of Europeans, I-Kiribati are still I-Kiribati.' Thus reassured, I went to have a look at I-Kiribati culture at the southern end of the atoll on the islets of Bairiki and Betio.

Being the administrative and commercial centres of Tarawa,

they are the most densely populated areas and they are not a pretty sight. Ugly concrete buildings and wooden shacks have replaced traditional thatched huts, there is refuse everywhere, and the lagoon is badly polluted. The intrusion of Western society is seen at its careless worst here in crowded slums and a general air of neglect verging on squalor. Where natives used to sing and dance, now they stay at home and watch videos featuring sex and violence.

Kiribati is among the ten least developed nations in the world, and a centralized state economic system looks like keeping it that way. Its most successful export is said to be applications for foreign aid, which has given rise to a cruel joke: a Samoan, a Fijian, and an I-Kiribati are each given a pair of iron balls. When the donors return, they find the Samoan playing bowls with them and the Fijian balancing one on the other. The I-Kiribati has broken one, and is sitting on the other writing a request for a replacement. But you take people as you find them, and I found I-Kiribati generally to be charming and hospitable, especially in the outer islands. A foreign diplomat suggested they were like adolescent children, but I found them much more appealing.

It is a minor miracle that they survived World War II. Betio was the scene of one of the fiercest battles in the Pacific, when US Marines captured it from a strongly entrenched Japanese garrison in November 1943. When the five-day carnage was over, the beaches and palm groves were strewn with the bodies of almost five thousand Japanese and more than one thousand Americans. The islet itself was totally destroyed. Not a house or a tree was left standing. On the southern shore, two massive eight-inch naval guns still point out to sea, as useless today as when the US Marines 8th Division stormed ashore from the lagoon beind them. The barrel of one is broken, the other is deeply scarred by bullets, and wild flowers are taking root on the gun platforms. I noted with interest that the guns had been supplied to the Imperial Japanese Navy at the turn of the century by the Vickers Armstrong company of England.

Further down the islet there is a similar relic, beside a concrete obelisk which is the only memorial to the American forces. The site by a small beach is littered with rubbish – beer cans, plastic bags, and war-time machinery half-buried in the sand – and a shattered blockhouse stinks with excrement. It would not take much to clean up the place, plant some coarse grass and flowers, and erect signposts, but evidently nobody can be bothered. This is a far-away place and the war was long ago.

According to Banana Joe, most foreigners in remote regions of the Pacific fall into three categories – mercenaries, misfits, and missionaries. 'I reckon I'm a misfit,' he said. He had drifted into Kiribati ten years before, a Californian surfer looking for the biggest waves he could find. What he found was a wife, and an opportunity to make money exporting shark fins and sea cucumbers to China. His courtship was unusual. One day he rescued a young woman who was being beaten by a man with a stick, and they escaped by jumping on a bus. The passengers were laughing and cheering; he was informed that he had taken the woman from her uncle, which was tantamount to elopement, and they were bound by custom to marry; and eventually that is what they did. His real name was Chuck, but he said: 'I like to think of myself as a South Seas trader. I just want to be a Banana Joe and raise kids here. It ain't paradise, but I can't think of anywhere else I'd rather be.' Tarawa was becoming too crowded for his liking, however, and he was planning to move to Tabuaeran, a remote atoll in the Northern Line islands. 'They tell me they got real big surf there,' he said.

SEVERAL TIMES each day I looked at the sky. Since my adventures in the Marquesas, I had become uneasy about flying around the Pacific in light aircraft, and the unsettled weather was a source of concern. My first experience of Air Tungaru did little to restore confidence, and the more I heard about it the more anxious I became.

It was a dark and stormy night (really) when I joined a group of friends in the lounge bar of the Otintaai Hotel after dinner. The wind was moaning through the sliding glass doors, and snapping angrily at tarpaulins on the terrace outside. At an adjacent table, awash with beer cans, local employees of Air Tungaru were getting methodically drunk. Our party included a young pilot from New Zealand who had just arrived to fly for the airline. I asked him whether its aircraft could fly in such weather. He said sure, the airframes were tested for cross-winds of up to thiry-three knots. I asked how strong the wind was blowing at the time, and he estimated forty knots. 'But don't worry, they can probably handle up to fifty knots,' he said. 'Also they have nagivation systems.' At this point the airline operations manager leaned drunkenly over from the next table, waving his finger in a negative gesture. 'Navs not working, no,' he said.

The navigation systems were not all that were not working in Air Tungaru. At the time its fleet comprised two Trislander aircraft, which were repeatedly running out of spare parts. A slightly larger plane was not flying because there had been a fire in the cockpit, and the pilot had used its only extinguisher to douse the flames. It was still grounded, waiting for a replacement extinguisher, when I left Kiribati a month later. Also the radio beacons on the islands, and the personnel supposed to operate them, were unreliable. This occasionally resulted in pilots flying blind in appalling weather and trusting to luck and judgement to find a speck of land in the biggest ocean on Earth. The simile of the needle and the haystack comes to mind.

A few weeks before, a Trislander had lost its way in a storm and the pilots radioed three islands in the vicinity for help in fixing their position. They got no reply. With their fuel running out, they sent a distress signal to Fiji, more than a thousand miles away, pulled out their inflatable life raft, and prepared to ditch. At the last minute, as they descended through low cloud, they spotted an atoll in the distance and managed to land on the beach. I wished I had not heard this story.

On the eve of my flight to Butaritari, I lay in bed listening to the wind gusting sheets of rain against the windows, and the lagoon surging against the rocks below. The only picture in my room was a gloomy oil painting in various shades of grey, depicting palm trees bending in the gales of a stormy night. I fell into a troubled sleep, disturbed by visions of an aircraft bucking wildly in a black sky.

The rain abated overnight, but in the morning the skies were still overcast and a stiff breeze was whipping across the lagoon. At the grandly named Bonriki International Airport (a runway and two grubby brick sheds by the lagoon) I learned that a flight to the southern islands had been cancelled due to bad weather. The passengers for Butaritari, however, were already being weighed in for departure. Weight, and the distribution of it, is an important consideration on small aircraft, hence each passenger was obliged to step in turn on to a baggage scale at the check-in counter. I regarded with misgiving several hefty locals tipping the scales at more than two hundred pounds.

The interior of the eighteen-seat Trislander aircraft waiting on the tarmac looked like an old coffin. It was narrow and dirty, suffused with unpleasant odours, and most of the fittings were broken. I tried not to think what the engine looked like. The I-Kiribati word for aircraft translates as 'flying canoe', which in this case was appropriate. As I installed myself in a rear seat beside the emergency exit (Anxious? Who, me?) a pilot began bleeding fuel from the wing tanks into a syringe, presumably checking for impurities. I recognized him as one of the drunken Air Tungaru crowd of a few nights before, and offered a silent prayer that he would not take a swig of the aviation fuel. He did not, in fact he seemed perfectly sober, and I was assured afterwards he was a good pilot.

I am not superstitious by nature, but a wee supplication to RLS had not gone amiss in the past, notably during my helicopter flight in a Marquesan rainstorm. So as we gathered speed down the runway, I quietly suggested to him that fair weather would be appreciated. Evidently our communications were excellent, because we had a relatively smooth flight and after about an hour Butaritari came into view off the port wing. The greater part of the atoll is submerged, or forms great sandbanks, leaving detached segments of land in the shape of a plough about twelve miles in length. Banking low over the lagoon, there was a fleeting vision of turquoise water, a rush of palm trees with thatched huts among them, and then we were bouncing along a runway of impacted coral.

There were only two vehicles on Butaritari, a truck belonging to the island council and another to the local co-operative store. Neither was at the landing strip, but one of my fellow-passengers called over an old man on a motor bike and asked him to take me to the Catholic guest house, where I had been advised to stay. The man smiled and murmured a greeting, placed my bag on his handlebars, motioned to me to sit behind him, and we puttered off along the edge of a coconut grove. It was in this manner that I arrived on an island of magic and laughter.

SIXTEEN

You are welcome in this place. This is your house

STEVENSON'S FIRST IMPRESSION of Butaritari was that he had wandered into a scene from the *Arabian Nights*. Traversing a silent village, in which most of the inhabitants were asleep, he mused:

. . . here some adventurous prince might step ashore among new characters and incidents . . . the impression received was not so much of foreign travel – rather of past ages; it seemed not so much degrees of latitude that we had crossed, as centuries of time that we had reascended.

The illusion remains intact. In the late nineteenth century the island was the principal commercial centre in the Gilberts, with about a dozen resident foreign traders. Having ceded that role to Tarawa after World War II, it has slipped back in Pacific dream-time to become a sleepy outpost of fishermen and vegetable farmers happily remote from the stresses of the twentieth century. During the week I spent there, I was the only white man on the island.

Riding along a coral path muddied by rain, we attracted a menagerie of pigs, chickens, dogs, and laughing children, respectively grunting and squawking in protest and cheering our passage with cries of *matang* (foreigner); and from every thatched hut in the palm groves came a smile or a friendly wave. It is similar to Fakarava in the Tuamotus, being a narrow strip of low-lying land bounded on one side by the sea and on the other by an enormous lagoon. The highest points are two trigonomet-rical stations which are barely ten feet above sea level. But the vegetation is more luxurious than on Fakarava, and in places as lush as a rain forest. From the main coral road by the lagoon, undulating paths meander through dense foliage and around fresh-water pools crowded with exotic fruit trees; fleeting visions of a tropical Garden of Eden, and every one pleasing to the eye and the spirit. I was deposited in the centre of a village near a large stone church. A handsome young man wearing a brightly coloured *lava-lava* sauntered up with an outstretched hand and a wide smile.

'Hello, I am Teataake the chief catechist. You are welcome in this place. This is your house.'

He gestured to a brick bungalow with an iron roof opposite the church, with a veranda facing the main road through the village and a rear porch a few steps from the lagoon. It was officially the priest's residence, but its last occupant had left the island four years before, entrusting the back-door key, and the spiritual care of the community, to Teataake. My lodgings comprised a large central room with two tables where I could eat, read, and write, and a bedroom with a louvred window overlooking the lagoon. I was provided with a mattress, clean sheets and a towel, shown a cold shower and (with some pride) a flushing toilet, and informed a woman would come shortly to cook me dinner. A plump, cheerful girl called Rakera duly appeared and produced an excellent stew of meat and vegetables with fried breadfruit, a tastier and probably more nutritious local version of chips. Teataake then reappeared and invited me to his home.

Like most of the houses in the village, Teataake's was a raised wooden platform covered with fine soft mats woven from pandanus leaves. Ironwood pillars supported a lofty roof of plaited pandanus, and in the evening or during inclement weather blinds of palm leaves were lowered. Thus in the heat of the day it provided shade from the sun, while remaining open to cool breezes. Apart from a few old chests and trunks, there was no furniture. In the evening it was illuminated by a neon light powered by an oil-fired generator, and until the blinds were lowered it looked from a distance like a brightly lit theatre stage.

The characters strolling around this scene were pleasing to the eye. The men were strong and handsome for the most part, with a tawny skin over muscular frames. Even in old age, when the spring in the step was gone, they retained an erect bearing. The very young girls, with their long black hair, dark eyes, and flashing smiles, were exceedingly beautiful; by puberty they began to lose their lithe grace, and middle age was a period of comfortable corpulence; but, the task of child-bearing over, many of the older women regained the slender figures of their youth and became elegant and even glamorous. I concluded their beauty came from within; an inherent good nature and happy disposition twinkling from mischievous eyes.

Stevenson recalled that some of the prettiest girls, and one of the most beautiful women he had ever seen, were Gilbertese. He found their charm enhanced by the *ridi*, a skirt of smoked fibres of coconut leaves like tarry string. Happily English fashions never became popular on Butaritari. Women have since found a compromise between tradition and modesty by adopting the *lava-lava*, a wrap-around of gaily patterned cloth, worn with blouses or T-shirts. This is also the usual garb of men. It is both comfortable and practical, so I bought one for the equivalent of two pounds, and moved with a liberty I had not enjoyed since leaving my kilt at home.

A few steps from Teataake's home was the *maneaba*, or speak-house. This is the traditional meeting place in Kiribati villages, and it is all things to all men (and women and children). It is a community centre in the real sense of the word, serving as a conference venue, a theatre, a sports hall, a social club, and a playground, frequently all at the same time. Essentially a larger version of their houses, it was filled with people who had come from outlying districts to celebrate the New Year. About a hundred folk were squatting in front of a small television set watching an American video film, drawn more by the images than the dialogue, which few of them could understand. Other groups were chatting or playing cards, some were reading, and infants were sleeping beneath mosquito netting strung from the supporting beams. People acknowledged my presence with smiles and nods of greeting, offering to make space for me on their mats. The place had a warm, cosy atmosphere, and I felt there was much to be admired in such a companionable society.

STEVENSON RECEIVED a less cordial welcome when he waded ashore from the *Equator* in July 1889. This was because most of the natives were in a drunken stupor following a ten-day binge which showed no signs of ending. It had begun when the traders persuaded the local king, Teiburimoa, to lift a *tabu* on liquor for celebrations on the 4th of July; unfortunately he had omitted to reimpose it, and every day the traders were besieged by surly natives baying for more drink. To the alarm of the handful of whites, the situation was getting out of hand. The scene was worthy of a comic opera, but it came close to ending in tragedy.

Stevenson's contemporary biographer, Graham Balfour, wrote: '. . . the arrival of the *Equator* fell at an unpropitious moment. For the first and probably the only time in his wanderings, Stevenson was in real danger of violence from natives.' Stevenson likened the mood in the trading posts to that of English garrisons before the Sepoy Mutiny:

The degree of the peril was not easy to measure at the time, and I am inclined to think now it was easy to exaggerate. Yet the conduct of drunkards even at home is always matter for anxiety; and at home our populations are not armed from the highest to the lowest with revolvers and repeating rifles . . . It must be thought besides that we were here in barbarous islands, rarely visited, lately and partly civilized. First and last, a really considerable number of whites have perished in the Gilberts

*. . . This last was the chief consideration against a sudden closing of
the bars; the bar-keepers stood in the immediate breach and dealt direct
with madmen; too surly a refusal might prove the signal for massacre.*

The flashpoints were the stores of Messrs Crawford and Messrs
Wightman Brothers, both of San Francisco, about half a mile
apart. Each had its tavern – the Land we Live in, and the Sans
Souci, respectively. Having arrived on a Wightman schooner,
Stevenson and his family were installed in the Wightman
compound, which they soon realized was untenable in a military
sense. After a drunken brawl at the Sans Souci, Stevenson wrote:

*It was a serious question that night if we should sleep ashore. But we
were travellers, folk that had come far in quest of the adventurous; on
the first sign of an adventure it would have been a singular inconsistency
to have withdrawn; and we sent on board instead for our revolvers.*

Captain Denny Reid of the *Equator*, described by Fanny as 'a
small, fiery Scots–Irishman' came on shore to be on hand in case
of trouble, and joined the Stevensons in public shooting practices
on the beach aimed at intimidating the natives.

The locals were not impressed. On the evening of the 23rd,
Stevenson recorded a disturbing incident:

*. . . dusk had fallen, the lamp had just been brought, when a
missile struck the table with a rattling smack and rebounded past my
ear. Three inches to one side and this page had never been written; for
the thing travelled like a cannon ball.*

The assault was repeated the next night, and Stevenson
concluded the missiles were stones aimed at frightening him. In
fact it made him angry, and precipitated an intervention which
ended the crisis. Mr Rick at the Wightman store had already
closed the Sans Souci, and Stevenson eventually persuaded
Muller, the German trader at the Land we Live in, to do
likewise. Mr Rick's wife, who spoke the native language,
probably averted a massacre by informing the befuddled King
that Stevenson was an intimate personal friend of Queen Victoria, and that if any harm should befall him a man-of-war would

be dispatched to exact terrible reprisals. The resolution of the traders and the fanciful threat of retribution had the desired effect, for the next day the *tabu* was reimposed, and on the following Sunday the King stood lopsidedly on the gravel floor of the church and solemnly abjured drinking.

The affair had a salutary effect on the traders, and was concluded by Stevenson 'with the approval of all present' helping to draw up a petition to the United States for a law against the liquor trade in the Gilberts:

. . . *useless pains, since the whole reposes, probably unread and possibly unopened, in a pigeon-hole at Washington.*

A century later, alcohol was still a problem in Kiribati. It was banned in at least seven islands, but elsewhere moderation was an unfamiliar concept. The week I arrived, the *Marshall Islands Journal* carried a report on its front page with the headline 'Tragedy in Tarawa'. The story read: 'There's a grave shortage of the people's favourite beer, Fosters, on south Tarawa. The Otintaai Hotel, which has multiple choices, is taking the opportunity to get rid of its New Zealand Steinlager, Fiji bitter and other brands . . .'

The folk on Butaritari didn't have a problem with alcohol, however, because usually there wasn't any. I discovered this when I asked Teataake where I might buy some beer to celebrate the forthcoming New Year.

'It's finished,' he said.

'Finished?'

'Yes. We had some, but some young men drank it.'

This had been weeks ago. There would be no more beer until the next steamer came from the Tarawa, and nobody knew when this would be. This was of no great concern, as almost everybody was teetotal. Teetaake said he knew of a store which might have some whisky, but it didn't. The island was effectively 'dry', and I faced the sobering prospect of celebrating hogmanay without a dram. It was to be a novel experience. For the time being, I was more concerned about finding the sites of the old trading stores. Teataake said he would have a word with a man who knew the history of the village.

Rakera was a little late in serving breakfast the next morning. This was because a shrieking wall of water was lashing the atoll, making all human movement somewhere between hazardous and suicidal. It began with a gentle sigh in the trees, followed by a spatter of raindrops. There was a distant but distinct roar like a jet engine, and within a minute a storm came howling out of the depths of the Pacific. From my bedroom window I watched the palm trees doing their Indian braves trick, their huge leaves streaming in the fury of westerly gales, and confused waves from the lagoon inundating the shore a few feet away. The world seemed to have been sucked into a maelstrom, through which Teataake's house and the *maneaba* were barely visible.

There was a thud at the front door. I opened it cautiously, and a screeching bundle of fur literally flew into the living room, careered into a chair, and collapsed in a corner. A bedraggled kitten regarded me reproachfully, presumably for not opening the door sooner. She proceeded to lick herself, spring into my lap, curl into a ball, and fall fast asleep. My next visitor was Teataake, who had come to apologize for the delay in serving breakfast. I assured him this was a minor concern, and enquired whether the storm was causing problems for the villagers.

'This is a big strong wind and the people are afraid, but they are glad it comes in the day,' he said. 'If it comes in the night, they are very afraid.' Looking outside, I could actually see the gusts of wind in terms of the sheets of water they carried. The storm lasted about an hour, but the damage was slight. A neighbouring *maneaba* had lost some of its roof, and a lean-to lavatory at Teataake's house had been demolished.

The priests who served on Butaritari had been conscientious historians, and I spent the rest of the morning browsing through their handwritten records stacked on shelves behind a big wooden desk. In the inside covers of a volume inscribed *Butaritari Village Book 1*, I found neatly typed excerpts from the diary of Captain E. H. M. Davis of HMS *Royalist*, concerning three visits in June and July of 1892 (three years after Stevenson). His list of *dramatis personae* showed that Mr Rick had moved from Wightman Brothers to Messrs Crawford, while Muller had set up on his own account, and King Teiburimoa was still muddling along as monarch of all he surveyed.

Davis found the King a weak man, easily led but willing to do well, and suggested to him a number of reforms 'for the better government of his island'. One of them concerned Mrs Rick (who had designated Stevenson a personal friend of Queen Victoria): 'Hearing that Mrs Rick, wife of a trader on the island, had gained a great influence over the King, which did not tend to his welfare or that of his subjects, I advised him strongly not to be guided by her any longer, and pointed out to him, now that Her Majesty had established a Protectorate over the group, he must ask more on his own responsibility – and he might rely on assistance from Her Majesty's ships visiting the islands.' (This was probably news to Teiburimoa, as Davis had proclaimed the protectorate at a ceremony on another island only a few weeks before.)

I was perusing this sequel to Stevenson's adventures when I became aware I was not alone. An elderly man had entered the house while I was reading, silently placed himself in a chair opposite me, and was waiting patiently for me to address him. Like most of the islanders he had a dignified mien. It was my place to welcome him; it would have been rude to ask what he wanted; that would become apparent in due course. Like the man on the flight from Hawaii had said: there is always plenty of time. When I looked up and greeted him, he said: 'History is important. It tells us where we come from and our place in the world.'

This seemed a reasonable proposition, but off-hand I could

not think of an appropriate response. I told him I had been
reading the journal of Captain Davis of the *Royalist*.

'Yes,' he said, 'that was in the days of Teiburimoa. He was a
foolish king. He drank too much.' It finally dawned on me this
was the man Teataake had sent to help me with my researches.

Bureimoa Tokrei was a sprightly figure with a sturdy frame,
and a shock of white hair receding from a noble forehead. He
was sixty-seven years old and most of his teeth were missing,
but the eyes in his nut-brown face were bright with intelligence.
He looked what he was: a Pacific island sage. He said he knew
where the two nineteenth-century stores had stood, and asked
which I would like to visit first. I suggested the Crawford
compound, which had been adjacent to Teiburimoa's palace.

The seat of royal dignity in Stevenson's day was a small
wooden building in the European style, with a corrugated-iron
roof, in a yard enclosed by walls. Before the gate lay a large bell,
two pieces of cannon, and a single shell, none of which was in
working order. The palace was deserted when Stevenson first
viewed it, but near by he found the court and guardsmen of
Butaritari sprawled in a *maneaba* by the pier, yawning in the
midday heat, their rifles and cutlasses scattered around them. In
their midst, lolling on mats, Stevenson viewed the grotesque
figure of their monarch:

*He wore pyjamas which sorrowfully misbecame his bulk; his nose was
hooked and cruel, his body overcome with sodden corpulence, his eye
timorous and dull; he seemed at once oppressed with drowsiness and held
awake by apprehension: a pepper rajah muddled with opium, and
listening for the march of a Dutch army looks perhaps not otherwise.*

The site of the palace was now a jumble of stones and rubbish
by a small cove, from which a jetty still protruded. The pomp
and ceremony of Teiburimoa's court had been reduced to a pile
of rubble, from which a little boy was fishing hopefully with a
line of coconut fibre. Near by in a grove of palm trees were the

ruins of a tall brick water-cistern which Bureimoa reckoned was all that was left of the Crawford trading post.

'The war between the American and Japanese soldiers broke this place,' he said. 'There were many bombs. They came from the sky and the sea and there were no trees left.'

I asked him where the other compound had been, and he led the way back through the village. After about fifteen minutes, he stopped and said: 'The other store, which must have been what you call the Wightman place, was here.' I looked up, and asked him if he was sure. He said: 'Yes, it is certain. This was the only other *matang* trading place in the days of Teiburimoa.' We were standing outside my quarters in the Catholic guest house.

So it was that for the first time in my travels, I found myself staying, by chance, in precisely the same spot as Stevenson. Writing up my notes by candlelight that evening, I thought of stones whistling through the dark, of hushed councils of war, and of Stevenson priming his revolver. My reverie was interrupted by a shower of pebbles pattering against the window beside me. Was history repeating itself? Hardly. I looked out to find a gaggle of children calling for the *matang* to come out and play.

APART FROM the endless sigh of the sea, the predominant sound in Butaritari is laughter. It is like a theme song. Until the last lamps are extinguished, it can be heard in the villages, and along the shores, and among the coconut groves. It is a far better and happier place than the dispirited community described by Stevenson, and along with Western Samoa and possibly Fakarava it was the only one I found of which this could be said. The twentieth century, by and large, has not been kind to Oceania.

The quality of religious devotion on Butaritari has also improved. Being lodged in the house of a Hawaiian Protestant missionary, Stevenson was compelled to endure Sunday services during which he struggled to stay awake:

I never heard worse singing . . . a plain expanse of tedium, rendered unbearable by heat, a hard chair, and the sight through the wide doors of the more happy heathen on the green. Sleep breathed on my joints and eyelids, sleep hummed in my ears; it reigned in the dim cathedral. The congregation stirred and stretched; they moaned, they groaned aloud; they yawned upon a singing note, as you may sometimes hear a dog when he has reached the tragic bitterest of boredom.

Yet he admired the vain attempts of the preacher to instil religious fervour in his congregation.

To see him weekly flogging a dead horse and blowing a cold fire was a lesson in fortitude and constancy.

The contrast with the Catholic devotions led by Teataake could not have been greater. The villagers were summoned to Mass on Sunday mornings by a little boy banging with a piece of iron on a rusty gas bottle outside the church. Inside, bright-eyed youngsters gathered around the pulpit, seemingly enchanted by the rituals of the Eucharist, while their elders squatting on mats behind them followed the proceedings with close interest. There were no pews or chairs, because I-Kiribati don't use them. The lofty church and its congregation were bathed in soft light from windows of louvred wood and stained glass, and sounds of the sea drifted in through the open front door.

The singing was enchanting. There was an innocence and purity of tone in the children's voices, blending with the rich baritones of the men, which I found uplifting. It is difficult for a godless Celt to admit, let alone describe, this almost spiritual sense of peace and harmony; I felt I was on an island of sanity in a turbulent world, which had discovered the essence of Christianity.

Teataake received nothing from the Church for his labours, but he and his family were amply rewarded by the community. Three times a week his parishioners gave him food, and at Christmas he received a bag of rice, six papaya, a two-week supply of dried fish, and some money.

'We do not need much money,' he told me. 'If we have no money we do not die. We can eat fish, breadfruit, and papaya, and we can drink sweet toddy from the coconuts. We are not like I-Matang who need money to smoke and drink tea. Our people are very kind. They give my family food and say, "Catechist, this is our gift to you," and I say, "Thank you very much."'

Despite his privileged position, Teataake felt it would be good for the village to have a resident priest again.

'We have no Father,' he said. 'You see, he can come and look at this place and tell us what we must do, if we must build something or like that. You see, he is in charge. If he says there is not enough money in the parish, he can say to the people please to make it big.'

Watching a group of youngsters emerging from the church after choir practice, the sound of their laughter mingling with singing from the *maneaba*, it occurred to me that the good folk of Butaritari were doing quite well on their own.

Outside Church activities, the principal occupations on Butaritari are gathering food and having fun. After Mass, Sundays are devoted to games in which virtually everybody joins in. On emerging from my house, I found a crowd assembled around the *maneaba*, and the chairman of the village council organizing the first event, a series of foot races along the main road for a distance of about fifty yards.

Teataake invited me to participate, assuring me it would be a rare treat to have an 'international' event, and my entry was greeted by the spectators with enthusiasm. The rough path was strewn with decaying coconuts and breadfruit, and the advantage of hardy bare feet over smooth-soled sandshoes on a muddy track became immediately apparent when I almost fell flat on my face on the starting line. When I looked up, I had a view of the backs of five young bloods striding into the distance. Fortunately my stumble had created a momentum, which carried into a semblance of a running rhythm, and I finished third. The line judge said: 'More far, you win. Shoes no good. Feet more better.'

Next up were the elders. The dignity of the deputy chairman of the *maneaba* was literally flung to the winds, to the delight of the spectators, when his *lava-lava* unravelled in mid-stride. Clutching at it wildly, and bravely maintaining his stride, he fought back to finish a creditable second in his underpants. A slow bicycle race followed, in which the object was to finish last, with the result that most of the competitors ended up sprawling in the mud. A squall then forced us into the *maneaba*, where the fun continued with hand-stand races. Several youths demonstrated remarkable agility in streaking along the floor upside-down, but a buxom young woman drew the biggest cheer of the day when a considerable part of her anatomy tumbled from her loose-fitting blouse, and she collapsed in an undignified heap.

'It's OK,' Teataake said with a grin. 'She has soft landing.'

At least nobody tried to fly. Stevenson observed this rare event during a festival of singing and dancing which had attracted performers from the neighbouring atoll of Makin. The leader of the visiting team, Karaiti, was a man who took an interest in new ideas and inventions, and he was intrigued when one of the traders told him about experimental flying-machines. Stevenson recorded their conversation and the ensuing events as follows:

'Is that true, George?' he asked. 'It is in the papers,' replied George. 'Well,' said Karaiti, 'if that man can do it with machinery, I can do it without'; and he designed and made a pair of wings, strapped them on his shoulders, went to the end of a pier, launched himself into space, and fell bulkily into the sea. His wives fished him out, for his wings

hindered him in swimming. 'George,' said he, pausing as he went up to change, 'George, you lie.'

I heard a similar tale in Tarawa, which ended badly. Two young men had watched a video film in which shipwrecked mariners were rescued by mermaids; convinced that these wondrous creatures existed, they rowed a canoe far out to sea, jumped overboard, and swam away from it until they were exhausted. The mermaids didn't turn up, and the youths drowned.

In the outskirts of the village there was a police station with a wooden counter and two cells, and a courtroom which had a concrete bench and a table on a dais, but I never saw anybody in either of them. Crime was evidently not a problem. Locksmiths were unheard of, there being few doors on the island let alone locks for them. The priest's house was an exception, but since the keys had been lost years ago, the handle of a spoon attached to a post by the back door served to gain entry. Everybody knew this, of course, but I was never once disturbed by an unwelcome visitor.

One day I was strolling through the village with Teataake when I heard what sounded remarkably like somebody playing a tuba.

'What is that sound?'

'It is a man playing a tuba.'

I looked at Teataake closely, but he did not appear to be joking.

'May I see this man?'

'Of course.'

We passed through a grove of coconut palms and pandanus trees to a clearing in which there were several platform houses. In one of them, sitting cross-legged on soft mats and wearing the ubiquitous *lava-lava*, a young man was coaxing with great concentration a traditional French melody from a battered old tuba. The result was as good as, if not better than, anything I had heard in provincial French towns. I gaped at the sight.

'Are there any more like this man?'

'Yes, many. Come to the *maneaba* in an hour and you will see our band practising for the New Year party.'

It was Bureimoa who explained how the Butaritari Brass Band had been founded at the turn of the century by an enterprising Swiss priest.

'It was Father Bernard, I think his other name was Trotwein. When he came here nearly everybody was Protestant. He wanted to have people in his church, so he started teams for football and cricket, and he sent to Europe for instruments for a band. Now everybody wants to be in the band, but we have few instruments left.'

An hour later, I entered the *maneaba* with Bureimoa and joined a circle of musicians sitting cross-legged on the stone floor. One of them rose, and politely offered me his seating mat. I counted four trumpets, three tubas, a trombone, two drums, a pair of cymbals, and a triangle. Bureimoa said that once there had been violins, saxophones, and an organ, but they had been lost or damaged beyond repair. Presently the bandmaster, a middle-aged man sitting beside me, began tapping a beat on the floor with a wooden baton, and the band launched into a jaunty tune. The scores lying on the floor before the ensemble identified it as 'Beau Sejour'. It was played with remarkable skill and sensitivity, and as the notes of a fine solo rose through the *maneaba*, a ragamuffin in a grass skirt smiled shyly at me and made a little dance entirely for my benefit, with sidelong glances to make sure I was watching.

It was hard to believe that Father Bernard had been the first and last music tutor on Butaritari; but I was assured his lessons had been passed down through several generations. There was only one printed sheet of music, for Albinoni's *Adagio*; the rest was written by hand on scraps of paper, and the passage of time had produced interesting variations on a theme. One melody was identified on different sheets 'Jeanne Dark', and 'Saint Dark; but I think the rendition would have pleased the Maid of Orleans anyway.

During a break in the rehearsal, the bandmaster said to me apologetically: 'We have very little music left.' When I offered to send some on my return to Scotland, an elderly man walked into the centre of the circle and made a brief speech. Bureimoa leaned over and translated: 'He is thanking you on behalf of the band for your presence, and for your generous offer of music from Scotland, and now the band will perform for you a little song composed by one man in our village.' As the band struck up a lively tune, the old man went into a jerky, energetic dance to shrieks of laughter from a crowd of spectators, then bowed to me with an elegant gesture and sat down. I kept my promise, and from time to time I like to think of fishermen on the other side of the world mending their nets to the strains of 'Marie's Wedding' and 'The Skye Boat Song'.

ONE OF THE ENDEARING qualities of I-Kiribati is the manner in which they greet foreigners without hesitation or suspicion. Despite an unhappy history of being hauled off by Peruvian slave-traders in the 1860s, and having their islands almost wiped off the map in World War II, most are prepared to give foreigners the benefit of the doubt. It seemed to me a triumph of optimism over realism. Over lunch one day, Teataake explained their philosophy:

'We are very happy when white men come to our village, but we see they have many different customs. Some of them join us in the *maneaba* and talk with us, and play our games, and it is good between us. But some of them only look at us and stay by themselves, and the people are afraid and say do not go to that man because he is not kind. I think the best with different cultures is to meet and talk and learn the other ways. Is it not so?'

I agreed this was a sensible approach, and he said: 'The people like you too much. They say you are kind, and you are a funny man, and they say the customs of Scotland are surely the same as our customs. Is this true?'

I considered the basic decency of most Scots, and then I wondered how one of these Catholic Pacific islanders would be received by self-proclaimed defenders of the faith in a Protestant pub in Glasgow.

'Well, up to a point,' I replied. 'Mostly yes, but there are good people and foolish people everywhere.'

It sounded a bit lame, but Teataake seemed satisfied. 'Yes,' he said, 'that is a truthful answer.'

I soon learned I was not, as I had supposed, the only foreigner on Butaritari at the time. There was an American schoolteacher serving with the Peace Corps on the island, and Teataake offered to take me to her. She lived on the outskirts of the village, in a two-roomed house of wooden poles which provided minimal shelter and not much privacy. When we arrived, I noticed that Teataake did not accompany me to the door. He said he would wait for me, but I told him it was not necessary, and he left.

The young woman's welcome was not effusive. She admitted me, but I was left standing while we talked, which the islanders would have considered the height of rudeness. She had been there almost a year, but seemed to have made no friends. When the locals asked her why she was so reclusive, she told them she was shy. I supposed it was difficult for a single woman to live here without inciting unwelcome advances, but she was not the kind of person who invited sympathy or companionship. I met her again by chance a few days later, strolling through the village with her mother who had come for a brief visit. There were no smiles or friendly greetings, and the mother was complaining about mosquito bites. I asked if they were going to the New Year celebrations.

'What celebrations?' the teacher said.

'There's a feast in the *maneaba* tonight, and another tomorrow.'

'Nobody told me,' she said. 'So I'm safe.'

I wondered why she had bothered coming here.

The main festivities were scheduled for New Year's Day, and the ceremonies on the preceding evening were given over to prayers, hymns, and collective resolutions for the coming year. The main theme of the speeches (as translated for me by Teataake) was to apologize for 'bad things' committed during the preceding year, and to atone for them in the next. The chairman of the *maneaba* set the tone by advocating temperance, notably concerning strong drink, and by urging parents to spend more time with their children and less time playing cards. Some of the men spoke in parables, and I liked the metaphor of one elder in calling for remembrance of the deceased.

'We are swimming today from one island to another,' he said. 'Some of our people will not reach the new island, so we must look back and remember them with love.'

The proceedings ended with a devotional song, the chorus of which, roughly translated, went: 'This is a good island, we thank God for making this island for us.'

The New Year began with a commotion outside my house. When I went to investigate, I found four young men wrestling in the dust amid a crowd of laughing children. It was an uneven contest, being three to one, and the loser was being bound hand and foot with rope and strips of cotton. His assailants were smiling, and I assumed it was a game. Then I noticed the youth being trussed up was crying; not in pain, but in rage and humiliation. I spotted Bureimoa on the fringe of the crowd, and asked him what was happening.

'This boy is drunk,' he said.

'Is he from the village?'

'He is my son.'

There may have been no commercially produced alcohol on the island, but there was toddy from coconuts. Consumed soon after the nut is opened, it is a sweet and refreshing drink, but left for a few days it ferments into a potent spirit. Bureimoa's son had been imbibing this local hooch throughout the night, and in the morning he had got involved in a fight with a boy from another village.

Having been tied up, he was deposited in Bureimoa's house and left there to contemplate his misdemeanours in full view of curious onlookers.

'This is our way,' Bureimoa said. 'He will stay like this until the drink leaves him.'

The youth's public disgrace was not over. He was subjected to a severe scolding by his mother, a formidable figure whom it would have been best not to antagonize. He made the mistake of arguing with her, and was promptly slapped and punched, quite hard. She then started on him with her bare feet, and got a few solid kicks in before Bureimoa intervened and drew her away, with some difficulty. After a while I felt I was intruding, and left. From my house next door, for the next half-hour I heard angry shouts interspersed with sounds of slapping, and the youth moaning in misery and shame.

The treatment seemed harsh, like the village stocks of medieval England, but Bureimoa said: 'In our society it is the custom. We do not call the police, because they will put the man in jail and the next day the family must pay money. Our way is to tie him up so he will not cause much trouble, and then it is finished.' In this case at least, the remedy was effective. Later that day I spotted Bureimoa's son sidling into the *maneaba*, and sitting alone in a corner. I went to him, and asked him how he was.

'I bad boy,' he admitted. 'Drink no good.'

His friends then gathered around and offered him salvation in the form of a pledge of sobriety, and a place in the village football team, which he gratefully accepted.

The star of the New Year's Day celebrations was a glamorous grandmother who entertained the assembly in the *maneaba* with a high-stepping dance routine, and a rendition of 'Happy New Year to you' in English, to the tune of 'Happy Birthday'. I gathered the song was a tribute to me, and I repaid the complement by teaching her the basic steps of a Scottish country dance. The band was in great form, and what we lacked in skill we made up for in enthusiasm. Before the ceremonial feast, young girls placed floral crowns on the heads of the elders, and I was similarly adorned. We looked like characters from *A Midsummer Night's Dream*: a wood near Athens had become a tropical isle, Oberon had been transformed into Bureimoa, and magic was in the air. I was duly enchanted by a little girl with big eyes, a dusky Peaseblossom who fell asleep with her head in my lap.

Stevenson brought a touch of wizardry to the islands with a magic lantern, an early version of the slide projector. The natives were spellbound by the flickering images, phantoms of a wondrous science conjured by the white man and summoned by strange music produced by his Chinese cook. Shortly before Stevenson's departure from Butaritari, the church was packed for his last picture show:

In the midst, on the royal dais, the lantern luminously smoked; chance rays of light struck out the earnest countenance of our Chinaman grinding the hand-organ; a faint glimmer showed off the rafters and their shadows in the hollow of the roof; the pictures shone and vanished on the screen; and as each appeared, there would run a hush, a whisper, a strong shuddering rustle, and a chorus of small cries among the crowd.

The modern equivalent is less romantic. One night there were no games in the *maneaba*, because an entrepreneur had brought an American video film from Tarawa and was charging a small entrance fee to watch it on a television set. The scene was much the same, with the villagers gazing at the luminescent screen in rapt attention, but the images were of a violent world in which murder and mayhem were the main attractions. Oberon had disappeared, and Rambo was king of the forest. The magic had gone.

I walked into the moonlight and sat by a cross above a small shrine which some priest had erected on the shore. I had come here before to listen to the night songs of the Pacific, the sigh of a silver lagoon, the rustle of palm trees, a mother crooning her child to sleep; but this time the ancient rhythms were broken by the sound of explosions and gunfire and screeching tyres from the video. Teataake told me that until recently there had been only one old projector on the island, and people used to come from outlying districts for a weekly film show in the *maneaba*. Then merchant seamen began bringing home video recorders for their families, and now there were about a dozen of them, and their owners were rarely seen at the *maneaba*. Thus modern technology was tearing the fabric of island life. Soon nobody would want to come and play silly games in the *maneaba* any more.

THE SCENES OF BATTLE on the video films were familiar to the elders. An American who witnessed the capture of Butaritari from the Japanese garrison in 1943 wrote in his journal: 'As the bombardment of the interior continued, mangled coconut trees arose in the air, and their tops came down slowly like shuttlecocks.' At Beach Yellow, the site of the old King's palace where Stevenson had waded ashore little more than fifty years before, American soldiers struggling waist-high through the shallows were cut down by two light machine-guns beside a seaplane ramp. It took them three days to capture the island, during which they lost sixty-four dead and a hundred and fifty wounded. Nobody counted the native dead.

A relic of the battle still lies in a cove by the wharf. It is the skeleton of a disabled Japanese seaplane which had been unable to escape, a Kawanishi Zero-2 Navy patrol bomber. Shortly before the Americans landed, its crew of nine draped themselves over the fuselage and wings, and committed suicide. Parts of the wings are missing, but the rest of the airframe is intact; for half a century it has stood in the shallows, a gaunt memorial to ritual death on an island of laughter. Now it is a playground for children, who clamber around the cockpit and jump from the broken wings.

I had heard stories in Tarawa of other aircraft having been shot down over the lagoon at Butaritari, and I asked Bureimoa if anybody knew where the wrecks were.

'Yes, maybe,' he said. 'You must ask Uatera the diver.'

I had left my scuba equipment at Tarawa, but Uatera had a small compressor for his divers who harvested sea cucumbers. He offered me the use of it, and sought out an old man who claimed to know of at least two sunken planes.

Our expedition set off in an outrigger canoe powered by a small outboard engine, with the generator balanced precariously on a cross-board. The old man stood in the prow, scanning the lagoon, as Uatera held on to his precious air machine and Bauro, one of his divers, steered us out across the lagoon. After a few minutes, our guide motioned us to stop. I peered into the water, but it was murky due to recent storms and there were no reference points on land or sea that I could discern. How the old man knew how to locate this precise spot was a mystery. Bauro drew in a lungful of air, jumped overboard, and disappeared. He had been gone for a full minute before he surfaced, grinning.

'Plane not far, not deep.'

Uatera started the generator, Bauro and I took mouthpieces attached to long yellow hoses, and we plunged into a silent, ghostly world. We finned down through a slow-moving blizzard of sediment and tiny organisms glinting palely in the receding sunlight, until puffs of sand signalled our arrival at the bottom. Everything was an opaque blur, the predominant colour white rather than blue or green. It was as if we were swimming in one of those little glass ornaments filled with water and tiny white flakes, which give an illusion of a snowstorm when you tilt them. The visibility was little more than an arm's length, and I felt the plane before I saw it. It was a Japanese single-seater with its nose buried in the sand, and it was remarkably intact. A few bullet holes in the port wing and fuselage, and the buckled propeller blades, were the only signs of damage. It was an eerie sight, this ghost from the past, conjuring images of its last flight over the lagoon, shuddering with the impact of armour-piercing bullets, trailing smoke, staggering from the sky. Perhaps it floated briefly before sinking to its lonely grave. I wondered whether the pilot had survived. Suddenly I was caught by a strong surge, and grabbed at the wreckage. I found I was holding the pilot's harness, the webbing still strong and firmly attached to the rear of the cockpit. I looked inside, but there were no signs of human remains. The plane was now crewed by sea urchins and trumpet fish. It had soared in the realm of birds, and now it was a fishbowl beneath the sea.

Murky water infested by sharks is not the safest place in the world to be, and I was alarmed when I felt a sharp tug on one of my flippers. It was Bauro, motioning me to a similar wreck a few yards away. It was the same type of aircraft, and I assumed they had been shot down at the same time. I supposed the pilots had been friends. I resisted the temptation to wrest a fragment from the wreck as a souvenir; it would have been like plundering a tomb. In any case I regard it as a privilege to explore Neptune's realm; its treasures should be admired and left undisturbed, not looted for useless ornaments.

*

THE SITE OF STEVENSON'S lodgings, and mine a century later, was delightful. By the shore there was a magnificent *eetai* tree which stood in a clearing of sand and crushed coral, from which an old wooden beam projected over the lagoon. This is where I would place a canvas chair to read and write up my notes. One morning after breakfast, I settled happily beneath the tree with a new-found treasure from the priests' bookshelf. It was a tattered old copy of a P. G. Wodehouse novel, in which the inestimable Jeeves extricates Bertie Wooster from another sticky situation at Steeple Bumpleigh – in fact it was the super-sticky affair involving Nobby Hopwood, Percival Lord Worplesdon, and old Boko Fittleworth.

After a while I was disturbed by a pig grunting on one side of me, and a troop of bright-eyed children playing on the other. I looked up to see two fishermen wading through the shoals with hand-nets, and a lone canoe with a triangular sail shimmering across the lagoon. Two frigate birds were patrolling the shore in perfect formation, and dropping like dive-bombers into the shallows in pursuit of a meal. It occurred to me that the title of Mr Wodehouse's novel was in tune with the scene. It was *Joy in the Morning*.

Stevenson spent six weeks on Butaritari, while the *Equator* roamed around the Gilberts buying copra. Apart from gathering material for *In the South Seas* he did little work, and spent most of his evenings in the convivial company of island traders in the Land we Live in, which he described as a kind of informal club:

It was small, but neatly fitted, and at night (when the lamp was lit) sparkled with glass and glowed with coloured pictures like a theatre at Christmas . . . here songs were sung, tales told, tricks performed, games played.

He left no record of venturing beyond the confines of the main village, so I was heading into unknown territory when Teataake offered to take me to visit his home village of Tabonuea. This is where I found the singing snowmen.

We arrived by motor bike to find the village assembled in the *maneaba*, celebrating the election of a new council. A group of young men was singing songs of their ancestors, accompanied by a guitarist who had been blind and crippled since birth. I noticed that no discrimination or favours were shown to him; he was just one of the boys. After I had taken my place on a fine mat, a young woman sprayed me with deodorant. I was not sure how to take this, but apparently it was a gracious custom rather than a comment on my personal hygiene, as the elders and musicians in turn were given the same treatment. Then some strange things started happening. First the singers were smeared with flour by an elderly woman, who was then struck on the head with a plastic cup by a man who ran away. Next a woman sneaked up behind an unsuspecting man and poured a pot of water over his head, to shrieks of laughter. The local catechist turned to me and explained: 'This is our way of having fun. People who do not know this custom can be unhappy.' As the tempo increased and the assembly disappeared in a flurry of flour, water, and deodorant, I could see his point. By the end of the performance, the singers were like perfumed snowmen. I tried to explain the simile to Teataake, but he had difficulty with the concept of snow.

On my last day in Butaritari, Teataake commandeered his friend's motor bike again for a trip even further afield, to the village of Keuea in the northern part of the atoll. We traversed a long causeway, with the lagoon on one side and tidal shallows on the other. A line of palms on a distant islet, framed by a huge sky, completed a panorama of exquisite symmetry.

Our destination was a hamlet of thatched huts by the edge of the lagoon, where we were invited to take coffee. There were the usual polite questions about who I was, where I came from, and what I was doing here, but by this time Teataake knew all the answers so I let him get on with it while I enjoyed my surroundings. We were sitting in a house with two men; behind us in another dwelling women were plaiting mats, and in another a girl was plucking at a ukulele. The hour of the evening meal was approaching, and the air was suffused with woodsmoke and the aroma of turtle meat and papaya simmering in black iron pots.

I strolled a few steps to the shore, and caught my breath at the view. Warm golden tones of the setting sun radiated over a long stretch of spotless beach, on which brightly painted canoes were drawn up. Three children were punting a raft in the shallows, dark silhouettes of happiness on a sparkling sea. The sky was a magnificent deep blue etched with piles of cumulus tinged with rose and gold. I stood there for a long time, drinking in the aching beauty of it all.

When at last I retraced my steps, Teataake said: 'What do you think of this place?' I took a while to answer. I knew I could never live here; I would become weary of a life which offered little more than fishing and playing games, even in idyllic surroundings. And yet . . .

I replied: 'I think this place looks like paradise.'

'You never said this before.'

'No, Teataake, and I doubt if I will say it again for a long time.'

A brief translation followed, and our hosts beamed with pleasure. As we were leaving, one of the men looked at me. I could see he wished to say something, so I waited. I-Kiribati have a peculiar way of looking at a foreigner, quietly drawing attention to the fact they are about to address him. To my surprise, he spoke with grave courtesy in halting English.

'When you come back this place?'

'I do not know, but I would like very much to come back one day.'

'When you come back this place, you stay this house. This my house, same you.'

On the long ride home through the gathering darkness, the

moon and early stars flitting across the tops of palm trees, I was silent.

'You are sad,' Teataake said.

'Yes, in a way. But I am happy too. It is difficult to explain. Sometimes there is sadness in great beauty.'

'You are a writer. Maybe you think too much.'

'You are a wise man, Teataake.'

The next morning, I was awakened by girls singing as they swept fallen leaves from around my house. When Teataake and Bureimoa came to bid me farewell, I was reminded of a comment by Stevenson on his sojourn among the fishermen of Hawaii. He wrote that he had drunk 'that warm, light *vin du pays* of human affection'. That remains my abiding impression of Butaritari, the island of laughter.

SEVENTEEN

It was OK in the old days, there were all sorts of crazy characters around

OLD KING TEM BINOKA was not a Merry Old Soul. He was a tyrant who ruled a triple-island kingdom in the Gilberts with scant regard for the colonial powers and even less for native subjects deemed to have transgressed his laws. Legends ascribe to him the quaint customs of playing bowls with human skulls, and of launching his regal canoe on a ramp of living bodies. An indeterminate number of wives did not impinge on his *droit de seigneur* to deflower the virgins of his realm, with the added refinement of sleeping on pillows of their pubic hair. He also liked to wear women's clothes.

The *Equator* was at sea, bound for the islands of Nonouti and Tabiteuea, when a fair wind determined a change of course for Abemama, the principal territory and stronghold of this fearsome despot. After mooring in the lagoon, the Stevensons awaited with interest their inspection by the royal personage who sped towards them in a man-of-war's gig. The corpulent figure which heaved its massive bulk aboard left a lasting impression on Stevenson:

We could never see him and not be struck with his extraordinary natural means for the theatre: a beaked profile like Dante's in the mask, a mane of long black hair, the eye brilliant, imperious, and enquiring: for certain parts, and to one who could have used it, the face was a fortune.

Tem Binoka's concept of fashionable attire was bizarre: he favoured naval uniforms, costumes of his own design featuring tailed jackets of green velvet and red silk, and women's dresses.

Stevenson thought the well-cut jackets suited him admirably, but:

In the woman's frock he looks ominous and weird beyond belief. I see him now come pacing towards me in the cruel sun, solitary, a figure out of Hoffmann.

It required a further visit of inspection the next day before Tem Binoka informed Stevenson he would be accorded the rare privilege of staying on Abemama while the *Equator* went about its business in the neighbouring islands. 'I look your eye. You good man. You no lie,' said the King. Stevenson considered this a doubtful compliment to a writer of romance, but accepted the invitation to choose a site on which the King would have lodgings built for them. He and his family stayed there for two months, in arguably the most curious setting of their travels.

I arrived on Abemama with my right hand holding on to the aircraft seat in front of me, and my left clutching an iron stove behind me. I was doing this to prevent the stove from hurtling on to an unsuspecting village through a cargo door which had flown open during our descent. When I mentioned the incident to the Air Tungaru pilot on landing, he seemed unconcerned. 'Thank you,' he said.

I had been looking forward to this visit, because the island boasted an establishment called the Robert Louis Stevenson Hotel. An American guidebook published the year before sketched an idyllic picture of thatched cottages by a lagoon, with portraits of Stevenson in the communal lounge. It was, the book said, the kind of hotel where the author might have stayed: 'If you imagine living a very simple Robinson Crusoe life but in a comfortable and very relaxing setting, you're at the RLS Hotel.' It sounded great. Unfortunately it was closed. In fact it was in an advanced state of decay, there had been no 'sing-alongs under the stars' for months, and its wooden huts were disintegrating into the bush from whence they came.

The alternative was a nearby hotel named after another distinguished British visitor of the nineteenth century, to which a Protestant pastor offered me a lift from the airfield in his truck. We had to make a detour, as the main coral road was blocked by a palm tree which had been uprooted by a gale-force wind the previous evening, and for several miles we scrunched along paths inundated with water and littered with debris from the storm.

The Captain Davis Hotel was a simple affair of two-roomed huts made from the spines of coconut trees, with a communal lounge and dining-room, in a clearing between the main road and the lagoon. On my arrival, I was invited to sign the visitors' book, a dog-eared school exercise jotter. The first entry was by the Chief Justice, who had come to adjudicate land and other civil disputes a year before. His lordship approved of the hospitality shown by friendly and efficient staff, but expressed reservations about the primitive shower and toilet facilities. A police officer who had come subsequently on official business wrote: 'No comment.'

The only other guests during my stay were two young women from the Finance and Home Affairs planning departments, Tahirih and Ruta, who had come to check on development projects. They were bright, jolly girls who shared a room in the main building, and I was glad of their company in the evenings when we would get together for dinner and they would tell me stories of Tem Binoka.

The hotel was situated in Kariatebike, the main village and government station, a scattering of brick buildings and wooden huts on either side of the road. Near by a low causeway spanned a channel through which the lagoon flowed to and from the sea in strong tidal currents. The scene was similar to Butaritari, but the atmosphere was different. There was none of the vitality, and little of the gaiety of Teataake's parish; the people here were more reserved, and their village had a subdued air, as if the spirit of Tem Binoka still walked the land. I had much the same experience as Stevenson:

We were rarely called into a house: no welcome, no friendship, was offered us.

There was only one white man resident on the island when Stevenson arrived. He was a fellow Scot: George McGhee Murdoch, the son of a painter and glazier from Greenock, who worked as a kind of factor for Tem Binoka; but Stevenson formed no high opinion of him. He observed that McGhee was a silent recluse, 'hearkening and watching his conduct like a mouse in a cat's ear'. There were now three whites on the island, living with native wives in varying degrees of isolation and eccentricity: a retired British colonial officer, an Irish adventurer who was proprietor of the defunct RLS Hotel, and a former NASA scientist who had worked on the early Apollo missions. The first two regarded each other with cordial distaste, and the third was drinking himself quietly into oblivion on vodka and beer.

I found Eric Bailey in the dishevelled domesticity of a pleasant wooden bungalow in the bush, surrounded by books and children and members of his wife's family who did odd jobs around the place. I had come across ex-colonial officers in outposts of the old British Empire before, and he was typical of the breed. After serving in the Palestine police and then for twenty years as an administration officer in Nyasaland, he had returned to England and taken up potting; unable to settle, he had resumed colonial duties in the Gilbert and Ellice Islands. On retirement he had remained in the islands, where he considered life to be cheaper, simpler, and altogether more agreeable than in England.

A tall, distinguished figure with a shock of white hair and a cultured, gravelly voice, he received me wearing a flowered *lava-lava* and a thick bandage over a leg ulcer: a cultivated English-man who had served and then forsaken his country, ending his days contentedly in the tropics with a half-caste family, a radio tuned to the BBC World Service, and copies of the *Guardian Weekly*.

He seemed to have no regrets about settling on a speck of coral in the middle of nowhere: 'The complications of living in England today are quite appalling. So many bits of paper. But land is fairly easy to buy here, and I cleared the bush and built this house in two years without having to submit a single sketch for it. It's a very free and untrammelled life here, you know. There's much to be said for it.'

Eric agreed that social activities on Abemama were limited, and he regretted that the traditional dancing admired by Stevenson was dying out. He advised me not to expect much from Tem Binoka's successor as Paramount Chief. 'He's a pleasant enough chap, but he's usually drunk,' Eric said.

It may be useful to explain here that kings were top of the native pecking order in the Pacific islands, who held sway over fractious tribal societies as long as astute alliances and force of arms maintained their authority. As often as not, they were drawn from the ranks of paramount chiefs, who in turn lorded it over a hierarchy of chiefs and local sub-chiefs. The Samoans added the refinement of high-talking chiefs – orators who perform ceremonial duties, engage in ritual debates and liaise with impressive dignity in affairs between their village chiefs and outside entities.

In this respect, Paul Bauro had inherited the royal and chiefly titles of his ancestor, Tem Binoka, but he was an unpopular man with little honour in his own fiefdom.

My introduction to the Chief was to be affected by his boon companion Brian Ormes, the Irishman who presided over the ruins of the RLS Hotel. I had heard a lot about Ormes from expatriates in Tarawa, and most of it was bad. He was a rough character, he despised the natives, he was forever getting into furious rows with the government, he was lucky not to have been deported years ago, and so on. I looked forward to an interesting encounter.

We met by chance the day after I arrived. I had gone for a stroll to the ocean side of the island, a wild place with a desolate kind of beauty. It was low tide, and I walked with difficulty across the exposed reef shelf to where a native was fishing with a rod and line, a lone figure etched against the sky and huge waves crashing on to the reef wall around him. Neither he, nor two women I saw fishing with nets in the channel, paid me any heed.

On walking back, I saw a white man who could only be Ormes crossing the causeway towards me: a gaunt figure in green corduroy trousers and open sandals, with a striped jersey tied around his waist exposing a thin torso covered with tattoos. On closer inspection, his chest was adorned with a large sailing ship, his arms with an assortment of daggers and snakes, and the fingers of his right hand with letters which spelled a woman's name. He had only two teeth that I could see, yellowish stumps in his lower jaw. Close-cropped sandy hair, a drooping moustache of the same colour, and remarkably pale blue eyes completed the image of an Irish rover down on his luck. Stevenson encountered such characters in his Pacific travels; every island had its assortment of adventurers and villains who were living 'on the beach', i.e. washed up on a foreign shore with little more than the clothes they stood in and colourful tales of past exploits. In Ormes I was pleased to find a descendant of this romantic tribe. I also noticed with interest that, in his lean frame and general aspect, he bore a passing resemblance to Stevenson.

He said he had been born in Dublin in 1932. His grandfather, who contributed Irish obituaries to *The Times*, had a library which included volumes bound in red leather of travels to Christmas and Easter islands. Ormes read them, and went to sea on a merchant ship at the age of thirteen. After serving in Malaya with the Royal Fleet Auxiliary, he went to Canada, where he joined the Army and fought in Korea. Then he drifted around for a while, 'got off here and there', and finally settled in the Gilberts in the early fifties.

'It started with a fight over a cold beer,' he said. I had asked him how he had come to own the hotel. 'There was a local guy who owned a guest house here in the late seventies. One day he refused to sell me a beer. We got into an argument and he pulled a shooter on me. So I took it off him, pulled his pants down, and shoved it up his ass.' Ormes secured a twenty-five-year lease on the site from the local council, and returned to inform the guest house owner he was trespassing. 'I told him to piss off, and when I sobered up I decided to build this place.' The RLS connection was tenuous: 'No particular reason, it just seemed a romantic name.'

In those days there were regular flights to Tarawa from Honolulu, and for a few years the hotel did reasonably well. Then the flights stopped, the supply of tourists dried up, and Ormes and his extended family (eight children from two local women) had been living hand-to-mouth ever since. But he had elaborate schemes for the future. He claimed that European Community experts had drawn up plans for restoring the hotel, and he intended to start rebuilding after the rainy season. He envisaged formal dinners by candlelight in the bar-restaurant, with lectures and discussions on the life and times of Stevenson and Tem Binoka.

We were sitting on canvas chairs in a lean-to shed amid the ramshackle remnants of the hotel, wreathed in fumes from mosquito coils. In the undergrowth, chickens were poking around the belly gun pod of a World War II American B-28 bomber and the central wing section of a Corsair F4U. A sudden squall hammered on the tin roof, and gusts of wind sweeping rain into our precarious shelter brought the interview to an end.

I returned the next day to have a look around the hotel. The gloomy interior of the bar and restaurant area was dominated by a large oil painting of Tem Binoka, dressed in one of his naval uniforms and looking remarkably like the Libyan leader, Moammar Gaddafi. The beaked profile and imperious eyes noted by Stevenson were there, but the mane of long black hair had been cropped into tight curls; the heavy-jowled face with its wide mouth looked at once sensual and cruel; the sight of him striding around in a woman's frock with a brace of pistols concealed in its folds must have been awesome.

To one side of the portrait was his royal standard painted on a woven mat, with its shark emblem (he traced his ancestry to a shark and a heroic woman); to the other hung the broken jaws of a large tiger shark. The walls were covered with faded photographs: here was the *Casco*, her sails billowing in a stiff breeze, there was Captain Davis in white tropical uniform and pith helmet proclaiming the Gilberts a British Protectorate at a flag-raising ceremony in Abemama in June 1892. Another showed an execution scene: ranks of sailors standing at attention as one of their comrades raised his rifle at a native standing listlessly by a palm tree. In another, the stern pride of a native warrior in his battle regalia: a breastplate of shark hide, shoulder pads and helmet of coconut fibre, and holding a long stave spiked with sharks' teeth. He looked like a dusky *samurai*. The boy King Paul Simon, a nephew of Tem Binoka, who eventually succeeded him, sat in a pillbox hat and bare feet scowling at the camera, surrounded by a retinue of fourteen men with frizzy hair.

We installed ourselves on the veranda, amid a jumble of old bottles, fishing tackle, and American and Japanese military helmets, and Ormes discoursed on the decline and fall of Kiribati since independence.

'It was OK in the old days. There were all sorts of crazy characters around, and you never knew what was going to happen next. Now it's kinda dead. The whites are wimps and the *kanakas* are drunks. There's no adventure, no danger, it's no fun any more.'

The figure slouched on an old sofa beside me was a complex character. His conversation was at once perceptive, opinionated, and profane. He was a romantic and a racist, an adventurer from the past ill at ease in the present. Once he said: 'The Gilberts are a state of mind rather than a country. There is no sense of national identity here, just individual islands.' In the same breath, he added: 'A constitution is fine for Brits, but it's no use for Stone Age fucking niggers.'

Less than a mile from the village, in a sheltered grove of pandanus, was the site of the settlement which Tem Binoka's subjects built for the Stevensons. Its main elements were two houses and two *maneabas*, which Fanny likened to basket-work bird cages on stilts, transported from the village by dozens of natives. Stevenson thought at first they were airborne:

It was singular to spy, far off through the cocoa stems, the silent oncoming of the maniap', at first (it seemed) swimming spontaneously in the air – but on a nearer view betraying under the eaves many score of moving naked legs.

Lloyd Osbourne was alarmed to observe Tem Binoka supervising the project by firing a Winchester in the direction of anyone he deemed to be slacking:

It was extremely disturbing at first to see that loaded rifle pointed hither and thither, and occasionally going off with a terrific report; but as nobody was ever hurt, and as the work certainly continued with feverish briskness, we were soon won over to think it quite a help.

They dubbed their settlement Equator Town, after their ship, and settled to a routine of writing, reading Gibbon and Carlyle, taking photographs, and playing music and cards. Stevenson and his stepson began writing *The Wrecker*, one of several novels on which they collaborated with mixed results.

Night was the time to see our city, Stevenson wrote, *after the moon was up, after the lamps were lighted, and so long as the fire sparkled in the cook-house . . . over all, there fell in the season an extraordinary splendour of mellow moonshine. The sand sparkled as with the dust of diamonds; the stars had vanished. At intervals, a dusky night-bird, slow and low flying, passed in the colonnade of the tree stems and uttered a hoarse croaking cry.*

Equator Town was dismantled the day the Stevensons left, and the site is now marked by a concrete plinth erected by a district commissioner after World War II. I was taken there by Ormes and his pal Paul Bauro, the last 'king' of Abemama in a line of succession from Tem Binoka's brother. I did not like him, and I was told he was not popular with his relatives and neighbours either. In theory, he retained his ceremonial title as custodian of the *Uea* (royal lands) which had been given in trust for the benefit of the people; in practice, he treated them as a private estate, leasing portions for copra production. Shortly after selling about a hundred acres of supposed trust land, his house burned down in mysterious circumstances. One of the few possessions he managed to salvage was a framed blessing from Pope John Paul II which assured him of 'continued divine protection'. Maybe his guardian angels had been off-duty that day.

Bauro and his wife were living temporarily in reduced circumstances in two tin shacks about the size of hen houses, but when we met he looked as if he had just come from a polo club. Dressed smartly in a light blue sports shirt and matching slacks, he was a smooth, well-groomed figure with receding dark hair slicked back over a light complexion. Ormes was delivering one of his racist diatribes: 'Gilbertese, I don't like the fucking monkeys. I've been here forty years and I never invited a *kanaka* into my house.' When I pointed out he was married to one, he said: 'Look at the alternatives.' Bauro, who apparently didn't count as a native, agreed: 'You know, when you mix with these Gilbertese people, they come and wake you in the middle of the night, so I don't mix with them.'

With this odd couple leading the way, I trekked through dense undergrowth to Equator Town. There was not much to see: a clearing in the woods, the small concrete memorial, and a depression in the earth which had been a fresh-water pool in which the Stevensons had bathed and washed their clothes. Now it was just a dirty puddle, and the area all around was strewn with decaying leaves and coconuts. Ormes considered it a disgrace: 'What this place needs is a benevolent dictator like Paul. The only thing these *kanakas* understand is fear.' Bauro graciously concurred.

Pending such a regime, the two entrepreneurs have grand schemes for clearing the place, declaring it a historical site, and staging *al fresco* black-tie dinners and displays of traditional dancing. Ormes thought it would be a good idea to transport clients from the airfield in stretch limousines, which he reckoned he could buy cheaply in Japan. We left their dreams in the forest and went to have a look at Tem Binoka's tomb.

Despite his fearsome reputation, Tem Binoka impressed Stevenson as the benevolent dictator his less worthy successor aspired to be:

He does not aim at popularity; but drives and braves his subjects, with a simplicity of domination which it is impossible not to admire, hard not to sympathize with . . . orderly, sober, and innocent, life flows in the isle from day to day as in a model plantation under a model planter. It is impossible to doubt the beneficence of that stern rule.

Not everybody shared this view. Not long before, the King had killed one of his wives for some offence and exhibited her putrefying body in an open box as a warning to others. Stevenson was aware of the incident, but he never saw Tem Binoka in an angry mood, and came to regard him as a gentleman and a scholar. His manners in the Stevensons' company were impeccable, he rarely drank much, and he copied their behaviour where he perceived it to differ from his own.

The King enjoyed the company of his guests, mutual respect

and affection grew between them, and when the *Equator* returned to take the Stevensons to Samoa he became melancholy. One evening they organized a fireworks display, but it was not a success:

It was a heavy business; the sense of separation was in all our minds, and the talk languished. The King was specially affected, sat disconsolate on his mat, and often sighed. Of a sudden one of the wives stepped forth from a cluster, came and kissed him in silence, and silently went again. It was just such a caress as we might give to a disconsolate child, and the King received it with a child's simplicity.

Presently Stevenson and Fanny retired, but Tem Binoka detained Lloyd Osbourne, patting the mat beside him, saying he wanted to talk.

'*I very sorry you go,*' he said at last. '*Miss Stlevens he good man, woman he good man, boy he good man; all good man. Woman he smart all the same man. My woman* (glancing towards his wives) *he good woman, no very smart. I think Miss Stlevens he big chief all the same cap'n man-o'-wa'. I think Miss Stlevens he rich man all the same me. All go schoona. I very sorry . . . you no see King cry before. King all the same man: feel bad, he cry. I very sorry.*'

Tem Binoka's sorrow was short-lived. He died two years later, at the age of forty-seven, without fathering children. Bauro said the family believed he died of syphilis. He was buried in an iron box in a shallow grave near Equator Town with a pistol, a sword, and five pillows of pubic hair.

The unmarked concrete tomb in an open area of sparse grass between the coral road and the lagoon is now in a sorry state. About a year before somebody had tried to break into it, either in the belief it contained treasure, or to remove the King's remains for magic spells. The top of the tomb was reduced to rubble, and chunks of it lie to one side. At my request, Bauro had brought along the portrait of his ancestor, and he posed with it for photographs; the beaked profile, the image of Dante in the mask, rose again and gazed imperiously over his former domain, but it was an illusion: Tem Binoka's power was long gone.

That evening I told the girls at the hotel about my visit to the tomb. They told me it was regarded as a sacred place with spiritual powers, and legend had it that any bird which flew over the grave would fall dead. People still believed in magic, and grave-robbing for charms was not uncommon. A few months before, a former manager of the publications and broadcasting authority had literally lost his head after drinking himself to death, when his skull was taken from his grave for *wauwi*, or bad magic for killing people. Love potions were used to reunite divorced couples, and those gifted with *te kaiwa* – the magic of seeing – were consulted to locate missing or stolen property. This last brand of magic was considered particularly useful during World War II, as the seers could supposedly predict where bombs would fall.

In fact, not many bombs fell on Abemama. The only action took place on the 21st of November, 1943, when sixty-eight Marines and ten sappers of the US 5th Reconnaissance Company landed from a submarine to scout for an assault force due five days later. When they learned from the natives that the Japanese garrison comprised only twenty-five men, the US commander strung a few naval mattresses from palm trees – a coded signal for gunfire from the submarine – and his Marines advanced. One of them was killed, so they withdrew and waited. Four days later, a native reported that the bombardment had done the trick; half of the Japanese had been killed or wounded, and the survivors had committed suicide.

ABEMAMA MEANS 'land of moonlight'. The startling clarity of the moon which bathes the atoll in ghostly luminescence provides a perfect backdrop for tales of the supernatural, and after dinner one evening Ormes informed me the RLS Hotel was haunted. We were sitting by the light of a kerosene lamp, a faint breeze was rustling the palm trees around us, and the harsh cries of unseen night birds mingled with the distant boom of the surf. I had learned to be sceptical of much that Ormes told me, but he told good ghost stories and the setting was perfect.

The first occult visitor had announced his presence ten years before by extinguishing lamps in three bedrooms used by Ormes and his family. There had been no wind, and the next morning Ormes checked the fuel and wicks. There seemed nothing wrong with them, but every night for a week they continued to flutter and die. 'I wasn't thinking about ghosts, I was just pissed off,' Ormes recalled. The main door to the building was locked and bolted, but one night one of his daughters cried out there was a man in her room. He grabbed a pair of knuckledusters (as one does) and went to investigate, but there was nobody there. The next night, Ormes saw something which made his hair stand on end.

He had gone outside to answer a call of nature, and as he approached the toilet shed the beam of his torch dimmed.

'I was sitting on the throne when I felt sort of funny, as if there was somebody near me,' Ormes said. 'I shone the torch out the door towards some chairs, and there was George' – Paul Baurio's father – 'clear as day in a white T-shirt, long khaki pants, and the plastic sandals he always wore.'

George and Ormes had been friends, but his visit was unexpected. He had been dead for six months.

'He was turned slightly away from me, with his legs crossed. He started to turn towards me and I was scared to see his face, I don't know why. I switched off the torch and shut the bog door, and I sat there for a few seconds. I thought, This is crazy, so I put on the torch and opened the door, but he was gone. I wasn't souped up, and even when I'm pissed I don't go around seeing things.'

A few days later, Ormes was sitting in the bar writing a letter when an old pendulum clock, which had not worked for years, began swinging and chiming furiously. His daughters, who had been sweeping outside, stopped and stared in astonishment.

'I said, "George, if that's you, you're pissing me off," and then a bottle opener came off the bar like a fucking bullet. I ducked, and it hit a suitcase. I ran behind the bar, but there was nobody there. By then I'd had enough, and I ran for it.'

He finally informed Paul, who summoned a Jesuit priest to perform an exorcism, and George had not been seen since.

Another of Paul's ancestors materialized five years later. An Australian who was managing the hotel saw a curious figure on the beach – a man wearing a white suit and a pith helmet, waving a black cane with a gold top. As he stared, the figure vanished. He asked some boys near him who the man was, but they said they had seen nobody. Later that morning Bill, the manager, was taking a shower when there was a knock at the door, and through gaps in the wall he saw the man in the white suit. When he opened the door, the man had disappeared. Paul was consulted, and he produced a photograph which the manager identified as the mysterious visitor. It had been Paul Simon, the nephew of Tem Binoka who had ruled Abemama at the turn of the century. 'Bill was anything but a superstitious bloke,' Ormes said, 'but he was a bit shook up that day.'

No other visitors from the spirit world had been observed, although an old guitar had an unpleasant habit of leaping off tables on the stroke of midnight and strumming harshly. I had been told that some natives still practised magic, and Ormes said he had witnessed bizarre rites in which a corpse had been placed upright in a chair with a bottle of beer in his hand. 'There's still some pretty weird voodoo stuff going on here, but nothing to make you really afraid, no clanking chains or vampires,' he said.

I fondly imagined that if the ghost of RLS turned up on my travels, he would announce his presence with discordant notes of a flageolet. This small wind instrument was Stevenson's constant companion, a source of endless amusement to himself and unmitigated torment to those around him. For hours at a time he would pore over sheets of classical music, and without fail crucify the compositions. Lloyd Osbourne recalled: 'There is an unconscious pathos in Stevenson's fondness for his flageolet. He played it so badly, so haltingly, and he was always poking fun at himself in regard to it . . . it was amazing the amount of pleasure he got out of the effort. The doleful, whining little instrument was one of his most precious relaxations. He played it persistently.'

The most familiar sound at their home in Samoa, he added, was 'that strange wailing and squeaking that floated down from his study . . .'

In my desire to be in tune with Stevenson, so to speak, I had brought along a recorder and the scores of a few old Scottish songs. Thus on moonlit beaches where RLS had murdered Bach and Mozart, I inflicted similar punishment on 'Ae Fond Kiss' and 'The Flowers of the Forest'. One evening I was tootling away in my room when my efforts were drowned out by an electronic synthesizer being played equally badly in the main building. At first the singing that accompanied the jarring music was pleasant, but as the evening progressed it degenerated into drunken screeching and yelling. The chords became numbingly repetitive, clashing with the throbbing of an oil-fired generator; swarms of mosquitoes had penetrated the netting around my bed, and the mattress was heaving with fleas. Sweating, bleeding from insect bites, and with a splitting headache, I fell asleep to dream I was back in the Marquesas.

On Butaritari, Stevenson had been thrilled by a performance of native dancing and singing which he said combined elements of opera and ballet.

The hula, as it may be viewed by the speedy globe-trotter in Honolulu, is surely the most dull of man's inventions . . . but the

Gilbert Island dance leads on the mind; it thrills, rouses, subjugates; it has the essence of all art.

I had been disappointed to miss a Christmas dancing show on Butaritari, but on my last night in the outer islands Tahirih and Ruta invited me to join them for a performance being given in their honour by villagers who lived near the airport. On arriving at the hamlet, we were allotted sleeping mats in a small *maneaba*, dinner was served in wooden bowls, then the dancers donned their costumes.

Stevenson was right. It was like an exotic opera, in which tales and legends dating from the era of Tem Binoka were acted out with gestures, songs and concerted clapping. An old man began the singing, and solo dancers moved back and forward with tiny steps, arms outstretched and making fluttering movements with their hands relating stories of birds and flowers and warriors from Samoa. The star performers were young men with superb physiques dressed in soft dancing mats, garlands of red and green flowers, and crowns of wild grass and coloured paper; in the dim light of a gas lamp, with beads of sweat trickling around eyes glazed with concentration, they looked like dusky Christs with crowns of thorns. Girls wearing skirts of smoked coconut leaves weaved among them, acting out an elaborate pantomime. We were treated to *tekamei* (standing dances) and *tebino* (sitting dances), all of them performed with a subtlety and precision which, as Stevenson observed, made the *hula* look second rate.

When the performance was over, to my despair the electric organ was produced by the girls from the hotel and one of their friends began shrieking a song in my ear which went through me like a knife. From the sublime to the vulgar; in the space of a moment, the spell woven by an ancient Gilbertese art form was broken and I had to endure the tuneless screeching of modern pop songs until the woman who owned the instrument was prevailed upon to pack it up and go home.

I spent my last night on Abemama sleeping beneath a mosquito net on the stone floor of the *maneaba*, surrounded by natives chatting quietly until the last lamp had died. Beyond our little circle of light, the bush was pitch dark but I could see moonlight shimmering on the lagoon. I read for a while by the light of a candle, lulled by wind sighing in the palms. It was at once the most primitive and the most agreeable night's lodgings in all my travels.

HAVING SURVIVED a succession of storms, rotten masts, and close encounters with submerged reefs in their voyages, the Stevensons had another narrow escape on the final leg of their passage to Samoa. The *Equator* had gone about her business in the islands while the Stevensons were on Abemama, but after a month had passed with no sign of her they had almost given her up as lost. When the *H. L. Tiernan* came in to trade, they considered booking passage on her, but the price was exorbitant, and Fanny was concerned about Captain Reid's dismay should he return and find them gone. Stevenson agreed, and the *H. L. Tiernan* sailed without them. Shortly after her departure the ship, lying becalmed with all hands asleep, was struck by a squall and turned turtle. Sixteen lives were lost, and the survivors almost died of hunger and thirst before reaching land in her whale boat. The *Equator*, when she eventually turned up, fared only marginally better. Fanny recalled: 'A succession of storms followed us to Samoa, where we arrived in the early part of December, having lost our fore-topmast and staysail in a squall that nearly sent us to the bottom. Had the *Equator* not carried a cargo of some fifty tons of copra, which served to steady her, nothing could have saved us.'

My passage to Samoa was less eventful, although the timing was equally unpredictable. The Air Tungaru flight which was to take me back to Tarawa was delayed by a few hours, but this was no hardship; I simply lay in the lagoon reading a book until the plane touched down on the grass runway beside me. On my return to the capital, however, I found there were no ships going anywhere in the foreseeable future. Thus I found myself again waiting for an Air Nauru flight, this time to Fiji with a connection the following day to Samoa.

The woman who confirmed my ticket at the 'Headquater Office' of Air Tungaru, a shabby bungalow at the end of a dirt track, said the check-in time was 7 a.m.

'But the flight doesn't leave until ten fifty,' I said.

'No, it leaves at nine.'

'But the ticket says ten fifty.'

'Yes, that is a mistake.'

'Well, if you were betting on it, what time do *you* think it will leave?'

She just smiled.

In the event, there was no need to hurry. The plane was two hours late in arriving, and was delayed for a further two hours while an engineer carried out emergency repairs to the auxiliary power unit. I supposed this was less vital to a modern aircraft than a fore-topmast to a nineteenth-century schooner, but I wondered. Happily the main engines seemed to be in better shape, and the next day I arrived on an island where Stevenson lived and died in a place he called 'beautiful beyond dreams'.

EIGHTEEN

You can't conceive what a relief this is;
it seems a new world

WHEN THE *EQUATOR* limped into Apia harbour in Samoa
on the 7th of December, 1889, an American trader who boarded
her observed a man of singular appearance. He looked about
thirty, although he was nine years older, with a sallow complexion, a scraggy moustache, and hair hanging down around his
neck 'after the fashion of artists'. He was barefoot, and wearing
a thin calico shirt, light flannel trousers, and a small yachting
cap. The trader, Harry J. Moors, recalled: 'He was not a
handsome man, and yet there was something irresistibly attractive about him. The genius that was in him seemed to shine out
of his face. I was struck at once with his keen, enquiring eyes.
Brown in colour, they were strangely bright, and seemed to
penetrate you like the eyes of a mesmerist . . . I needed not to
be told he was in indifferent health, for it was stamped on his
face. He appeared to be intensely nervous, highly strung, easily
excited. When I first brought him ashore he was looking
somewhat weak, but hardly had he got into the street when he
began to walk up and down in a most lively, not to say eccentric,
manner. He could not stand still.'

RLS had arrived at his final destination.

The immigration officer who welcomed me at Faleolo Airport
on the main island of Upolu was the first in my travels who did
not demand to see an onward ticket. I had gone to some trouble
and expense in Fiji to acquire one, but I need not have bothered.
On learning my nationality, he was more interested in discussing
the strengths and weaknesses of a Scottish rugby team due to
visit Western Samoa in a few months' time. We had a pleasant

chat about various players likely to be in the opposing teams, before he stamped my passport with a one-month visa and assured me I should have no difficulty in extending it if I wished to stay to watch the game. I thought: I like it here.

It was not immediately apparent on leaving the airport which side of the road people drive on in Samoa. At first the road was narrow, and my taxi driver stayed firmly in the middle; when it widened he seemed to prefer the left, until an oncoming vehicle forced him to swerve to the right; then he reverted to left of centre. Fortunately it was late at night and there was little traffic, otherwise I might have come closer to the spirit of Stevenson than intended. As we hurtled along the winding coastal road, my first view of Samoa was a succession of brightly lit thatch houses without walls clustered around village greens, as in Butaritari, like little theatres enacting silent dramas. The outskirts of Apia had a pleasingly ramshackle aspect, with old wooden buildings evoking the ambience of the South Seas in the colonial era. It was easy to imagine Stevenson riding home through the bush on his favourite Samoan-bred pony, Jack.

Apia's two main hotels are named after famous residents. Aggie Grey's, at the eastern end of the bay, was founded by the half-caste daughter of a Lincolnshire chemist who had arrived in Samoa in the same year as Stevenson. Aggie made her fame and fortune selling hamburgers to American servicemen during World War II, and developed her snack bar into one of the best-known hostelries in the Pacific. After her death in 1988 it was extensively rebuilt, and its old-fashioned charm was sacrificed for luxurious accommodation for the package-tour crowd. My guidebook suggested the hotel at the other end of the bay was quieter and more popular with the locals (which meant it was peaceful during the day and raucous at night) but it was its name that decided the matter. It was called the Tusitala Hotel. It did not have much old-fashioned charm either, but I was spared Aggie's elaborate entertainments for busloads of tourists, and it was fun in the evenings when a largely Samoan crowd would gather to dance to live music in a huge barnlike structure by the lagoon.

There was the odd drunken brawl, of course, but I found this more entertaining than the rarefied atmosphere at Aggie's. One night I paid a hefty entrance charge to watch a 'traditional' dance-show at Aggie's, and it was awful – a loud, glitzy production with fire-dancers leap-frogging into the swimming pool to a crescendo of drums in a grotesque parody of Pacific island culture that owed more to Hollywood than Polynesia. Aggie's daughter-in-law, a woman of a certain age with rouged cheeks who looked about as Samoan as Margaret Thatcher, was forever swanning around among the dancers, playing the *grande dame* in a Chinese dress (perhaps her geography was uncertain) with diamonds sparkling on her fingers. It was pathetic, but the American tourists loved it.

On returning to the Tusitala Hotel, I found a dance troupe from the neighbouring island of Savai'i giving a performance to raise funds for their village. Entrance was free, but patrons could express their appreciation by leaving a donation in a cardboard box. From the ridiculous to the sublime; here was the essence of Polynesia which enchanted the early navigators, an intricate and lyrical mime of island life acted out by children and elders clapping, swaying, and dancing to the rhythm of a single guitar and a boy drumming on a log with sticks. Girls in green and white shift dresses and boys in matching *lava-lavas* performed subtle dance routines, creating images of birds and lovers, as children around them sang of legends and old men and fat women in the rear ranks clapped and swayed in unison. The sight and sound of them made the feet tap, the eyes shine, and the heart soften. There was a riotously funny mime by young men in Mother Hubbard dresses and flowery hats, mocking the prudish piety of the early missionaries; then ten of their muscular elder brothers came out brandishing machetes and performed a kind of midair sword dance, the long blades flashing and clashing as the dancers leaped and whirled to the beating of the log-drum. The mainly Samoan audience roared its approval, and coins and notes poured into the cardboard box. The Americans at Aggie's, I thought, had been cheated.

APIA IS A COLOURFUL little town, bustling with good-natured crowds in a setting which evokes its history of traders and adventurers and squabbling colonial powers. The predominant building materials are still wood and iron, which with their tendency to rot and rust in the tropics give the place an agreeably run-down look. Its costume of once elegant colonial structures has become threadbare; in places it is coming apart at the seams, and haphazard attempts to patch it up make it all the more charming. The cornerstone of this architectural jumble is a rambling two-storey structure housing the Prime Minister's offices and the Supreme Court, which stands at the corner of Beach Road and Leifi'ifi Street. It is a wonderful old building with rickety staircases, full of the romance of the old South Seas. When a foreign film crew came to make a television drama about Stevenson's life in Samoa, rival ambassadors were portrayed viewing the arrival of the *Equator* from the upper verandas. A sense of tradition is maintained by a flag-raising ceremony outside the building every weekday morning. Shortly before 8 a.m. the Police Band of Western Samoa marches around the corner, resplendent in powder-blue tunics and *lava-lavas* and white pith helmets, and plays the national anthem while the flag is raised.

There are few modern buildings, and most manage to be fairly discreet – with two glaring exceptions. While I was there, I was invited to attend the official opening of the new Central Bank building on reclaimed land on the waterfront. A succession of speakers lauded it as a symbol of the new Samoa, a brave and striking vision of future prosperity in harmony with a rich cultural past. I wondered which planet the architects had come from. They claimed the building was supposed to resemble a *fale*, or traditional Samoan house; all I saw was a monstrous cage of glass and lime-green concrete, as much in tune with Samoan culture as a space launching pad. There was worse to come. On an adjacent prime site, Chinese workmen were constructing a seven-storey government building in the post-Mao repressionist style, a grim tower block with all the charm of a Revolutionary Guard barracks. The twentieth century has been late in disfiguring Apia, but it is making up for lost time. I consoled myself with the thought that at least these blights on the landscape would not be occupied by faceless bureaucrats in grey suits. The day after I arrived, the *Samoa Times* reported that there would be no more parties in government offices, because fights had broken out in at least three departments over Christmas.

STEVENSON WAS FOREVER changing his mind. While sailing from Abemama, he wrote to Colvin that he did not intend staying long in Samoa and he wanted to be back in England by June; at first he was not impressed with Apia or its people, and considered taking a winter home in Madeira; but within a few weeks he wrote to another friend that he was so pleased with the climate he had decided to settle in Samoa. He tried to explain his fateful change of heart in a letter to fellow author Henry James:

I was never fond of towns, houses, society, or (it seems) civilization . . . the sea, islands, islanders, the island life and climate, make and keep me truly happier.

Within six weeks of arriving, he had bought four hundred acres of land on a high plateau two miles behind Apia for $4,000. Most of it was impenetrable jungle, but after clearing a few acres the Stevensons had a small cottage built pending the construction of a larger house.

We see the sea six hundred feet below filling the end of two vales of forest. On one hand the mountain runs above us some thousand feet higher; great trees stand round us in our clearing; there is an endless voice of birds; I have never lived in such a heaven.

This was the site of the Vailima estate, where Stevenson would spend the last years of his life; the mountain above was Mount Vaea, where he would be buried.

While the house was being built, Stevenson sailed twice to Australia, and made another circuitous voyage with Fanny through the Gilbert and Ellice Islands and the Marshalls on the *Janet Nicoll*, a six-hundred-ton iron steamship. They called at more than thirty atolls, but rarely spent more than a few hours on each, and Stevenson later wrote of this cruise: 'Hackney cabs have more variety than atolls.'

The mansion into which they finally moved in April 1891 was by far the grandest private residence ever seen on the island. Built entirely of wood, painted dark green with a red corrugated-iron roof, eventually it had four rooms on the ground floor and five upstairs with wide verandas on both levels. The chief feature was a main hall about sixty feet long and forty wide, with walls and ceilings of varnished redwood from California, in which a hundred people could dance with ease. The library was lined with hundreds of volumes – principally on Scotland, France, the Pacific, and military history – whose covers had been varnished to protect them from the climate. Stevenson insisted on having a fireplace, probably the only one in the tropics; it was rarely used, and never drew properly, but it made him feel at home. His study next to the library upstairs was relatively spartan, with only a small bedstead, shelves of books, a table and two chairs, and a rack of half a dozen Colt repeating rifles (these were uncertain times).

Here the Stevensons would entertain guests at native feasts, dinner parties, and public balls in rooms blazing with lamps, amid the glitter of glass and silver, attended by barefoot Samoan house servants padding silently over waxed floors and antique rugs. Not another house or sign of cultivation was visible; the Stevenson mansion stood in splendid isolation in its wild estate. Lloyd Osbourne recalled: 'In Vailima there was always a sense of spaciousness; of a big and lordly house set in a park; of wide vistas open to the sea and the breeze. About it all was a rich, glowing, and indescribable natural beauty, which never failed to cause a stranger to exclaim aloud . . . the dignity, solidity, and air of permanence of Vailima was impressive. It dominated the country like a castle.'

Graham Balfour, Stevenson's cousin and biographer, who lived at Vailima for more than two years, wrote of its profound peace: 'At this height the beat of the surf was plainly to be heard, but soothing to the ear and far away; other noises there were none but the occasional note of a bird, a cry from the boys at work, or the crash of a falling tree. The sound of wheels or the din of machinery was hardly known in the island: about the house all went barefoot, and scarcely in the world could there be found among the dwellings of men a deeper silence than in Stevenson's house in the forest.'

It was more than a house: it was like the stately home of a Scottish highland chief. Louis and Fanny frequently remarked on the similarities of Samoan tribal society to the clan system of eighteenth-century Scotland; at Vailima, Stevenson assumed the role of a paternal chief towards his retinue of house servants and plantation workers, approving marriages and imposing fines for misconduct. The illusion of feudal Scotland was fostered by the adoption of kilts in the Royal Stuart tartan, worn on Sundays and holidays.

Every day, the household gathered for prayers, written by Stevenson and translated into Samoan by Lloyd Osbourne, who had become fairly proficient in the language. Stevenson dismissed religious dogma with its supernatural visions of heaven and hell; according to Osbourne, Tolstoy had a profound influence on him and did much to formulate his views on Christianity as a sublime ethical formula which alone could redeem society.

It was Stevenson's habit to rise early, at least two hours before the rest of the household was astir, to begin writing in the coolness of the morning. Shortly after dawn one day he wrote to Colvin:

The morning is such a morning as you have never seen; heaven upon earth for sweetness, freshness, depth upon depth of unimaginable colour, and a huge silence broken at this moment only by the far-away murmur of the Pacific and the rich piping of a single bird. You can't conceive what a relief this is; it seems a new world.

STEVENSON'S BRAVE NEW WORLD lasted less than four years. After his death, Vailima was occupied successively by a retired German businessman, colonial administrators, and the Samoan head of state. In recent years it had fallen into disrepair, battered by tropical storms and neglected by a government with neither the funds nor, apparently, the enthusiasm for restoring it. In Samoa, as in most of Polynesia, if a thing is worth doing it can wait till later; if it's not, it can be conveniently forgotten.

Then along came three wealthy American businessmen, who had been Mormon missionaries on the island, with a project to rebuild Vailima as a literary museum to mark the centenary of Stevenson's death. They were led by Rex Maughan, who had bought the Southfork Ranch featured in the American television soap *Dallas*, which said much for his extravagance but little for his taste. At first there were alarming reports that they intended to convert Vailima into a kind of theme park, with mechanical dolls of Louis and Fanny in the house, and cable cars running up to their tomb on Mount Vaea. Maughan conceded after a chorus of protests that the cable car scheme was not 'economically feasible or aesthetically pleasing', but doubts remained.

A Samoan at the tourist information bureau told me: 'I am very angry about them. I think it is a business-related venture. They are not doing this because they love the people of Samoa, or want our government to have money. It is they who want to have more money by cooking up something funny.' I asked an engineer whom I met at a dinner party what he thought about it. 'The problem is nobody really knows what's going on, what they're going to do,' he said. 'For us it is the residence of the head of state, a place of respect, like your Buckingham Palace. How would you feel if they made Buckingham Palace a museum for a Samoan writer?' Clearly there was a problem of communication here, so I went to see Seiuli Paul Wallwork to find out what was going on.

As the Director for Youth, Sports, and Culture, Paul was usually more involved with the national passion for rugby than the Vailima project. The walls of his office were adorned with sporting trophies, and British press reports of Western Samoa's victory over Wales in the recent rugby World Cup. Inevitably we chatted about the forthcoming visit of the Scottish team, but when the conversation turned to Vailima he was reassuring. I asked him about the mechanical dolls.

'God forbid,' he said. 'Stuff like that is out of the question. It's going to be a straightforward literary museum where people can learn not only about Stevenson but also about the Samoan people and culture of that period. The Head of State will have an office there, and facilities for holding official functions. We have the final say on all of this. It's clear to us there was a deep mutual affection between Stevenson and the Samoan people. He was more than a writer to Samoans, he was like a father. We are becoming nostalgic for those days, and very emotional about this project. It will be in good taste, and above all it will show respect, you can be sure of that.'

The Americans had already established their credentials as philanthropists by donating $100,000 for the construction of a school on the neighbouring island of Savai'i – thereby halting the logging of a rain forest which was to have funded the school. Paul seemed sincere, and as one of two Samoan directors on the five-man trust supervising the project, he assured me the end result would be a memorial that admirers of Stevenson would be proud of. Work had just begun, and the place was in a bit of a mess, but I was welcome to have a wander round it if I wished.

In Stevenson's day, the only access to his estate was a rough footpath which led across the hills to the other side of the island. This was now a surfaced road which passed Vailima on its way up to cloud forests on the central summits, and thence down to the south coast. Paul arranged for a car and driver, and a woman from his office to show me around. Climbing out of Apia, the air became cooler and fresher as we passed schools, churches, and small stores. Houses became fewer and more substantial, as we entered the rarefied atmosphere of wealthy residents who had followed Stevenson's example in settling on the plateau. It is still a lovely place to live, with massive hills clad in rain forests sloping gradually up on either side and the sweep of the Pacific sparkling far below. Even with the noise of occasional passing vehicles, the distant murmur of the surf can still be heard. The estate had shrunk from its original four hundred acres to seventeen, the People's Republic of China had constructed a typically graceless embassy compound across the road from Vailima, and the Australians had built a more pleasant enclave a few yards beyond; but Vailima still dominated the landscape, and lush foliage shielded its privileged position from its new neighbours.

The main gates were closed, and we drove on to a small access road leading into the estate. The first thing I noticed was that the house had changed shape and colour; a wing had been added, part of the lower veranda had been enclosed, and the whole was a dirty white with a roof of pale blue. The next thing I noticed was that it was falling to pieces. This process was being hastened by workmen ripping away sections of the roof in a crescendo of hammering and banging. I had fondly imagined a quiet stroll around the grounds, contemplating the most imposing residence in Samoa and conjuring up images of RLS restlessly pacing his study. Instead I saw a derelict house from which his 'spirit intense and rare' had long departed. His maxim about it being a better thing to travel hopefully than to arrive came to mind.

The interior was equally forlorn. Water was dripping from the ceiling, forming puddles on flagstone floors, vines were creeping through wire mesh on the windows, and doors hung lopsidedly from broken hinges. The fireplace was there, but it was empty and cold to the touch. The only furniture was a large ornate dining table, broken in several places, and a dusty old billiard table. Stevenson played billiards only rarely, and with more enthusiasm than skill. A visitor to his Swiss mountain retreat in Davos in the early 1880s recalled: 'Once only do I remember seeing him play a game of billiards, and a truly remarkable performance it was. He played with all the fire and dramatic intensity that he was apt to put into things. The balls flew wildly about, on or off the table as the case might be, but seldom indeed ever threatened a pocket or got within a hand's-breadth of a cannon. "What a fine thing a game of billiards is," he remarked to the astonished onlookers, "once a year or so."'

Early in 1893, Stevenson began coughing blood, and was confined to his study. To amuse him, his stepdaughter Belle Strong taught him the deaf and dumb alphabet; and for several days he continued work on *St Ives*, a romantic novel set in the Napoleonic Wars, by dictating it to Belle with his fingers, achieving between five and seven pages of manuscript a day.

This image was in my mind as I entered the study. It still commanded fine views of the sea, and to the left the hilltop which Stevenson had marked for his tomb, but inside it was just a bare, dirty room. The scene of Stevenson's burning desire to continue writing through bouts of severe illness was a forlorn, empty corner of a derelict house. I walked slowly down the great staircase of Californian redwood, pausing on the bottom step to look at a corner of the hall where I knew Stevenson had breathed his last, but there was nothing there. It would have been irrational to expect anything else. When a house is long abandoned and gutted of its contents, its atmosphere and its memories do not linger. Still, I had come so far, and I was disappointed to have seen so little. The magic had gone.

It was a relief to emerge into the sunshine, and to hear birds singing when the workmen took a break. A century before, the front lawn had been lined with jasmine, roses, and gardenias; beyond were orchards of mango, lemon, and orange trees; among them grew bananas, avocados, breadfruit, and hibiscus in perpetual bloom; there were hedges of fragrant limes so fruitful the Stevensons gave them away by the sackful, and others bearing pineapples weighing up to eighteen pounds. The lawn had been maintained, and a few flame trees provided a splash of colour, but otherwise the estate had reverted to its natural wild state. I found the remnants of a dry-stone wall, which had separated the lawn from a paddock where the Stevensons had kept their horses and ponies, but I failed to reach the stream where they had bathed. I emerged badly scratched from futile attempts to beat a path through the undergrowth to find the woman from Paul's office regarding me with bemusement.

'There is another way,' she said. 'Come, we can take the car.'

The other way was *Ala Loto Alofa*, or 'the road of loving hearts'. When a civil war broke out in Samoa in 1893, a Paramount Chief whom Stevenson had befriended was defeated, and twenty-seven of his chiefs were imprisoned near Apia. For months Stevenson visited them regularly, bringing supplies of food, tobacco, and *kava*, and when they were released at the end of August the following year they built an access road to Vailima as a token of gratitude. The fact that chiefs engaged in labour normally consigned to commoners was a singular mark of esteem for their benefactor. Within a month they had carved a broad path for about a quarter of a mile through the bush, and erected a wooden sign in Samoan. It said: *Considering the great love of his excellency, Tusitala, in his loving care of us in our tribulation in the prison, we have made this great gift. It shall never be muddy, it shall endure for ever, this road that we have dug.*

The track skirting the northern boundary of the estate had endured for at least a century, and on the day I drove along it, it was not muddy. The chiefs' signboard had been replaced by bronze plaques with inscriptions in Samoan and English, saying: *This is the road of loving hearts hewn by the people of Samoa for Tusitala — Robert Louis Stevenson whose resting place lies on Mount Vaea above.* Beneath it were verses from his requiem. I thought the original dedication was better, and made a note to suggest that it be restored.

Stevenson chose the name Vailima, meaning five waters or rivers, mainly because he liked the sound of it; he had a vague notion there were five streams on his property, but in fact he discovered only three. The path the chiefs built led to the principal stream, to the west of the house, below the confluence of two tributaries. I stepped gingerly over a heavy wooden beam spanning the shallow, fast-flowing brook; to the left, signs pointed to two trails leading up the mountain to Stevenson's tomb, to the right another indicated nature trails. Having decided to leave the tomb until my last day in Samoa, I struck through the forest to the right. After a few paces I was stopped by a massive fallen tree trunk, a roar of rushing water, and a remarkable sight. The stream, which had been innocently tumbling down its shallow course through the forest, suddenly became a cataract plunging sixty feet down a sheer rock face into a narrow gorge. There had been no warning of the fall; I retraced my steps and looked again – but from the bank there was nothing to alert the unwary rambler that he was on the brink of a precipice.

I had with me a volume of Stevenson's letters, which contained a map he had drawn of the area. The spot where I was standing was marked: *Large waterfall into deep gorge where the heat of the fight was*. The reference was to a tribal battle which took place before Stevenson arrived, during which the gully had been filled with dead bodies. For all that had changed in the depths of the forest, it could have happened yesterday: war clubs smashing skulls, spears flashing through the trees, the cries of the vanquished as they tumbled over the edge of that fearsome cataract. The images rose, filled the mind with horror, then vanished as two gorgeously hued birds glided through shafts of sunlight over the water.

On the other side, at the foot of the remnants of a botanical garden closer to the house, I found the place I had been looking for. 'A stream on one side of the clearing,' Lloyd Osbourne wrote, 'splashed musically in a series of cascades and ended in a glorious pool, as clear as crystal, in which we bathed.' The sight which emerged at the foot of a steep bank was inexpressibly beautiful. Amid luxuriant foliage, the stream became a spray of glittering curtains playing over massive rocks into a natural bowl of translucent water; a stone barrier with an old iron sluicegate, which I assumed had been built at the turn of the century, maintained the depth of the pool at about three feet. I was sweating from my short hike, and the temptation was irresistible: I stripped off my shirt and muddy sandshoes and plunged into deliciously cool water; I swam beneath the surface to the largest rock, and laughed with delight under the shock of its waterfall; I drifted with the eddies to the barrier, and lay against it with the flow bubbling around me. Not another soul was to be seen. I felt like Adam waiting for God to produce Eve, and content to admire His other creations in the meantime. The sadness of the house of five rivers ebbed away, I became hopeful the renovation project might restore a sense of Stevenson's presence, and in short the world seemed altogether a better and happier place. The magic had come back.

NINETEEN

The loveliest people in the world, moving and dancing like gods and goddesses

THE POLITICAL SITUATION in Samoa when Stevenson arrived was confused, to say the least. Essentially there were four paramount chiefs at the head of powerful clans, of whom two or three were vying for supreme power at any given time. In these endeavours they were encouraged, opposed, or ignored by three contending colonial powers which had no clear idea of their own policies towards Samoa let alone anybody else's. The resultant imbroglio was like a game of three-dimensional chess, with native pawns scrapping at the behest of illusory kings and being attacked by foreign knights who had difficulty deciding which side they were on. It was a recipe for disaster: the country was on the brink of civil war, and when it erupted Stevenson was in the thick of it.

When Colvin expressed concern for his safety, he replied: 'Why, you madman, I wouldn't change my present installation for any post, dignity, honour, or advantage conceivable to me. It fits the bill; I have the loveliest time. And as for wars and rumours of wars, you surely know enough of me to be aware that I like that also a thousand times better than decrepit peace in Middlesex?'

Stevenson's enthusiasm for the war he had tried to prevent by mediating between the rival chiefs came from a part of his character which is not widely known. Fanny once made a passing reference to it: 'One side of my husband's character was almost unknown; the profession of letters was a second choice, his ill health making what he preferred, the career of a soldier, impossible. His library had many books on military tactics, fortifications, etc., on any one of which he could have passed a thorough examination.'

In the event, his involvement in the hostilities was confined to acrimonious disputes with the colonial administrators and secret councils with the contending chiefs in a vain attempt to prevent bloodshed. Stevenson favoured Mataafa Josefa, a worthy claimant to the Samoan throne whom he regarded as a kind of Bonnie Prince Charlie rising against foreign oppressors. But Mataafa fared no better than Stewart, and after a few skirmishes his forces were routed. The chief's remains now lie in a mausoleum in the grounds of the parliament building on a flat, wind-swept peninsula at the western end of Apia.

I arranged to meet Mataafa Faasuamaleaui, the great-grandson of Josefa's brother, who had inherited the clan title of paramount chief. He was a heavily built man with receding grey hair, and the same quiet dignity Stevenson had admired in his ancestor. On a drive to his village at Amaile in a remote corner of Upolu, he explained how Western Samoa had managed to retain its culture and traditions.

Samoans regard their land as the cradle of Polynesia, at once the scene of a mythical genesis and an enduring example to other Pacific island nations. Honour, dignity, respect, courtesy, and obedience still have the utmost significance in the *fa'a Samoa*, the Samoan way of life, a complex but well-defined social order in which everyone knows where they fit and how they are expected to behave. Allied with the security of the *aiga*, the extended family system, and a fairly relaxed attitude to life in general, it produces people largely content to leave things the way they are. 'It is deep in us, this respect,' Mataafa said. 'There is no need for policemen in villages, because it is for the chiefs to keep order in their places. Our way is changing, but it is changing slowly.'

So was the landscape. After following a badly rutted road

along the coast for about twenty miles, we struck inland and began climbing through jungle-clad hills to a mountain pass where clouds drifted in ghostly shapes through virgin rain forests. Far below, valleys of cultivated land ran to the sea, but in the highlands there were few signs of human encroachment. This was the Samoa I had read and dreamed about; less spectacular than Tahiti, less forbidding than the Marquesas, but with an ethereal beauty only a poet could capture in words. Then we turned a corner and found a fleet of excavating machines building a reservoir; and we passed out of yet another shrinking dream world.

The scenery improved again on the long descent to the south coast, where horses and ponies were more numerous than cars, and the villages had the familiar aspect of rural hamlets gathered around playing fields. Amaile lay at the end of a dirt road. A chestnut horse was grazing on the green, a few pigs and chickens were shuffling around the undergrowth, and we could hear the laughter of children as we walked to the main *fale*, a raised platform beneath a thatched roof supported by wooden pillars.

After women had served us food, the elders began to gather and approached their chief with deference verging on reverence. Where they smiled and shook my hand, they crouched before Mataafa and kissed his. The village *tulafale* (talking chief), an old man bearing the fly whisk symbol of his office, began the proceedings by bidding us welcome and apologizing that they had not had sufficient warning of our coming to prepare a *kava* ceremony in our honour. Two whitened sticks like bones, fashioned from *kava* roots, were placed before each speaker in turn as he paid homage to Mataafa and brought him up to date with village affairs. I understood nothing, but watching the elders listening gravely to their chief and occasionally laughing at some witty remark, with the surf booming against the distant reef, I reflected that Stevenson would have found the scene familiar. It was as if the twentieth century had never happened, and on our return to Apia we might find Imperial German warships in the harbour.

As we rose to leave, the two *kava* sticks were placed in my jeep. Mataafa said one was for him and one for me, but he wished me to have both. 'These are very important symbols of our village life,' he said. 'When you are far away you can remember our ways here.'

Rupert Brooke may have missed the 'lost' Gauguins he was seeking in Tahiti, but in Samoa he found something which enchanted him even more: '. . . the loveliest people in the world, moving and dancing like gods and goddesses, very quietly and mysteriously, and utterly content. It is sheer beauty, so pure that it's difficult to breathe in.'

In Western Samoa, the people still have a rare dignity that sets them apart from other Pacific islanders. With handsome, bronzed features, they walk tall and gracefully like some kind of Polynesian master race. The image is most memorable in rural areas at dusk, when the light becomes soft and hazy with the glow of the setting sun and woodsmoke from cooking fires. One senses a quietness in the land and the people as small groups stroll barefoot through the misty twilight to bathe and gossip in the tepid waters of the lagoon.

I had found a beach cottage to rent at Vaiala, a village on the outskirts of Apia, and it was one of my greatest pleasures to join this nightly promenade to the sea, and lie in the shallows beneath stunning sunsets as my neighbours chatted around me. Often in my travels I had felt lonely, but in Vaiala this was a physical impossibility. Samoans are a gregarious people, who do not like to be alone. When they see someone on their own, they naturally assume he would like some company; so I was frequently approached by strangers enquiring where I was going, why I was in Samoa, and so on. It is a sad reflection on society in general that travellers tend to become wary of such encounters, fearing: I am going to ask you for money; I want to sell you something; I am going to beat the shit out of you and rob you. In Samoa, it is more likely to mean: join us for a swim; come to my house and meet my family.

Yet there is paradox in the Samoan character revealed by a high suicide rate, particularly among young men. A pastor told me the *fa'a Samoa* produced as much anguish as wellbeing with its strict and demanding code of conduct, which aroused feelings of guilt and shame if its standards were not met.

'The feeling is that if I do something wrong and disgrace my family, I would rather die,' he said. 'Even if a son or daughter has done something disgraceful, it makes the father feel small and want to disappear rather than continue living. This is a great shame. It is unforgivable, but it is the custom.'

The most common form of suicide among young men is drinking Paraquat, a particularly unpleasant and prolonged way of shaking off one's mortal coil, in which the victim burns to death from the inside. A local magistrate suggested it was an attempt to induce remorse among parents who had inflicted punishment seen as harsh or unjust. He told me of the case of a young man who had been scolded by his father for not preparing a ceremonial feast properly, and his new bride had overheard. The son felt angry and ashamed, and drank a bottle of Paraquat; he lived long enough to regret it, but died in agony three days later. Fiame Naomi, the Minister of Education, was scornful. 'Basically it is a cry for attention, and it happens because our men are wimps,' she said.

The squad of rugby players who splashed around the lagoon outside my cottage every evening after training in a nearby stadium were anything but wimps. The Vaiala team were the national champions, and one weekend I went to support them in an international seven-a-side tournament featuring teams from Fiji and Tonga. The star of our team was a prop forward with the dimensions of a small house and the momentum of an express train. In full flight he was a glorious sight, and opponents who attempted to stop him were left feeling as if they had been mangled by a combine harvester. I shuddered to think what he and his mates would do to the touring Scotland team. Fortunately I left Samoa before the flower of Scottish rugby was duly harvested.

Among the most whimsical of Samoan pursuits is *kirikiti*, the local version of cricket. Stevenson was informed that shortly before he arrived, the gods of the chief islands of Upolu and Savai'i had played a match against each other; since then they had been at war, and occasionally the sounds of battle were heard to roll along the coast. The game as played today by mere mortals is less ferocious, but equally mystical. The rules are obscure to all but the most dedicated *aficionados*, the pattern of play is unpredictable, and the outcome is anybody's guess. Three-sided bats keep things interesting since nobody, not even the batsman, has the least idea where the ball will end up. Entire villages join in, and serious competitions can last for days. For a Scot, it is as incomprehensible as the English game, but it is a lot more fun.

Returning from a hike in the hills one day, I came across two teams slugging it out on a village green. The home team in blue *lava-lavas* was Tanugamanono, and their opponents in red *lava-lavas* were Vailima, so I stayed to cheer on 'Stevenson's team'. There were about two dozen players on each side, including a wild-haired cheerleader who acted as a kind of master of ceremonies at a vaudeville show, leading his team in silly antics designed to unsettle the opposition. Each time a batsman was dismissed, he would lead the fielders in a high-kicking dance routine, mimicking the actions of riding a horse or a motorbike, then running backwards and falling down. At this point, music blaring from loudspeakers would switch to the pop song 'I got you, babe'.

Rain did not stop play. When a squall which had been looming over the mountains broke over us, it just made the game more amusing, with the barefoot players slipping and sliding on the uneven grass field. A spectator in the Vailima pavilion, a wooden frame covered with canvas, explained the scoring rules: a ball struck to the boundaries (a nearby road, a church, and the front gardens of adjacent houses) scored one point; beyond the boundaries, two points; into a surrounding coconut plantation four points; and out of sight, six points. This was a one-day match, to be decided over three innings. As the game reached its climax, Tanugamanono required four runs, with three batsmen remaining, to win.

Vailima's hopes rose when one of the opposing batsmen swung wildly at the ball, missed his footing, and collapsed on his wicket. But the next ball was cracked high into the air, in the direction of a garden boundary. A Vailima fielder, running backwards with his eye on the ball, fell into a hedge from which a large pig emerged with indignant squeals. The ball flew on, over the hedge, ricocheted off a palm tree, bounced on a tin roof, and disappeared through the open window of a house. This mighty shot was adjudged a four, and Tanugamanono were declared the winners.

The closing ceremonies were as entertaining as the game. After shaking hands, and applauding both sets of spectators, the teams sat facing each other, about twenty yards apart. The captains in turn rose to address their opponents, and my neighbour explained: 'This is very important custom, to say thank you for friendship, no fighting and everything good.' I mentioned that the speeches seemed to go on for a long time. 'In Samoa there are many words to say thank you,' he said. Then the fun began, with each team amusing the other with songs and dances. The star performer was a member of the Vailima team, a massive fellow with an enormous belly like a Sumo wrestler, who pranced around with dainty steps, making delicate fluttering movements with his hands like an ungainly porker in a Disney cartoon.

The final act was a beautiful song, which the teams sang in unison as they parted. I can still see this image: the Vailima players walking away in the gathering dusk, their hosts standing in a group on the playing field, waving and continuing to sing. The song was called 'Farewell, my friend'. Samoans may not be familiar with the finer points of the game as played overseas, but they are second to none in sportsmanship.

Strolling back to my cottage, I saw a cruise ship with its lights ablaze towering over the Apia waterfront. It had docked only that morning, and it was due to leave in a few hours. I pitied its passengers having come so far, and seen so little of Samoa. I felt a lot sorrier for them before the night was out.

THE SAMOAN ARCHIPELAGO is in the middle of the South Pacific hurricane belt, and the months of December and January are prone to storms packing winds over 100 m.p.h. It was now January, and the weather was unsettled. I had seen dark clouds building up over Savai'i to the west during the day, but there had been no storm warnings, and I was looking forward to a Saturday night out on the town with a few friends. They included Salesi, the younger brother of the United Nations official I had met years ago in Namibia.

It began with a gust of wind, and a few raindrops. We had just finished dinner in a cheap and cheerful Italian restaurant in the suburbs of Apia, and were discussing where to spend the rest of the evening. Another gust whipped through the courtyard of the restaurant, bringing a shower of rain, and somebody suggested going to the Tusitala Hotel where a dance band was playing. As we drove along the waterfront in my rented jeep, we noticed that the wind was increasing in strength and waves were beginning to spray over the sea wall. By the time we reached the hotel, violent gusts were tearing at tarpaulins which had been lowered over the open side of the *fale*, and the crowd inside had moved into the recesses of the building. Somebody said there had been a storm warning on the radio, and somebody else said a hurricane alert had been broadcast in American Samoa, but nobody seemed unduly concerned; the place was packed, the band was playing, and the locally produced Vailima beer was flowing. For half an hour, the band battled valiantly against the rising noise of the wind, then the lights went out.

There was a chorus of cheers and laughter, but the roar of the wind in the darkness was suddenly ominous, and I began to feel uneasy. After a few minutes an emergency generator kicked in, and for a while the revelry continued beneath flickering lights. In the hotel garden, the branches of a large tree strung with festive lights were dancing crazily like some demented monster in an enchanted forest. Ten minutes later the lights went out again, the bar closed, and the clientele began drifting out into the night. There was a drunken yell, and a bottle smashed at my feet. We decided it was time to leave.

Salesi proposed we have one for the road, so we headed through a blur of torrential rain to a strip of agreeably seedy bars along the waterfront. The Love Boat was closed, but Otto's Reef next door was still blasting out rock music, so we went in; but we had barely ordered a round of drinks when the power cut out, and a furious gust of wind ripped away tarpaulin covers around the front terrace, sending chairs and glasses flying. Looking out, we could see the spray of huge waves crashing over the sea wall, and staggering figures illuminated in flashes by car headlamps. Through the shrieking of the storm came screams, curses, and the sound of breaking glass.

'Wheee,' Salesi cried as a bottle flew through the air.

'Ka-boom,' somebody else shouted as a table crashed to the floor.

'Jesus,' the barman intoned as the table became airborne and smashed into a wall beside us. Things were getting out of hand, but Salesi was enjoying himself.

'Hey, Gavin,' he shouted into my ear. 'Bet this makes you feel at home, just like Glasgow on a Saturday night, eh?'

'Aye, but we'd better go before the police turn up.'

'What?' he screamed.

I took him by the arm, and we fought our way to the jeep. After finding his house and then my cottage more by good luck than judgement, I bolted the storm shutters and went to bed. I fiddled with the radio, in the hope of hearing a reassuring voice saying it was really not so bad and it would soon be over, but it was dead. Then I tried reading for a while, but the wind had swelled to a tumultuous roar which overwhelmed everything but my mounting sense of insecurity. I have experienced winter gales in Scottish mountains, and I hate and fear them above all else, but this was worse; it was as if all the hounds of hell were baying at my door.

Stevenson described similar feelings when a storm lashed Upolu in December 1890:

We went to bed with mighty uncertain feelings; far more than on shipboard, where you have only drowning ahead — whereas here you have a smash of beams, a shower of sheet iron, and a blind race in the dark and through a whirlwind for the shelter of an unfinished stable. I have always feared the sound of wind beyond everything. In my hell it would always blow a gale.

I was not exactly quaking, but my house was. I discovered this when I lay down and felt an interior wall by my head trembling. At this precise moment there was a sickening ripping sound and I leapt out of bed assuming the roof was coming off. In fact it was a tree being stripped of its boughs in the garden, but it was the final blow to my failing courage. I dressed quickly, grabbed an overnight bag, and climbed into the jeep.

The Tusitala Hotel may not have had the rustic charm of my cottage, but it was built of bricks and mortar.

Crawling back along the seafront, I realized this was now a hurricane: the rain was horizontal, and hefty timber beams and sheets of corrugated-iron were flying through the air; it was a howling black maelstrom, at once exhilarating and terrifying. Then my headlights picked out a wondrous sight: three demons brawling in the middle of the road. They turned out to be drunken youths who could barely stand, let alone throw punches, but still they grappled with each other. I saluted their tenacity, and crept past them. At the hotel, an American friend kindly allowed me to share her room, and a maid presented us with a note from the management apologizing for any inconvenience, and suggesting guests might wish to avail themselves of room service until the weather improved. We ordered champagne.

In the morning the storm was over, but Upolu was enveloped in an eerie, dirty grey shroud with only a faint glimmer of light on the northern horizon. Apia was like Beirut after a bad night, the streets strewn with debris and buildings splattered with vegetation like shrapnel. A helicopter which had been roped down near the shore was lying at a crazy angle, smashed beyond repair, and the cross-island road was blocked by fallen telegraph poles. My cottage was intact, apart from a missing veranda rail.

I learned later that we had been hit by hurricane Lin, which had formed over Savai'i ten miles to the west, but there had been no serious casualties. Fortunately we had been subjected only to her adolescent tantrums as she gathered strength before whirling off to inflict her full adult fury on an empty expanse of the Pacific.

TWENTY

Of a sudden the sweet, clean smell of the sea was gone

PAGO-PAGO, the main port and entry to American Samoa, is known as the armpit of the Pacific. This is due partly to its position at the head of an elbow-shaped bay surrounded by mountains, and partly to its tuna-canning factories, which emit an incredibly foul stench. Its other notable feature is Mount Pioa, known as Rainmaker Mountain, which dominates the entrance to the inlet like a massive fortress, trapping rain clouds and dumping every last drop on the harbour area. The overall effect is of a marine slaughterhouse with a hole in the roof.

It was never the most fragrant place in the world, judging by Stevenson's observations when he arrived from Apia in 1891 in the company of Harold Sewall, the American Consul-General, for a three-week visit.

A long while before we were fairly in the jaws of the harbour, of a sudden the sweet, clean smell of the sea was gone; there fell upon the boat instead a flat, acrid, and rather stifling odour of damp; it had been raining much of the day, the woods were all quite moist.

Another British writer, who passed through twenty-five years later, captured the oppressive mood of Pago-Pago in a short story. Somerset Maugham's 'Rain', a tale of a puritanical preacher and a prostitute drawn together with fatal consequences, is a classic portrait of a desultory town festering in the tropics beneath the ramparts of a broken volcano.

Modern guidebooks are no more flattering, pointing out that American tutelage has transformed a traditional Samoan society into a welfare state heavily dependent on employment in local government, thus depriving its citizens of their pride and cultural identity. Poor old Uncle Sam had fostered another breed of unhappy mongrels relying on scraps from Washington. My trusty *Lonely Planet* guide also advised against bathing anywhere close to the harbour due to a high level of contaminants, sewage, and garbage in the water.

Having read all this, I was prepared to detest the place. In fact, I thought it was splendid. Maybe that is because I feel at home in grubby parts of the world. In the same way that in my youth I preferred the honest grime of Glasgow to the pretentious airs and graces of Edinburgh, I found Pago-Pago with all its pungent odours more interesting then the gleaming sterility of places like Singapore.

For a start it has the most dramatic natural setting of any harbour I had seen in the Pacific. Rainmaker Mountain towers magnificently over a narrow inlet leading to the bay, where the northern shore is a sheer wall of thickly forested rock, a vertical jungle climbing to a razor-backed ridge which forms the spine of the long, narrow island of Tutiula. Pago-Pago and its neighbouring communities lining both sides of the harbour are ramshackle enough, but they are bustling with life and industry. I enjoyed the cacophony of sleek purse-seiners discharging their catches at the canneries, and hydraulic cranes winching mountains of black nets from their after-decks to a repair facility on the quay. These were modern, powerful vessels equipped with spotter helicopters, which ranged far over the Pacific for months at a time to fill their holds with up to one thousand seven hundred tons of fish. The rest of the tuna fleet comprised Korean long-liners, which looked like rust buckets by comparison. No fewer than seven of them were impaled on rocks on the northern shore, their shattered hulls testimony to the fury of hurricane Val two years before. Dead ships in a smelly port; at least the place had character.

So did Sadie Thompson's restaurant and liquor store, named after the cheerful harlot in Maugham's story. Sadie was reputed to have been based on a real character among the author's fellow passengers on the steamship *Sonoma*, who were delayed in Pago-Pago by an outbreak of measles while *en route* from Honolulu to Papeete. The story goes that she plied her trade in a two-storey wooden frame house near the wharf, owned by a half-caste trader. The building is said to be the same in which the restaurant now occupies the upper floor, and it certainly corresponds to the description of it in 'Rain'. An enclosed staircase leads up one side of the building to a door with a brass nameplate, inscribed: *Miss Sadie Thompson*. Within, subdued lighting and tasteful decor in various shades of red re-create an atmosphere with which she would have been familiar. It was in the bar next to the restaurant that I met Gallo. His real name was Damir Mislov, but everybody knew him as Gallo. He was a squat, powerful man with dark eyes, conversing with a big man with blond hair in a language I could not identify. I asked him where he was from.

'From the war,' he said.

'Which one?'

'Croatia.'

I had not expected to come across many Croatians in American Samoa, but apparently the place was full of them. Gallo told me he was the captain of the *Big Z*, one of a fleet of eleven Croatian purse-seiners based in Guam, ranging the Pacific and off-loading their catches in Samoa, Guam, the Philippines, and Indonesia depending on prices. I asked him how things were going in the old country.

'That's stupid war. For me, what I think, it's stupid war. I not political, for me my country number one, but for me in the world every war is stupid. Not only this war. Why kill people? We all die anyway.'

I agreed it seemed pretty pointless, and Gallo warmed to the subject.

'Why they shoot churches, museums, it's stupid. Every trip we send some money for Croatia, not for the war, but for the kids who don't have homes. Now is no time for fight. Now is twentieth century. I like work, I like work hard, I like make money. More fish I catch, more money I make. Believe me if this stupid war stop, Croatia grow up full speed. Croatia people work hard. Serbia people same like us. They not too bad, they just got wrong government is their problem. Normal people they don't want war, they want work and life. I know a couple Serbia families. I talk with them, they say they like living Croatia, this war bullshit.'

At this point a man called Mike, a former editor of the *Samoa News*, leaned over to shake Gallo's hand.

'I fought in Vietnam, and I lost two brothers there,' he confided. 'Samoa had nothing to do in Vietnam, but our people died there. When people fight, nobody wins.'

Gallo concurred: 'Nobody wins.'

Our little international gathering having reached agreement on the futility of war, Gallo offered to show me around his ship. Strolling along the darkened quayside, he told me of his life at sea.

'I finish architecture school, that's my really job. But fishing is in my blood. My grandfather, my father, he not want, but for four years I captain. Is hard job, mostly every day I flying five, six, seven hours in helicopter looking for fish. You think it's easy, it's hard. Sometimes bad weather catch us, but we just put bow in waves and slow down engines. Then it's up to God.'

The divine protector of the *Big Z* has his own quarters on the main deck. Stepping through a bulkhead, I was arrested by the sight of a shrine at the end of the corridor, a tableau of religious statues and symbols illuminated by red candles. In the mess, a small Croatian flag was fixed above an alabaster relief of the Last Supper, and on another wall an elaborate crucifix hung between a girlie calendar and a portrait of a ghostly Christ guiding a sailor through storm-tossed waters. I thought: This is a ship which faith would take through hurricanes.

Gallo showed me a video film taken during a recent voyage. Fishing for tuna in the Pacific is like a combined forces operation. First the air force (the helicopters) identify the target, then the navy (the purse-seiners) close in for the kill, and finally the marines (the fishermen) bounce around in speedboats shepherding the prey into nets a mile long and six hundred feet deep. It did not look like a great job, but at least it was far from the killing fields of Bosnia.

Gallo told me his ambition was to set up his son in the tourist business.

'This is future for Croatia, working for tourist. Adriatic coast not for industry, still very clean. But big hotels is not future. On my island we got little boat. We go fishing together, that's good for you. You in big hotel, you sit in room, that's not good for you. You come my island October, you gather olives to make oil, you can write book about that.'

It seemed like a good idea. There are worse ways of passing time than gathering olives on an Adriatic island. Like shooting people, for example.

THERE WERE TWO PLACES in American Samoa I particularly wanted to see: a small island off the eastern edge of Tutuila and a fishing village on the north coast, both of which Stevenson visited on a circumnavigation of the island by whale boat. Aunu'u Island lies about two miles across a windy channel from the village of Auasi, which is where I found Tino standing by the quayside. He was wearing a baseball cap and a smile, and he seemed pleased to see me. 'You want to go island? You need boat? I take you, one dollar. We go now, come.'

Tino said he was an engineer by trade who had married a

woman from Aunu'u and settled there, making a modest living from farming and ferrying people to and from the island. I stepped gingerly into his tiny aluminium skiff, squeezing on to a narrow centreboard along with a large lady in a floral-patterned dress, a box of fish, and two cartons of noodles. Tino gunned the outboard engine, and we skipped over the waves at the harbour mouth into the channel. I was grateful for an unseasonal spell of calm weather, but even so the long swells rolling in from the Pacific rose substantially higher than our craft. Tino was not in the least concerned. 'Sea calm today,' he said. 'Just you must balance boat, everything OK.' I noticed a gash in the bow, where the metal was badly buckled.

'What happened here?'

'Big wave,' Tino said with a grin.

My silent prayers for a safe passage were granted, and soon I was sitting on the steps of an old church perusing Stevenson's account of his visit in my copy of *Vailima Papers*. An old man mending nets by the seashore had waved a friendly greeting, but otherwise my presence was barely acknowledged by the few residents strolling around a small village of iron-roofed bungalows. Aunu'u is a tranquil island with more birds and ducks than people, a kind of volcanic nature park of low hills covered with banana plantations, and surrounded by remarkably clear blue water. Since Stevenson passed by its population has swelled from two hundred to about six hundred, and it has acquired a pick-up truck and a couple of shipwrecks, but otherwise it is much as he observed it.

A broad, well-defined path runs around the island in a rough figure of eight, the two circular portions joining on a plateau overlooking the village. Shortly after I began hiking along it the sky darkened, the wind freshened, and rain slanted in from the sea. I was thoroughly soaked, but still in jaunty mood, when I came to a path leading to a forest lake. Ducks were splashing among the reeds, and I was tempted to slip in for a swim, since

I could not get any wetter anyway. I consulted my guide book, which identified the spot as Pala Lake. It said: 'This beautiful and deadly looking expanse is a sea of fiery red quicksand . . .' It added that during the rainy season locals came here to shoot ducks, and actually swam out to retrieve them; but to avoid being sucked to their doom they had to remain horizontal at all times, and propel themselves using only their arms. I decided to bathe elsewhere.

Continuing around the exposed ocean side of the island, I began to wish I had invited somebody in the village to accompany me. On a clear day with cheerful companions, the walk would have been pleasant and full of interest. Squelching alone beneath a lowering sky, with the ocean booming to my left and the wind moaning through deserted plantations to my right, I felt vaguely uneasy. After about half a mile, the path veered inland and became a corridor enclosed by dense vegetation, rising steadily to an open plateau where one branch led back down to the village and the other on a circuitous route of a large lake in a volcanic crater.

Here I came across the first person I had seen since leaving the quayside. He was a dark, powerful man, hacking at a banana tree with a large machete. A hunting rifle lay on the ground beside him. He offered no friendly greeting, and his English being no better than my Samoan, I reverted to sign language to learn the gun was for shooting birds. He showed no interest in me, and clearly wished I would go away. So I went, somewhat dispirited, down the jungle path skirting the lake, which offered a wild and exotic prospect of still water with a curious reddish tinge, dotted with low islets.

It seemed nothing had changed here since Stevenson reported:
  . . . the water of the lake is said to be red and to redden bathers. We reached the western summit of this basin by a low place shelved in wood; our way was still in the midst of woods, so that we had little idea of the nature of the country, only walked in airless heat among

cocoanuts and great ipis dark as ivy and rugged as chestnuts. From a
little in front sudden crepitations of surf began to strike at intervals
upon our ears . . .

The scene which he then described, at the eastern end of the
lake where it drains into the sea, was breathtaking. A century
later, I stood mesmerized by the savage beauty of it. It was as if
a gigantic claw had ripped away a section of cliff, leaving two
bastions of rock guarding a stormy cove in which the sea
heaved, boiled, and rebounded from caverns with the muffled
roar of artillery. My guidebook cautioned against venturing close
to a rock shelf above this cauldron, and it soon became apparent
why. As I stood at what I thought was a safe distance, a rogue
wave towered over the cove, overwhelmed the shelf, and lapped
at my feet. Had I been on the shelf, these words would not have
been written.

My way now led through an old forest, which according
to legends was frequented by *aitu*, or bad-tempered spirits.
Passers-by were supposedly forbidden to call out or make loud
noises, lest they disturbed the supernatural residents. This was a
seriously gloomy, haunting place, but not wishing to offend
anyone past or present, I stifled a desire to whistle a merry tune
to speed me on my way. I had in mind something like 'Marie's
Wedding', you know, the one that goes: 'Step we gaily, on we
go . . .' An unaccountable edginess was still with me. Not a
breath of wind stirred this deep thicket of gnarled trees, twisted
by age into fantastic shapes, some of them dead and whitened
like old bones. Sudden stirrings and rustlings in the forest
startled me. I found myself turning round, sensing I was being
followed, and I yelped when a toad hopped on to my right
foot. All I needed was a bit of swirling mist to imagine that
around the next corner I would find a wicked witch in a
gingerbread house, with a soul as black as her cooking pot.
Evidently Scots beef was not on the menu that day, for I emerged
unscathed, and with a sense of relief, on to the plateau and my

homeward path, just as the skies began to clear. Cresting the rise, I had this vision: Stevenson emerging from the bush, standing on the path with hand on hip, and saying: 'Well, what kept ye, laddie?' Obviously it was time to relax and have some lunch.

Fortified by a snack of spring water and sticky buns made with coconut milk, I sauntered down the hill in sunshine, light of heart. A flock of wood pigeons flapped about in appreciation of an enthusiastic rendition of 'Marie's Wedding'. The remainder of the hike was a delight, past hedgerows and along a sandy shore where islanders were catching reef fish for dinner.

On my return to the village, I found Tino lounging in a *fale* with his family. A distinguished-looking gentleman in a *lava-lava* was introduced as his father-in-law, the High Talking Chief of the island. On discovering the purpose of my visit, the chief requested that I photograph him. Wearing his ceremonial necklace, and carrying an intricately carved wooden staff and fly switch, the emblems of his authority, I thought he cut a splendid figure and told him so. He beamed with pleasure, and I was assured of his hospitality should I ever return. My last image of this chameleon isle was young boys playing on body boards in the transparent water of the little harbour. For fun, a boatman threw two of them a rope and towed them in a plume of spray to the edge of the channel, evoking squeals of delight. I bet they weren't afraid of the wicked witch in the forest.

THE CENTRAL RIDGE of mountains on Tutuila is a watershed in more ways than one. On the one side lies a mongrel America, and on the other vestiges of old Samoa. From Pago-Pago a busy road along the south coast passes through communities of Western-style houses, with a dreary succession of supermarkets and fast-food restaurants; over the mountains, half a dozen switchback roads lead to isolated rural hamlets reminiscent of Western Samoa. The scenery is also grander on the sparsely populated northern shore. Here narrow roads hug a wildly eroded coastline, with on one hand cataracts plunging down sheer cliffs and on the other heavy seas battering rocky coves. From this perspective, the shoulders of Rainmaker are buttresses of vertical jungle wreathed in clouds which create a mystical effect of smoke rising from fires in the clefts and ravines.

At the end of one of these roads at the eastern end of the island lies the village of Aoa, where Stevenson camped for two nights and mused on the legendary exploits of Aeneas. He first viewed it from the sea and instantly felt transported to the shores of classical Greece.

Nothing lacked but temples and galleys, and our own long whale boat sped to the sound of singing by eight oarsmen figured a piece of antiquity better perhaps than we thought.

My first view of this fabulous bay, from the top of a mountain pass, was partly obscured by a mess of stinking garbage scarring the slope before me. Pacific islanders have an uncanny knack of picking sites of outstanding natural beauty to deposit their refuse. In fairness, they have been doing this for centuries with no ill effects, since their traditional waste of coconut husks, fish bones, and the like were biodegradable and enriched the soil. The concept that beer cans, detergent bottles, and other unsavoury items are less ecologically acceptable does not seem to have caught on yet. But it is difficult to admire a grand view when one is gagging with a foul stench, so I drove on down to the bay. On the way an elderly man and a youth carrying machetes smiled and waved as I passed. Further on, a dog lying in the middle of the road refused to move, and I was obliged to drive around him. I liked the style of this place.

A small village of wooden bungalows had strung itself along the shore, but otherwise the scene was as Stevenson described it: a shallow bay in the shape of a horseshoe, enclosed by low hills covered with thick vegetation and dominated by a conical hill at the head of the vale. It was low tide, and the sound of the surf came on the breeze from the mouth of the bay. I parked my car by the village green and strolled across a sandy track to a beach strewn with rocks. It was midday on Saturday, and all was peace and quiet. A woman walked past with a sack of breadfruit, and smiled and said hello. Barefoot children were investigating something mysterious beneath a rock in the shallows. A man dressed in a red *lava-lava* waded slowly out towards the reef with a fishing net over his shoulder. Half an hour later he walked back again, his net empty. The silence was disturbed only by the distant surf and birds trilling and chuckling in the forest behind me.

I unpacked some lunch, and browsed again through Stevenson's notes in *Vailima Papers*. On his first night here, the boatmen had performed songs and dances by the light of a lantern outside his tent, but it was the ethos of ancient Greece that moved him to lyrical descriptions of his surroundings. I laid my book aside in the sand, its blue cover imprinted with Stevenson's signature, and was struck again by the curiosity of carrying it to the place which had inspired its author. His words lying there conjured up his image, and I wished more than ever I could summon him for just a few moments. Before me the bay opened out into a vast expanse of sea and sky, and I could not decide which was the more compelling vision: Stevenson's gaunt figure pacing the beach, or Aeneas' battered fleets on the horizon.

Like Stevenson a century before, I was enjoying my solitude. Going into the village would have broken the spell, so I went instead for a stroll along the western shore of the bay to where a cleft in the hills led to a smaller hamlet in an adjacent cove. This is where I found Theresa. She was standing on a rock, her dark hair streaming and a red frock clinging immodestly to her hips from swimming, an enchanting portrait of Polynesian childhood. She greeted me with laughter, and led me with shining eyes to a rock pool where her friends were playing; and for half an hour I played the roles of diving platform and sea monster for a gaggle of brown-skinned children. Each to his own fable, I thought. Stevenson could keep his Greek heroes. I was happier playing at being Peter Pan.

When I returned to the bay of Aoa, it was still enveloped in quietness. I walked slowly back to my car, and left it to its illusions.

TWENTY-ONE

Literally, no man has more wholly outlived life than I

I SPENT MORE THAN A MONTH in Western Samoa, and for most of the time I was within sight of Mount Vaea. Occasionally, while driving over the cross-island road, I caught sight of the sun reflecting on the white cement of Stevenson's tomb near the summit, but I resisted the temptation to visit it until my last day. I knew from his last letters that he had gone there willingly. Wearied by a lifetime of illness, worried about providing for his family, and fearing that his creative muse had deserted him, in the end he had longed for death.

Stevenson accomplished an immense amount of work in 1892. He finished *The Wrecker* and *The Footnote to History*, wrote most of *The Beach of Falesa*, and all of *Catriona* (the sequel to *Kidnapped*), which he considered his best book. In April of the following year he was still in good humour, writing to Arthur Conan Doyle:

I hope you will allow me to offer you my compliments on your very ingenious and very interesting adventures of Sherlock Holmes. That is the class of literature that I like when I have the toothache. As a matter of fact, it was a pleurisy I was enjoying when I took the volume up; and it will interest you as a medical man to know that the cure was for the moment effectual.

The mood at Vailima began to change a few weeks later. Lloyd Osbourne recalled that there were times when Stevenson was terribly on edge with nerves, when he would fly into a passion over matters of little consequence, and when jaded and weary he would give way to fits of irritability that were hard to bear: 'The sad part of life in Vailima was the consciousness of that physical martyrdom; of that great striving heart in so frail a body; the sight of that wistful face, watching us at tennis, which after but a single game had ended – for him – in a haemorrhage; the anguish which underlay that invincible optimism, and which at rare moments would become tragically apparent; the sense of a terrible and unequal struggle . . . that was the shadow of Vailima.'

The first clues that Stevenson's 'spirit intense and rare' was beginning to break appeared in a letter to S. R. Crockett, a Scottish minister, in May 1893, in which he complained of being confined to an upper room of the house because the rest of the family was suffering from influenza.

I sit here and smoke and write, and rewrite, and destroy and rage at my own impotence, from six in the morning till eight at night, with trifling and not always agreeable intervals for meals.

Soon he was deprived of his cigarettes (his favourite brands were Capstan and Three Castles) and his French wine, which he found gave him splitting headaches. To Henry James, he wrote:

I have had to stop all strong drink and all tobacco, and am now in a transition state between the two, which seems to be near madness . . .

Another source of concern was his finances. In a flippant mood six years before, he had asserted that wealth was useful for only two things – a yacht and a string quartet; apart from these, he maintained that an income of £700 per annum was as much as anybody could possibly wish. Since then, royalties from his books had been bringing him six times this amount, but the running costs of Vailima (Fanny and her children contributed nothing to its upkeep) and his generosity to friends overseas left him barely breaking even.

It is a matter for conjecture how much comfort Fanny was to him in this gloomy period. She also suffered from recurrent bouts of depression and real or imagined illness, and their friends in Samoa regarded her behaviour as eccentric. The natives called her Aolele, 'flying cloud', because they observed dark clouds crossing her face. Harry J. Moors, the American trader who negotiated the purchase of Vailima, and who was no great admirer of Fanny, felt that Stevenson needed to get away from his family for a few weeks.

'True, his marriage was a happy one; but I make bold to say that neither was his character bettered by it, nor his art benefited. He was very fond of his wife, and easily led by her; Fanny was like a king – she could do no wrong. Mrs Strong, too, was headstrong and talkative, and generally got her way with him . . . It became quite evident to me that if Stevenson was to give us of the best that was in him, he must get away from the restraints and annoyances that he was subject to in Vailima.'

Moors failed to persuade Stevenson to pack his bags for a spell in a remote island, and at the beginning of 1894, Stevenson began to be preoccupied with his own death. In January, he wrote to a friend:

If I could die just now, or say in half a year, I should have had a splendid time of it on the whole. But it gets a little stale, and my work will begin to senesce; and parties to shy bricks at me; and now it begins to look as if I should survive to see myself impotent and forgotten. It's a pity suicide is not thought the ticket in the best circles.

He had marked the summit of Mount Vaea for the site of his grave, but as he contemplated being entombed there he yearned for Scotland:

I was standing on the little veranda in front of my room this morning, and there went through me or over me a wave of extraordinary and apparently baseless emotion. I literally staggered. And then the explanation came, and I knew I had found a frame of mind and body that belonged to Scotland . . . highland huts, and peat smoke, and the brown swirling rivers, and wet clothes, and whisky, and the romance of the past, and that indescribable bite of the whole thing at a man's heart . . .

On the 3rd of December, Stevenson worked hard all morning

on *Weir of Hermiston*, a tragic Scottish novel which his friends considered a masterpiece, and in the afternoon replied to personal letters. He had been seen gazing long at the summit of Mount Vaea from the windows of his study, and Fanny was filled with a sense of foreboding; but when he came downstairs at sunset he was in a buoyant mood, talked of a lecture tour to America he was eager to make, and played a game of cards with his wife to dispel her melancholy. He said he was hungry, and asked Fanny to help him prepare a salad for the evening meal. They were on the veranda, and Stevenson was chatting gaily, when suddenly he put both hands to his head and cried out: 'What's that?' Then he asked quickly: 'Do I look strange?' As he spoke, he fell to his knees beside Fanny and lost consciousness. His body was carried into the great hall and laid in an armchair that had once been his grandfather's.

Lloyd Osbourne at once saddled a horse and galloped, hatless and coatless, into Apia and returned with the resident doctor and a British naval surgeon, but there was nothing to be done. A narrow bed was brought into the centre of the room and Stevenson was laid on it, his head supported by a rest gifted to him by Sir Percy Shelley, a son of the poet. The Samoan retainers who had formed part of the Tusitala clan sat in a semicircle on the floor with sorrow-stricken faces fixed on their dying chief; some knelt on one knee, to be instantly ready for any command. Stevenson's laboured breathing became slower, and at ten minutes past eight in the evening it was over. The large Union Jack that flew over Vailima was taken down, and laid over the body. Messengers were dispatched to the chiefs who had known Stevenson. One of the first to arrive placed a precious fine mat on the bier and said simply: 'Our beloved Tusitala. The stones and the earth weep.' Then the household staff began reciting the prayers for the dead, and their wails, hymns, and sonorous chants in Latin and Samoan rose from the house until midnight.

Stevenson had often asked Lloyd Osbourne to build a path to

the summit of Mount Vaea, but his stepson, sensing its purpose, had prevaricated. Now the task had to be done in a matter of hours, and it was. Before dawn, the woods resounded to the ringing of axes as forty Samoans hacked a trail up the steep face of the hill, and shortly afterwards Lloyd Osbourne led a party of house servants to the top to dig the grave.

The morning broke cool and sunny; a beautiful day, rare during the rainy season. At one o'clock a body of powerful Samoans bore away the coffin, draped in a tattered red ensign that had flown on Stevenson's voyages in many a corner of the South Seas. The rugged path taxed the pall-bearers' strength to the utmost, but the coffin was carried high; it would have been shameful to have borne it other than on their shoulders.

Fanny outlived her husband by twenty years. In accordance with her wishes, her ashes were interred beside him after she died in California in February 1914.

MY QUEST WAS ALMOST OVER. For eight months I had been roaming the Pacific in search of an elusive spirit, and I had been amply rewarded. In remote communities I had found the same simple goodness and kindness that had enchanted Stevenson; I had discovered that paradise exists in the South Seas, and that the essence of it is love among people who have little else to share. I felt at once privileged and saddened to have glimpsed a way of life which may soon be remembered only in old tales. As for the Tusitala who had drawn me here, there had been fleeting moments when his image had appeared before me with startling clarity, and I had experienced a sense of fellow-ship. I could have no complaints.

I had one last journey to make. I had always imagined that I would climb to Stevenson's tomb alone; I sensed it would be an intensely personal experience, and I would have no desire for a companion. However, in Samoa I met Rachel, a young woman from New Zealand, whose father was serving on the islands as a judge. The day after we met, I took her to the rock pool on the Vailima estate, and somehow we fell into each other's arms. (Magic still happens in enchanted places.) On my last day, I asked her to accompany me to the tomb.

We drove to the road of loving hearts, and walked across the wooden plank to the mountain side of the stream, where two paths led to the summit. I decided to take the longer, more circuitous route, which should have taken us about an hour. In fact it took two hours; unknown to us it was officially closed because of the recent hurricane, which had uprooted massive trees and blocked the trail through dense rain forest in many places. I was glad to have Rachel with me; often it required a helping hand to clamber over the fallen tree trunks and to climb steep rocky inclines slippery and treacherous with rain. The sky was overcast and we had to shelter from sudden squalls, but when we reached the shoulder of the mountain the air was sultry and still. We were strolling along a grassy avenue in the upper reaches of the forest when Rachel called out: 'There it is.' I looked up, and there was the white sepulchre in a clearing at the end of the trail. 'You go on,' Rachel said. 'I'll wait for you here. Call me when you want me to come.' I appreciated her thoughtfulness, and proceeded alone.

The site is not actually the peak of Mount Vaea, which stands a few hundred yards to the west; but the small plateau commands magnificent views across green-clad mountains to the sea, where the faint murmur of the surf drifts up in an eternal requiem. After Stevenson's death, the chiefs tabooed the use of firearms on the hillside, that the birds might sing undisturbed around his grave; and today the air is still sweet with bird song. Somebody had placed on the tomb a cross of two small branches tied together with bark, to which was fastened a bird of paradise flower. Beneath it on the plinth lay two crimson ginger flowers.

My search for Tusitala was over, but there was no sense of

achievement. Instead, there was pathos as I read Stevenson's requiem, inscribed on a bronze plaque:

> *Under the wide and starry sky,*
> *Dig the grave and let me lie.*
> *Gladly did I live and gladly die,*
> *And I laid me down with a will.*
>
> *This be the verse you grave for me;*
> *Here he lies where he longed to be;*
> *Home is the sailor, home from the sea,*
> *And the hunter home from the hill.*

When Stevenson wrote those lines in San Francisco, long before a Pacific voyage was contemplated, he could not have imagined he would be buried on a South Seas island. A year before his death, addressing the Scottish Thistle Club in Honolulu, he moved members of his audience to tears with a lament:

I feel that when I shall come to die out here among these beautiful islands, I shall have lost something that had been my due – my native, predestined, and forfeited grave among the honest Scotch sods. And I feel that I shall never attain to my 'resting grave' unless it were to be on one of our purple hillsides, under one of our old, quaint, and half-obliterated table-tombstones slanting down the brae . . .

Recalling those lines, I thought it seemed a pity that Stevenson was not 'where he longed to be', and that his last wishes remained unfulfilled. I thought of his restless spirit, and concluded: If Father Damien of Molokai could be brought to his native Belgium long after his death (and probably against his wishes), perhaps it was time for RLS to come home from the hill.

I felt a parting gesture was called for, and so I raised my arm in the gesture of a toast and delivered a salute in the broad Scots dialect with which Stevenson would have been familiar. The air was perfectly still, but as I dropped my arm a slight breeze stirred the leaves of a tree near the grave. Within seconds it grew to a strong wind, which whipped across the plateau and scattered fallen leaves around my feet. It was not a storm wind, but rather an exuberant, impish gust which played briefly around the tomb; and then as suddenly as it came, it was gone.

Descending by the more direct path to the rock pool, I thought of another part of Stevenson's requiem, written in San Francisco almost fifteen years before his death, which is not inscribed on his tomb. This is what he wrote:

You, who pass this grave, put aside hatred; love kindness; be all services remembered in your heart, and all offences pardoned; and as you go down again among the living, let this be your question: can I make some one happier this day before I lie down to sleep? Thus the dead man speaks to you from the dust: you will hear no more from him.

EPILOGUE

I wonder exceedingly if I have done anything at all good; and who can tell me? and why should I wish to know? In so little a while, I, and the English language, and the bones of my descendants, will have ceased to be a memory! And yet — and yet — one would like to leave an image for a few years upon men's minds — for fun.

— RLS, in a letter to Sidney Colvin, 29th of May, 1893.

INDEX